MANAGING FOR THE FUTURE

Managing for the Future

Alf Chattell

St. Martin's Press   New York

First published in the United States of America in 1995

Printed in Great Britain

ISBN 0–312–12431–7

Library of Congress Cataloging-in-Publication Data
Chattell, Alf.
Managing for the future / Alf Chattell.
p.   cm.
Includes bibliographical references and index.
ISBN 0–312–12431–7
1. Industrial management.   2. Economic forecasting.   I. Title.
HD38.C43186   1995
658.4'06—dc20   94–43720
                                                          CIP

To my family and to all those dedicated
to 'pushing the envelope'

Contents

List of Figures

Preface

The business world is in the midst of a radical transformation. To accept the future it appears we must let go of much of the past. We must see much that is familiar from a new perspective and we must see the new as a sign of tomorrow. As it becomes increasingly clear that tomorrow's business organizations will bear little resemblance to those of the past, a revolution in thought is required. The successful enterprises of the 21st century cannot be understood piecemeal – new thoughts, perceptions, styles, and ways of doing things are required.

As old certainties ebb away to be replaced by ambiguity and unfamiliarity, interest in the conditions for success in the nineties and beyond intensifies. Executives are becoming increasingly concerned to understand what it will take to ensure that their companies have the foresight and ability to continuously transform themselves to better 'fit' the requirements of a rapidly changing world. They are seeking new models of how their businesses will look, feel and function in the future, and how their roles as functional and general management are being changed. There are few who remain unconcerned with understanding what has to be done today to reshape their businesses to be amongst those who will succeed in the nineties and beyond.

My own interest in tomorrow's organization has its origins in an early conviction that information technology was going to have a major impact on business and society as a whole. A period with Peat Marwick in Canada, designing and implementing real-time business systems, confronted me with the major, and difficult, human and change implications of information technology. An episode with a major UK company illustrated and brought home the major problems senior management have in conceiving strategic business alternatives that have little in common with the business practices of the past. On joining PA Consulting in the UK, I was exposed to the challenges facing senior business management seeking to transform their businesses but lacking alternative models with which they could work. At Nolan, Norton & Company in London, as new models began to emerge, the challenge was to reconceive the fundamentals and characteristics of businesses that would succeed in an Information Age. In 1988, I joined Towers Perrin International, the major human resource consulting firm. This took me into the wider human and organizational issues surrounding the relationship between information technology and organizational effectiveness. In 1990, I joined

Price Waterhouse in London where I co-founded the Organization and Change Management Group – a multidisciplinary group addressing the complex questions of turning the principles of organization and business process transformation into practice. In 1994 I joined Ernst & Young Management Consultants, to work with others to bring the best of thought and practice to those companies committed to reshaping their businesses to succeed in the nineties and beyond. This book is a result of those experiences – almost fifteen years of direct observation and involvement in the field.

This book is for those executives and managers who are passionately concerned with what has to be done today to reshape their businesses to succeed in the turbulent nineties.

I have therefore set out to make a contribution to the thoughts of the thoughtful. It is not my intention to provide definitive answers to what are complex issues – there are still too many open questions. Rather, the objective is to provide management, and all those concerned with the evolving role of business in all our futures, with a thought-provoking guide to the characteristics of what might be called 'tomorrow's organization'. The book therefore aims to shed light on the characteristics of the successful organization of the nineties and beyond, and on the transformations that are required to bring it about. It is perhaps above all a participant's guide to the future that is rushing towards us all.

A central theme of the book is that fast responses, innovation, adaptability and customer orientation have become the key behaviours of tomorrow's successful organization. The book argues that these capabilities depend on a radical change in the form and character of the organization and that this in turn depends on addressing each of several dimensions of the organization simultaneously. The book brings together what appear to be the essential organizing concepts required to bring out the recognizable patterns that will characterize tomorrow's successful organization. By so doing the reader might be better able to address the complex task of thinking afresh about organizations, current and future. The emerging characteristics of each dimension of tomorrow's organization are brought together in order to provide a basis from which executives can formulate appropriate responses in terms of alternative approaches to: the business process; the customer; the management of people; organization design; the uses of information technologies; the shape of their organizational cultures; the management of the business; and their roles as managers. The book sets out to provide a holistic perspective on tomorrow's organization. The hope is that readers may be enabled to integrate their responses in a coherent way – in a way that will enable them to shape their companies to better 'fit' the requirements of a rapidly changing world.

I have recognized that understanding the future shape of organizations requires multidisciplinary perspectives and a multidisciplinary explanation. The book offers such a view and one that spans all aspects of how tomorrow's organization might look, feel and function. To do this, it combines perspectives from disciplines such as general management, marketing, business strategy, operations management, finance, systems theory, psychology, sociology, philosophy, human resource management and information technology.

The turbulent nineties require fresh perceptions of what it makes sense to do and why. The book offers a recognition that a major consequence of this is that tomorrow's organization is rich in its own language, and new phraseology and imagery is required to escape from the confines of the old. This language appears to be very different. I have not tried to avoid the new language – recognizing its necessity – but rather have tried to explain it, and by so doing, make tomorrow more familiar. The slim reliance on case examples is intentional. It is the author's belief that these suggest that copying is better than really thinking through and understanding what is going on and what is taking shape.

The 'Introduction' summarizes the issues and challenges raised in the nineties. It highlights the need to question fundamental assumptions, and argues for a revolution in thought based on new multidisciplinary perspectives, and on a holistic understanding of how tomorrow's organization will need to look, feel and function.

Chapter 1, 'The new Performance Imperatives', describes what has to be different if an organization is to maintain leadership under conditions of continuous change. The chapter emphasizes the imperatives of fast responses, adaptability, innovation and customer satisfaction.

Chapter 2, 'Embracing the Customer', is concerned with how all aspects of organizations are being reshaped to ensure the delivery of distinctive responses to individual customer needs. It describes: the creation of value as a unique interaction between producer and the customer; customer participation in the design, creation and integration of lifestyle-enhancing products and services; the roles of tangibles and intangibles in the shaping of customer value; customer experience design as the integral consequence of the entire production, delivery, selling and after sales process; and the transformational implications of delivering unique customer satisfaction.

Chapter 3, 'Delivering the Right Response at the Right Time', is concerned with how the entire organizational process needs to be transformed to deliver the right response at the right time to highly unique and transient customer needs. It describes: the fundamental role of process transformation in creating and sustaining competitive progress; the redesign of business processes to provide individual solutions to individual customer needs; the wider dimensions of process transformation; and the organizational process dynamics required to ensure the success of tomorrow's organization.

Chapter 4, 'Creating Entrepreneurial Structures', is concerned with what organizations need to look like, and how they will need to work to enable the behaviours required by the turbulent nineties. It describes: the importance of redefining relationships with customers, markets, suppliers, competitors and partners; the issues surrounding the mobilization of the knowledge, ideas and full resources of the organization; the transformations required to reduce the inertia bred by long lines of communication, layers of management and the compartmentalization of expertise; and the characteristics of the new 'complex' organizational structures.

Chapter 5, 'Change-Seeking Culture', is concerned with how the culture of tomorrow's organization needs to look if it is to enable the organization to respond fast enough to the world as it is and will be. It describes: the assumptions of change-seeking and change-resisting cultures; the levers of cultural change; the issues in challenging assumptions and key organizational beliefs; and the essential beliefs about management, products, services, administration, production methods, distribution, employee motivation, and customer satisfaction.

Chapter 6, 'Leveraging the Individual', is concerned with how the roles and management of people are being transformed to enable them to make their fullest contribution. It describes: why people, as individuals and as groups, are increasingly being seen as the key to success; the issues involved in encouraging creativity, innovation and experimentation; the importance of expanding people's perspectives; the importance of redefining inflexible roles, standardized procedures and narrow responsibilities in favour of broader boundaries for people; and the transformations required in management and what it means to be managed.

Chapter 7, 'Living with Continuous Change', is concerned with how the assumptions and processes of management are being redefined to equip the organization to live with continuous change. It describes: the issues faced by managers charged with successfully managing for the future of their organizations; how they can equip the organization with the means to continuously transform; the groundrules for managing in tomorrow's organization; and the groundrules for participation in the organizations of tomorrow.

Chapter 8, 'The Enabling Infrastructure', is concerned with how information technology is being used to enable tomorrow's organization to operate effectively. It describes: information technology as a fundamental element of the fabric of tomorrow's organizations; information technology as a powerful force enabling innovation, closeness to the customer, fast responses and adaptability; the roles of information technology in enabling tomorrow's organizations to embrace the customer, deliver the right response at the right time, exhibit entrepreneurial behaviour, embrace and respond to change, amplify the capabilities of their people, and to live with continuous change.

Chapter 9, 'The Soul of the Organization', is concerned with the social, philosophical and psychological factors which give shape to and energize tomorrow's organization. It describes: the wider social purposes and roles of tomorrow's organization; its attitude to shaping the future, and the posture it adopts to enable it to shape the future; its fundamental concern with human values and the furtherance of the human condition; the social dimensions and purposes of management in tomorrow's organization; and how tomorrow's organizations engage their people in its creative purposes.

Chapter 10, 'Resolution', summarizes what is required to sustain success and to ensure growth into the future.

Weybridge, Surrey, England   ALF CHATTELL

Acknowledgements

This book is the result of many influences. I have been very fortunate to have worked with a great number of very able and challenging colleagues representing the widest range of professional disciplines. I have also had the pleasure of working closely with individuals who represent the widest range of business, consulting and academic backgrounds, approaches and perspectives. And there has been the vast opportunity I have had to work with many international organizations wrestling with the many and complex challenges of the late 20th century.

There are too many people whose influences I could name and too many who would not recognize their direct and indirect contributions. However I am grateful in particular to Mark Thomas, founder of Performance Dynamics, and to Alan Little, Ron Camp and Tony Askew for their encouragement when the will flagged. Thanks also to Samantha Slee for the artwork. And without my assistant, Sonia Allison, there would have been much less sunshine along the way.

Introduction

'Every act of creation is first of all an act of destruction.' (Picasso)

IT'S NO LONGER CLEAR WHAT WE SHOULD INVEST IN

The business world is being transformed creating unimaginable possibilities for those able to let go of the past. Uncertainty and instability do not signal the end of any certainties and predictabilities, they signal the arrival of a new game. The wrong response is to retreat to familiar waters, hang tough, get back to the 'basics' and await the return of normal conditions.

Boundaries have been placed with unbounded possibilities. The 'traditional' boundaries – the physical, territorial, technical, social and psychological assumptions which bounded what was done, why, where and how – are invisible to new competitors who only know new 'rules' and who see the continuous redefinition of them as part of an exciting new world of growing speculations and horizons.

Predictability has been replaced with unpredictability. Forecasting and planning ahead have become a hazardous process of betting the business on the unpredictable behaviours of customers who no longer need most of the products and services on offer. Increased customer choice arising from floods of high quality products and services, means customers are no longer constrained to the dependencies and loyalties of the past.

Stability has been replaced with instability. Investment strategies which lock organizations into one response to a predicted future, lock them out of a future where the ability to respond differently becomes more important than the ability to predict. As customer demand becomes a volatile hard-to-catch blip, the long-horizon product and process development cycles of the past exclude organizations from a short-horizon world.

The massive has become the intangible. As markets increasingly fragment into unique one-customer niches, entire organizations and industries built on assumptions of economies of scale, wrestle with the implications of the transformations required to achieve economies of scope. As customer definitions of what meets their needs become more individual, complex and intangible, the self-referential organizations of

1

the past struggle to redefine deeply held assumptions which can only ensure success in a world which no longer exists.

Every organization is now being subjected continually to a variety of crashing waves from the future (see Figure 0.1) – waves of complex interacting cycles, uncertainties, instabilities and technological and competitive surprises that turn the 'nothing much changes except when we want it to' world of the past into a now already distant fantasy.

As customer needs, wants and expectations become unique in time and space, the concept of customer life cycles gives way to unique customer encounters, development cycles give way to real-time responses and economies of scale give way to the search for economies of scope – the leveraging of capabilities into the enhancement of unique customer lifestyles. As the unique increasingly becomes the only valuable outcome an organization can create, it must be capable of reconfiguring its processes, capital, human and other resources each time the customer is encountered – the alternative is rapid irrelevance. The ability to rapidly reconfigure a growing array of tangible and intangible resources becomes the only way to be in a position to grasp the opportunities in an increasingly 'now you see it, now you don't' world. To meet conditions of fast change and unpredictability where each response has increasingly to be unique, tomorrow's organizations must rapidly get to the point where the cost and time of letting go the past – the last learned response, the last delivered product – is less than the net gains available in a once-off, no

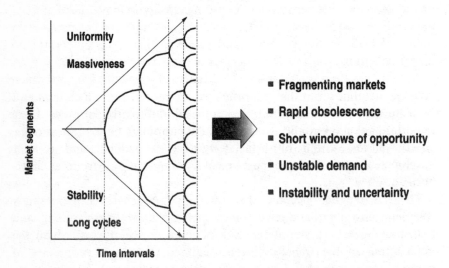

Figure 0.1 *Crashing waves from the future*

lead-time world. The rate at which organizations can leave the past behind becomes one of the key differences between those who will win and those who will lose.

The future does not lie in old certainties or in the elimination of ambiguity and complexity. Rather the need is for approaches which see the steady state as the dead state, and which see dynamic instability both as a basic survival requirement and as the primary source of new possibilities and opportunities.

We are all witnessing the passing of an old paradigm, and we are having difficulty in finding both the pattern and the bits that will make up the new. As we struggle to uncover, understand and master the required new patterns of thought and behaviour, we run the risk of reaching the condition Toffler called 'Future Shock', a state of confusion that arises when the past offers little guidance to dealing with the present and the future. Future Shock can only be avoided by transforming the powerful assumptions of the Industrial Age into new unconscious and instinctive ways of dealing with a world that bears little resemblance to that of the past.

The dilemma that confronts us is that we are all faced with making investments in the future, but that future looks very different from the past. When Toffler said, 'There's no one to copy any more', he was echoing at least two important aspects of the dilemma – the patterns of the past no longer apply, and we are now faced with making investments in something that doesn't yet exist. It is therefore difficult to know what assumptions to base investment decisions on. So what can we do?

OLD APPROACHES WILL NOT WORK

We are in a time when the past offers few signposts. The old certainties of management and what it means to manage are being swept away. Long-held business process and technological assumptions no longer make any sense, and entire industrial legacies built on and around them are being swept away by new and unexpected competition. Complex social relationships between employers and the employed, and between organizations and their communities are in a state of rapid flux. As seemingly age-old assumptions about jobs, careers and the nature of work becoming increasingly constraining, deeply rooted principles of organization design are being thrown away. Fundamentals such as definitions of skills and the educational and developmental processes by which they are acquired and maintained, are becoming deeply irrelevant. An entire world of meanings, values and expectations are being swept away on a tide of change.

In the space between the passing of an era and the successful transition to what is already taking shape, lies the task of intellectually, emotionally and spiritually grasping the new. The task of synthesizing apparent chaos to provide a picture of the new – and one which 'fits' the organization to a new scheme of things – is the challenge facing all. As Peter Drucker pointed out, 'what management needs is not more or better tools – for we already have many more than we can use – but simple organizing concepts'. In other words, we need the means to bring readily recognizable, and new, patterns out of the apparent chaos.

The 'architecture' of tomorrow's organization is not a supercharged version of the old paradigm. It is not the cow path electrified through the use of information technology or through high tech electronic images of yesterday's business. Nor is it an assemblage of management fads. The challenges of the turbulent nineties require a revolution in thought, outlook, and practice. The demands of the turbulent nineties require fresh perceptions of what it makes sense to do and why.

The complex question of understanding the nature of tomorrow's successful organizations requires us to look behind and beyond our preoccupations with the structures, parts and mechanisms, and with our apparent confinements within them. It calls for a new and holistic perspective on the intellectual, conceptual, behavioural, psychological, scientific and social cocktail required for organizations to generate the dynamic behaviours required to prosper in turbulent conditions – conditions which have gone well beyond the operating limits of traditional functional organizations and their old paradigm professional disciplines. The either/or perspectives derived from scientific rationalism have their role to play. But they tell us little about the holistic, systemic nature of the organization at work, its energies and life forces – and very little about its dynamics, and its dynamic interplays with the boundaries of the past, the present and the future.

In a time when it is the behaviour of the organization as a whole that is important – how it adapts, adjusts and responds to challenge and change – it is how these behaviours are produced that is the important issue. The need now is to see the 'whole picture'. Clinging to the neat and convenient inherited points of view confines us to a largely sterile observation and fascination with the parts – a study which tells us as little as anatomy does about the complex social behaviours of the creature carefully dissected on the laboratory table top. An insistence with seeing the constantly evolving thing in motion we call a business through the traditional monochromatic

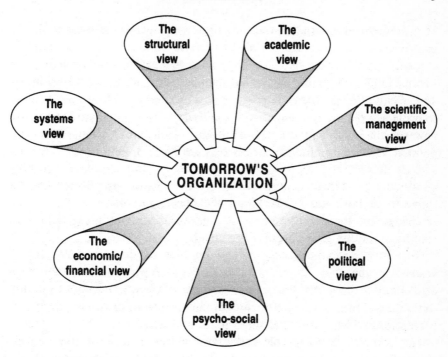

Figure 0.2 *Management disciplines are only points of view*

lenses of scientific management paradigm professional disciplines, is to confuse the eye with the thing being observed (see Figure 0.2). Understanding the thing observed requires analysis, intuition, imagination and everything else that is human to be in play at the same time. Anything less is to insist on being overwhelmed by the real-time events of a complex real-time world.

RIDING THE WAVE

The quality of the existence of any organization is defined by its abilities to extend the boundaries of its customers' lifestyles. Where once, customer lifestyles could be described in about three categories, there is now an almost infinite variety – and they are all rapidly changing all the time. Products and services are no longer stand-alone items defined in terms of their own intrinsic merits. They either fit in with a lifestyle, and by so doing enhance it, or they do not. They are not defined in their own terms, they are defined in terms of their ability to extend the possibilities open to customers. The processes by which lifestyle enhancements are defined, design, created, integrated and supported are perhaps now much more central than the tangible part of the package the customer can hold in her or his hand. Whereas in the past the product was the front-line, and the process was merely the means to the end, now the means and the end are inseparable – and both are critical to an organization's ability to sustain success. Sustaining lifestyle-enhancing capability in continually changing circumstances rests on the ability to redefine and re-create both the product and the means continuously. This continued redefinition and re-creation of both the product and the means imposes insurmountable challenges to the day-to-day structural, social and technical certainties and assumptions of yesterday's organizations.

Tomorrow's organizations depend on their abilities to continuously transform what they do and how they do. They depend on their abilities to transform at the rate determined by the environment, and not at the rate determined by self-satisficing internal bureaucratic priorities. They see their competitive capabilities as being a holistic expression of everything they know, all the intangible and tangibles resources they have at their disposal, a state of mind, future-oriented human talent, and a distinctive management process. The ability to transform is therefore a function of the total ability to change every aspect of business – and in particular the difficult 'soft' stuff of attitudes and assumptions – as and when required by changes in conditions which redefine the conditions for success. The key management issue for tomorrow's organization is not how to perfect what has already been learned, proven and applied, the issue is one of how to manage a process of complex and continuous change to ensure the capacity to stay in tune with a fast changing world is never exceeded by real-world conditions.

Tomorrow's organizations require a capacity for transformational regeneration which far exceeds that usually associated with organizational change. An entire regeneration of the organizational mindset is required if the necessary radical changes in all aspects of structures, assumptions, assets, processes, skills and technologies are to be achieved. If the organization is not only to stay ahead but be in a position to define the future, this ability to change must extend beyond the boundaries of the organization. Only by being able to reconceive what it does and how it does it – and with whom – can organizations hope to avoid being condemned to react by 'rolling with the punches', and, by purposefully riding the waves of the future (see Figure 0.3), participate in the creation of the future. The alternative to organizational designs that are able to

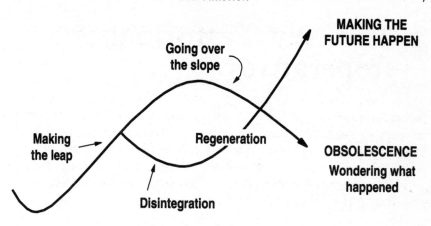

Figure 0.3   *Riding the wave*

change – not merely to absorb the punches (although that can be useful), but to enable the generation of appropriate behavioural changes – is to inevitably be overwhelmed by events.

Because transformation is inevitable, the issue is not one of if, it is one of to what and how. We are all engaged in a voyage of exploration and discovery – by definition, we cannot fully predict the process or its outcomes. What is clear is that the only organizations with a future will be those who have decided that the only place to be is in the forefront of making the future happen. Indeed, the almost universal concern in business with transformation already suggests that increasing numbers of organizations are committed to being amongst those with the foresight and ability to continuously transform themselves to better 'fit' the requirements of a rapidly changing world.

As someone once said, 'change always proceeds, with or without an articulated theory – but we can work to improve its course and its results. The choice then is which type of company we choose to become: one that makes things happen, one that watches things happen, or one that wonders what happened.'

1 The New Performance Imperatives

'Every product and every activity of a business begins to obsolesce as soon as it is started.' (Walter Wriston)

THE CHALLENGES

Complex social and technological changes are rapidly redefining every assumption that has shaped business thought and practice since the industrial revolution began in the late 18th century.

Product life cycles are trending towards the instantaneous, meaning that product-specific processes destroy the capital that enabled them in a very short period of time. Markets are trending towards unique customer-specific niches demanding the ability to deal with rather than eliminate diversity. With new forms of variety being required all the time, know-how needs to be continually re-created and re-applied to meet the needs of fast changing niche markets. The traditional concepts and realities of market domination are fast being called into question. Ready access to world-class production and information technologies means that there are few technical limitations to bringing any product or service to any market from a new source at almost any time. This is already happening with increasing frequency, and as it almost always accompanied by new management approaches, the resulting capabilities and standards of quality present the existing players with stunning new competitive pressures. As newcomers transform definitions of customer value to include design excellence, usability, corporate image and ethics, unique-ness, touch and responsiveness, the ability to redefine the game becomes the competitive high-ground. The growing demand for customized products that closely match individual customer expectations – themselves evolving fast and unpredictably – increases the absolute importance of a recognition that organizational survival depends on being able to change fast, rather than being able to defend a position.

Building the defensible position is a game of statics. The risk is being left holding the junk of yesterday's technology, processes, knowledge, expertise or products. The static positional games of 'competitive advantage' reflect yesterday's mindset. The business world is perhaps now best characterized as a war of movement where corporate Maginot Lines offer little other than a lesson in folly for future generations. Building competitive defences reflects the mindset where control of territory was wealth. This is in an era where it is he who does most with less that wins. It is an era where the 'territorial' cake is not fixed, but capable of perhaps infinite expansion. The rigidities of control and domination approaches are also of little use in a world that is fast coming to base 'competitive advantage' on the ability to dynamically reconfigure everything quickly, and in a world where being fleet of foot and nimble are essentials for survival.

In a world where everyone is aggressively searching for the best practices wherever they can be found, and where innovations, ideas and breakthroughs rapidly find their way across increasingly transparent organizational boundaries, resting on the laurels of past success is as good as resting with them. Without the ability to identify the opportunities and threats in a changing world, and the ability to fast-cycle the required new products and services into the right markets at the right time, the only option will be to stand aside and yield the future to eager and fast-changing global competition.

Being in the right place at the right time is a key to keeping ahead of the competition. Anticipation of competitor and customer actions makes the difference between riding the waves of the future and being crushed by them. Seeing what is likely to happen before it does, makes it possible to be in the right place at the right time, and lessens the prospect of being swept aside by the tides of change. Being able to adjust organizational behaviour rapidly to deal with surprise makes it possible to stay in the game of sustaining distinctiveness in fast-moving restless markets.

Conditions of continuous change make success dependent on being able to realize possibilities with short half-lives of opportunity. It also means doing so where the precedents of history are more likely to confer disadvantage than advantage, and under conditions where fast change is required to sustain the capability to meet potential before it no longer exists (see Figure 1.1). The realization of transient possibilities is perhaps the number one leadership challenge. Meeting this challenge increasingly depends on fast responses, innovation, adaptability and customer orientation.

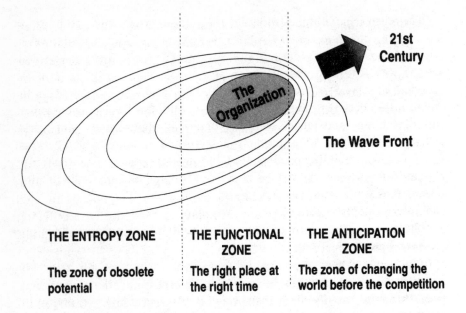

THE ENTROPY ZONE	THE FUNCTIONAL ZONE	THE ANTICIPATION ZONE
The zone of obsolete potential	The right place at the right time	The zone of changing the world before the competition

Figure 1.1   *Meeting potential before it exists*

CUSTOMER ORIENTATION

'Everyone sells intangibles in the marketplace, no matter what is produced in the factory'. (Levitt)

As Drucker pointed out, 'profit can only be earned by providing something that a customer accepts as value and is willing to pay for as such'. Drucker went on to say that, 'what the customer sees, thinks, believes and wants at any given time determines whether value is being created'. In other words, no organization has any right to exist beyond the moment its ceases to create distinctive value for customers – whether or not they have free choice. The complication is that not only is the customer a moving target, the target is now intangible – value is less and less economic, it is increasingly psycho-social.

The universe of the traditional organization revolves around itself and its historic role as the reliever of scarcity. The challenges of production, administration and organizational politics frequently assume greater importance than responding to the requirements for tomorrow's success.

The customer, despite modern rhetoric, is frequently seen as an inanimate economic target that has to be captured and held. However, this approach that sees markets and customers as economic transactions is giving way to a customer-oriented high-touch world. The value of the product or service is increasingly the result of intangibles arising from the relationship between the producer and the customer. Replacing customers as transactions and targets with customers as relationships which arise from the creation of shared values, means moving organizational purposes from building products to building a rapport with the customer. Organizations everywhere are already working to fundamentally redefine themselves to ensure they can identify and deliver on every aspect of a complex customer value equation.

Listening to the voice of the customer is becoming and increasing feature of organizational life everywhere. Instead of customers having products and services made available to them, they are increasingly being directly involved in their design. Everyone from top to bottom in growing numbers of organizations is being given the responsibility to listen to the customer, and being asked to ensure that the information is fed back into product and service designs, and into the production and delivery process required to create what the customer needs and wants. Listening to the voice of the customer accelerates organizations towards to the intangibles market – away from the one of products to the one of what products and services do to reflect customer values. In so doing, listening to the voice of the customer draws the organization from a high mass industrial product-based past to a low mass intangible future based on meetings of minds. However, for tomorrow's organizations, customer orientation is about more than listening to the customer and the benefits this can bring (see Figure 1.2). It is about a predisposition to bring about positive advances to the customer's lifestyle. This means going beyond the preoccupation with products as a means of fulfilling needs or of reflecting customer values. It means reconceiving products and services as customer aids to lifestyle simulation. Products and services are already moving quickly from being static lifestyle accompaniments to being the tools with which ideal-seeking customers can explore the present, simulate the future, uncover new possibilities and by so doing understand, realize, and if necessary, redefine their ideals.

Customer orientation is not that part of the business process that precedes the product or service. Nor is it that part of the business process which comes after to support the imperfect product or service. Customer orientation does not stop at the organization's boundary, or at the boundary between the product and the customer. For tomorrow's organizations, the product or service are the business process in motion. Products and services are the way the organization participates in the customer's lifestyle day by day. Tomorrow's organization sees its reason for being in terms of the realization of customer ideals. It sees it means as intelligent companionship.

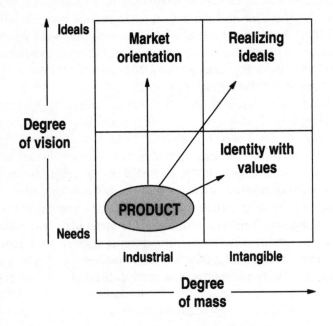

Figure 1.2   *Realizing customers' ideals*

ADAPTABILITY

'Evolution is chaos with feedback.' (Joseph Ford)

Complex social revolutions mean that sustained success depends on leadership in bringing intangible value to choosy and fickle customers. The rate of change, the intensity of competition, new products and new technologies are redefining leadership positions as fast as they can be created. The result is that the only companies who will survive and be around to have a future, will be those that can master the arts of continuous regeneration, and who are able to extend these arts throughout all aspects of the organization – from ideas generation to the delivery of distinctive lifestyle-enhancing satisfactions. The ability to generate ideas is of little use without the ability to realize them, and where each new idea limits the ability to express the next one.

Having a future depends on extending the zone of the possible. In other words extending the zone of the possible beyond the confines of the present (see Figure 1.3). Many organizations have a form of process tunnel vision. They are well tuned to their current vision of the world, and whenever the specifics of their vision change, they simply rebuild the tunnel. This is fine when the rate of change is slow and the new target is stable enough to justify the cost of building a new tunnel. However, when the rate of change is fast, their physical and capital structures lock them out from the new. Having set themselves up to defend one particular prediction of the future, they lock themselves out of the inherently unpredictable future. Strategies and tactics which confine what is possible to a particular prediction will inevitably result in the organization being absorbed by the future. Strategies and tactics which increase the zone of the possible turn change into the opportunity to increase the ways in which the organization's creative capacities can be expressed.

The ability to still do useful things when conditions change is a good measure of organizational adaptability. All organizations can be surprised by events. Those whose usefulness diminishes as a result, lack the required levels of adaptability. Those who are overwhelmed by events, were dead wood awaiting the first storm to clear the way for new growth. The ability

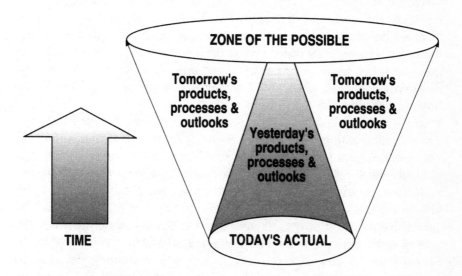

Figure 1.3 *Extending the zone of the possible*

to take in new information, acquire new skills, incorporate new ideas fast, introduce new technology successfully, and replace experience and assets as required, are at the basis of the ability to reconfigure in many ways, and are amongst those things that make the difference between a precarious, and a pre-emptive existence.

The strategies and tactics of competitive domination are devices designed to confine the future or to restrict its possibilities. While on the face of it being means of enabling the organization to meet its goals, they are in fact ways of ensuring it is not round long enough to see them. By attempting to cast the net of the present over the future, the organization is offering the competition unrestricted access to it. Far from disabling the competitors, competitive domination disables the organization by fostering a culture of self-confining isolation. However long it takes, it is only a matter of time before it is shocked by the waves of events passing it by, and before its unreadiness for change declares open season to fast-moving, future-seeking competitors.

No organization can be adaptive if it has locked itself into yesterday's opportunities and yesterday's ways of doing things. Only by developing capabilities that extend the range of the possibilities it can create, can it be positioned to create a future. Competitive progress depends on minimizing the costs of acquiring the new and of discarding the old. It is about how we see the world and what it costs to see the world differently. Anything that increases the costs of change – such as obsolete assumptions and most applications of information technology so far – increases the cost and decreases the likelihood of having a future. Competitive progress becomes a process of searching out what will bring tomorrow's success and transforming the organisation into one which is at home with new ideas and practices – and one which is mature enough to constantly challenge views and assumptions about the whys, whats and hows of growing into the future.

Organizational change is not something that can be done through periodic intervention. Ultimately, it can only come from within, and it can only result from a predisposition to see change as the norm. This in turn can only result from a far-sighted process of equipping the organization and its people to challenge what has been learned in the past, and to be able to apply new learning with distinction in the mind of the customer. A central issue for tomorrow's organizations is how to create the necessary management, cultural, social and technological architecture to enable the organization to absorb new ideas, practices and technologies quickly enough for them still to be useful, and without reducing the ability to change in the future.

Adaptability is fundamentally rooted in the anticipation of change. By being in a position to absorb the unexpected, whether this is fluctuating demand, new competitive practices, shifts in customer tastes, or changes in raw material costs, the organization can continue to evolve towards the future. The many recessionary shocks that recently hit the world economy are less likely to be a result of the inevitability of cyclical forces, and more likely to have been the result of a failure to anticipate them, and a failure to prebuild the capacity to adapt. Long-term changes and long-term cycles, Kondratiev or not, are not only inevitable, they are an essential part of forward growth and development. While it is not possible to predict the future, anticipating it is a way of preparing the abilities required to take it in one's stride. Seeking the future out helps create the kind of place tomorrow's organization needs to be – far-sighted, open, flexible and able to redefine the rules of the game.

Tomorrow's organization is one that believes that growth and success in the nineties and beyond will be dependent on its adaptive capabilities as expressed through its evolving purposes, products and services, and through its evolving means of production and delivery. Stage one in the development of those capabilities might be achieving a balance between the ability to operate in ways which meet in full the conditions of the time while at the same time retaining the scope to operate in other ways should circumstances change. For tomorrow's organization, however, its adaptability rests on developing a total organizational capability that meets the conditions for competitive success when the permanent condition is one of constant change – the ability to change is not something it keeps in reserve. Its measure of adaptability is its ability to stay at the forefront when change is at its most turbulent.

INNOVATION

'Idle dreamers have given true visionaries a bad name.' (Robert Fritz)

Experiencing the unexpected is the watchword of tomorrow's organizations. What will happen next is not known, but being prepared for the unexpected increases the chances of handling it with style and aplomb. Whether it is technological breakthroughs, or new competitors with exciting new product or process innovations that render everything obsolete overnight, thriving on quantum change is fast becoming an everyday survival requirement.

Innovation is one of the very important reflections of the life-forces of tomorrow's organizations. The continuous redefinition of products and services, and the ways in which things are thought about and done, is one of their central and most obvious behavioural characteristics. The ability to create the discontinuities necessary to achieve quantum changes in outcomes is one of the most vital expressions of their innovative capabilities. Grasping the new and discarding the old is what they expect their people to see as mission number one. The continuous regeneration of all aspects of the organization is not only seen as vital, innovation is seen as its essential force. The capacity to undergo quantum change as and when required, is seen as a basic requirement if the organization is to avoid the equally past-preferring slow decline or rapid crash into history. Generating the new and the unexpected has become a minimum requirement for survival in a fast-moving competitive global marketplace.

The innovations required to succeed in the turbulent nineties are not the localized ones of original ideas applied through work-arounds or work-withins of the existing system – though these must always be more than welcome. Nor are they those that sometimes result from buying and installing the latest computer system, acquiring an innovative company, or from poaching the thought leader from some other company. The innovations required are profound and represent a complete redefinition of what value – economic and otherwise – is, and how value can be created and re-created.

The organizational innovations – of which tomorrow's product, service and process innovations will be an expression – require the redefinition of what today's organizations do and how they do it. The necessary redefinitions have their foundations in the ability of the organization and its people to routinely reconceive existing combinations of resources, knowledge, assumptions, values, technologies, processes and skills. It has its foundations in the constant ability of ordinary people to assimilate the new and to discard whatever of the old no longer makes sense. To make innovation a routine of the organization is therefore complex – given where most start from. To become deeply innovative requires fundamental and complex change. To sustain it requires a different organizational paradigm.

Organizational and management assumptions that do not go beyond 'supporting' innovation to being the stuff of innovation, are no more than organizational sticking-the-toe-in-the-water. Unless the familiar is viewed with suspicion, or perhaps better with curiosity, past positions and glories will continue to exert their influence over the present long after their usefulness has ceased. Expectations that are not continuously self-adjusting to welcome and be changed by the new, will inevitably turn the latest invention or technology to the service of the past. Organizations which depend on innovation through complex management process often make the mistake of assuming that innovation is something that is poured into organizations. Successful innovation in organizations has its source in people and managers who, rather than being dedicated to preserving positions, are dedicated to bringing about the future. In tomorrow's organizations, management's role has got little to do with managing the present world of existing resources, assets, processes and assumptions. It has everything to do with making them a force for the future (see Figure 1.4). Innovation of and in organizations can only ever be an expression of a deep commitment to creating the future.

Peters and Waterman described innovative companies as:

> *not only being unusually good at what they do but as being especially adroit at continually responding to change of any sort in their environments. As the needs of their customers shift, the skills of their competitors improve, the mood of the public perturbates, the forces of international trade realign, and government regulations shift, these companies tack, revamp, adjust, transform, and adapt . . . In short, as a whole culture, they innovate.*

The ability to innovate is not about keeping the organization ahead of the competition. It is about redefining the future to be a better place for the organization, its people and its customers. By redefining the future, the organization is never in the morale-sapping game of catch-up. It is in the more exciting game of wave-hopping. The continuous transformation of capabilities that is expressed when innovation is a vital organizational force, is a key to being at home in a changed and changing world. A belief of tomorrow's organization is that change and discontinuity are windows on the future, but ones open only to those whose basic instincts are those of total innovation. A measure of this instinct for innovation is the rate at which the organization is continuously renewing its know-how and challenging and regenerating its capabilities in anticipation of the inevitability of the unexpected. Tomorrow's organization does not see its prospects for the future in terms of the control or ownership of resources, or in the inevitably transitory technological advantage, or in the belief that the occasional breakthrough will guarantee the future. It sees its future prospects in terms of its ability to be a wellspring of innovation applied towards the creation of a more abundant future for its customers and its people.

The ability to change shape quickly to apply new knowledge and ideas is the obsession of tomorrow's organization. The distinctiveness of what it

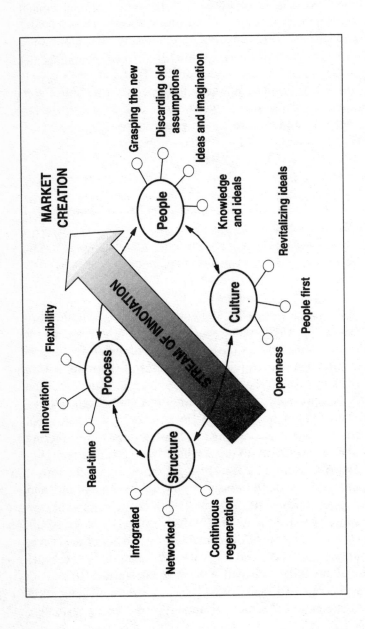

Figure 1.4 *Innovation as a pervasive dynamic force*

sells in the marketplace at any instant in time is the measure of its ability to have changed quickly and successfully the last time. Its prospects for distinction in the future are measured by its total organizational capacity for fundamental change, and by its imagination, spirit and belief in the future. An organization's capacity for fundamental change is the stunning combination of culture, organization, technology, processes, management and people.

The issue for those who aspire to being tomorrow's successful organizations, is the organizational gestalt of how and what they need to be, and the spirit with which they need to go about doing it.

FAST RESPONSES

'Now, here, it takes all the running you can do to keep in the same place. If you want to get somewhere else you must run at least twice as fast as that.'
(The Red Queen)

How fast do you have to run to avoid the obsolescence of products, processes, know-how, distributive channels and assumptions about markets and customers? The answer is fast and all the time. As the pace of change increases, by the time a position of excellence is slipping it is too late. Not to run all the time is to not to appear after the next wave of change.

Running fast means several things. It means being committed to and able to move from identifying customer needs to satisfying them faster than the competition, and faster than the best in whatever industry – that may be where the competition will come from tomorrow. As Stan Davis pointed out, time has joined the ranks of price, quality and service in determining market niches. Products and services that are delivered fastest to the customer increasingly put customer's time back in the customer's control. The transformation of design, development, production and delivery processes to enable them to be rapidly changed, gives the organization more time to exploit short-lived opportunities. The rapid introduction of new practices and technologies extends the time the organization has to operate at distinctive levels of performance. The ability to rapidly match products and services to changing customer tastes combined with the ability to create and deliver them at the moment required, increases the probability of the customer and the organization being in the same place at the same time.

Delivery of products and services to customers fast is already an essential capability. The current level of interest in time-based competition and just-in-time techniques reflects the growing importance of fast responses to increasingly time-sensitive customers, and the central importance of reducing time consumption throughout the entire business process. Delivering satisfaction to time-sensitive customers means reducing the time-lag between the identification of customer needs and the creation and delivery of a customized response. While this means reducing the time it takes to do things, the measure is the amount of time the customer is on hold – the time between the customer needing to do something and being able to do it.

The business process re-engineering movement is one of the ways in which attention is being focused on the time-critical business activities. Time-critical activities are those which determine the ability to meet customer needs as and when they occur. Re-engineering, although a new and rapidly evolving discipline, has begun to address all aspects of the business cycle: the time to identify needs is being reduced; the time taken to turn identified needs into solution designs; the time taken to translate design ideas into products; and the time it takes to deliver the satisfaction to the customer. Re-engineering is already beginning to blur the distinction between products and services. As the time between identified need and its fulfilment compresses, so the product development/delivery cycle gradually moves towards becoming a real-time experience. Indeed, as overall cycle time diminishes, the distinction blurs. This is perhaps the real meaning of the 'Service Economy'. In its truest sense, services do not replace manufacturing, they become expressions of the same thing – real-time experience.

World-class fast responses typically require a radical rethink of the business process end-to-end, and a rethink that turns notions of product development, production, distribution, and the delivery processes upside-down. The radical reductions in product and process cycle times required if the company is to distinguish itself in the face of dynamic competitors, requires more than streamlining or contouring existing processes. Reducing the time to identify needs, the time taken to turn identified needs into solution designs, the time taken to translate design ideas into products, and the time it takes to deliver the satisfaction to the customer, are seldom the result of 10 per cent reductions in time and 10 per cent improvements in efficiencies. Accelerating the 'traditional' business process is not the issue. Notions of business processes consisting of simple unidirectional flows and beginnings and ends – the 'supply chains' and 'value chains' with their heavy industrial age connotations – must be discarded and replaced with notions of the dynamic assembly of nodes of capability. What needs acceleration is the rate at which the best node of capability can be identified and brought into the value-generating equation. And what needs acceleration is the rate at which each node anticipates the future, discards its past assumptions and maintains a high rate of continuous forward evolution (see Figure 1.5). The 'business process', far from being a backwater means to an end, is the crucible where the past and the waves of the future collide. Tomorrow's organization occupies a zone of continuous metamorphosis where the time it takes to regenerate determines organizational survival.

TRANSFORMATIONAL THEMES

The performance imperatives of customer orientation, adaptability, innovation and fast responses are provoking a fundamental rethink of every aspect of the business cocktail. The issue is, what does it take to have fast responses, to be innovative, to adapt and to be customer oriented?

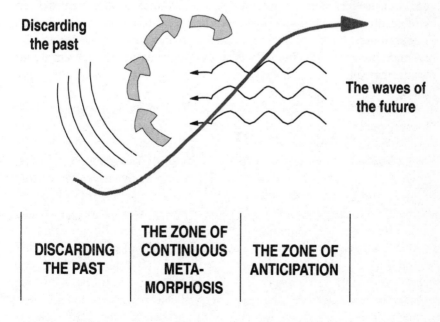

Figure 1.5 *Discarding the old, embracing the new*

Put another way, what has to be different if a company is to maintain leadership when the conditions for sustained success rest on world-class responsiveness, customer satisfaction, innovativeness and adaptability?

Tomorrow's organization is characterized by the investments it makes in capabilities. It is less concerned with investing in particular products than it is with investing in the ability to conceive, design, produce and deliver them. It is more concerned with creating the capabilities required to enable the business to prosper in an uncertain and rapidly changing world, than with building its future on the outcomes of a single prediction. In other words, tomorrow's organization is characterized by its commitment to enhancing its ability to perform excellently within the unstable dynamics of an unforeseeable future. Rather than concentrating everything on addressing each product opportunity and its production requirements as they arise – the shanty town strategy – tomorrow's organization invests to build the capability to address opportunity before it arises.

The nature of the challenges faced by tomorrow's organization, and the nature of the responses it must make, are the consequences of the arrival of a new paradigm of business. This paradigm shift is not restricted to any one dimension of the business system. It is not about culture or systems, or people or organization being the magic of business. It is not about the additive effects of culture, systems, people and organization – important as these are. It is about the multiplicative effects of these. It is about a radical change in their form and character. It is about new models of what organizations are becoming. It is about a fundamental organizational transformation.

2 Embracing the Customer

'Service can be described as the integration of two actors.' (Alvin Toffler)

STAGING THE PERFORMANCE

Tomorrow's organizations are in the business of creating lifestyle-enhancing possibilities. Their aim is not to dictate, control or sell customer lifestyles – it is to co-create customer futures. Their medium is the product or service and the process by which they are created. The medium is not passive – it is one that enables customers to discover and extend the physical and mental boundaries of their own lifestyles. As new high quality, high touch, customer tailorable and customer-specific products and services flood into the market, we are fast getting to the stage where the product or service specification is relatively unimportant. We are fast getting to the point where it is the ability of the product to dynamically empower the customer to enhance his or her lifestyle that makes the difference between active, highly-prized companion and passive low-value commodity.

What is fast becoming important, is the extent to which the product or service reflects, enhances and fits with the customer's evolving lifestyle. To customers with fast-changing needs, static physical products and static designs run the risk of being deadly embraces – something that gets in the way after its short period of usefulness has passed, or when it has served its limited purpose in moving the customer forward. Two challenges arise. The first is to design and deliver what fits a complex customer lifestyle at a moment in time. The second is to enable the customer to dispose of it, or redesign it, when it has fulfilled its role in taking the customer to the next level of lifestyle evolution.

Product design and delivery is becoming indistinguishable from service design and delivery – the technical quality of both has to be a given for the producer to even be short-listed. Traditional approaches to both product and service design are already too slow and too confining – even with intensive market research, products and services run the risk of being overly general and bland. Traditional approaches also reflect the notion that design is static and that the product or service is its sole expression.

They risk pinning the relationship with the customer on one design that can never have more than fleeting relevance. For tomorrow's organizations, the process of design is the product, and the process of continuous design is the cornerstone of continued connectedness with the customer's lifestyle. The basis of connectedness with the customer is becoming less an issue of communicating a designer's idea or 'solution', it is rapidly becoming centred in a process of continuous dialogue between two people both intent on uncovering or defining what is going to make a difference to both.

The concerns of tomorrow's organizations shift from the tangible ones of control over resources, capital, technology, people and customers, to intangible ones such as customer-specific knowledge, a sense of timing, sensitivity to the customer, intent, and the ability to build a rapport. The sense that the customer has of being listened to and responded to as an individual by an organisation which is concerned about what the customer values, will increasingly determine if the organization has any customers. This will mean letting go of the obsession with the product – its technical quality must be a given – and replacing product obsession with an obsession with distinctive relationships with evolving customer lifestyles. The organizations that maintain their connectedness with what the customer is learning will be the only ones with any prospects of having a future (see Figure 2.1).

Figure 2.1 *Staging the performance*

Maintaining connectedness with the customer requires knowledge of where the customer's lifestyle is at any point in time. The aim is a mutual attraction where the organization and the customer are committed to the same goal – extending boundaries to mutual benefit. Forecasting, interviewing, guesswork and periodic market research will increasingly be of little use. Longer term, there are perhaps only two ways forward. The first is to make every customer encounter a designing experience for both the organization and the customer – the 'solution' is not prejudged by a particular product or service. The second is to put designing tools at the disposal of the customer, and by providing the means of access to the best in the world, enable the customer to self-realize a preferred solution. By putting designing in the shop window, the organization becomes increasingly reflected in its customers, and its customers can become the mirrors in which the organisation can see and judge its own appearance and appeal.

Loyalty is as desirable and attainable an asset as it ever was. But loyalty is no longer bred of habit or acquired by precedent – nor is it the steady state of passive allegiance. Loyalty that results from the lock-in strategies characteristic of many loyalty schemes will disappear the moment customers sense that they are being crudely manipulated. The sense that the customer gets that the organization is committed to the goals of extending boundaries and increasing possibilities, is the only source of long term loyalty. And that can only come from increasing the customer's lifestyle designing power, not from convincing the customer to confine it. In the longer term, loyalty can only come from continued mutual development – organizations that are not developing fast will inevitably be left behind by customers who are. Embracing the customer is not about feathering the cage – it is about opening it.

Embracing the customer creates a need for a 'high contact' organization – one where everyone is dedicated to be in tune with the customer and to extending the organization's understanding and customer-serving capabilities. For the customer to get the sense of being personally recognized – and not merely detected or transacted – the organization needs to have its entire customer relationship instantly available at the point of contact with the customer. By increasing the scope and sensitivity of customer contact, the goal is to make it possible for the customer to feel he or she is being seen as unique. By having the organization sensitized to the customer, the organization in total is predisposed to mobilize whatever resources and capabilities are required. By putting its designing capabilities to the fore, it is predisposed to deliver the one solution that will uniquely satisfy the customer's needs. For tomorrow's organization, customer contact is the vital factor that brings the organization into action. Customer contact is also the unique co-ordinator of the organization's actions and its ability to deliver the unique one-time-only customer response.

Maintaining connectedness with the customer's lifestyle absolutely depends on maintaining a complex relationship between 'customer' and 'producer'. As this has less to do with the specific characteristics of a product at a specific point in time, and more to do with the effectiveness of the design process in keeping the organization and the customer engaged in a mutually rewarding dialogue, the more that the business process must operate on a human rather than institutional wavelength. In the not too distant future, the time lags usually associated with product and service design, production and delivery will seem 'geological' – and just about as relevant to day-to-day living. The more that the effectiveness of the connection the organization can make with its customer is dependent on the immediate response to unique customer needs, the more that design, production and delivery must occur simultaneously. The issue for tomorrow's organization becomes one of how to make what used to be worlds apart in time, space and thought – marketing/design/R&D, production and delivery – into an instantaneous high contact surface that senses, simulates and creates unique experience through the integration of the world's best into evolving customer lifestyles.

Instantaneous feedback arising from close design-oriented connections with the customer accelerates organizational learning. The designing capabilities of the organization move from being the means of expressing what the organization thinks it knows about the customer, to being the means of combining what the customer and the organization know. More importantly, each design encounter redesigns what the organization knows – the organization learns and is changed by what it learns in real-time. The faster it learns and is changed by what it learns, the more relevance it can incorporate into its next customer encounter.

Embracing the customer is an expression of the design orientation of the organization. This is not a process of surrounding the customer with what is known, nor is it a process of packaging the product with a series of lifestyle adjuncts. It is about enabling the customer to make a difference. For organizations concerned with having a future, enabling the customer to make a difference is not a once-off event – most products and services can only make a difference once. It is about redesigning the relationship between producer and customer to allow the organization to make its distinctive contributions in new ways.

MEETINGS OF MINDS

The opportunity to create lifestyle-enhancing possibilities depends on means-independent relationships with evolving customer purposes. Since building these relationships depends on touching the customer through involvement, tomorrow's organization is more concerned with customers as wholes than as segments. Given the central importance of designing to the forward development of the relationship, the required mutual recognition cannot be achieved when the image of the customer has been derived only from small series of low-resolution scans. A high definition image is required (see Figure 2.2). This high definition scan must go beyond the simple economic or social contexts, and create a real contact between customer ideals and how he or she can be empowered to discover, extend and realize them.

The starting point needs to be to put the human back into the concept of customer. Anything less than being able to view the customer as a human whole, with a dynamic nature, an evolving lifestyle, and a future to which they aspire, will immediately announce the fact that the organization is stupid. A holistic and visceral understanding of customer behaviours is increasingly a basic requirement if the organization is to configure its approach and offerings in a way that results in a meeting of minds between the producer and customer. Only from a position of being

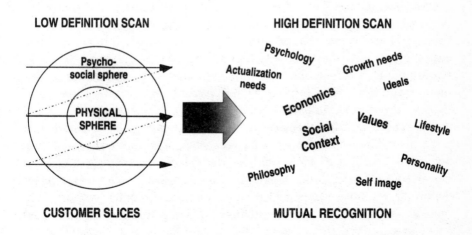

Figure 2.2 *Meetings of minds*

engaged with the customer's immediate needs can the organization develop its understanding of how it fits with and enhances a customer's lifestyle as a whole. Only from this position will the organization be able to make sense of the variety and complexity of the customer's behaviour, and will the customer be able to make sense of the organization's response. This is not easy, nor can it ever be fully achieved, but a designing approach will make progress possible. Designing becomes the means of the customer and the organization both making progress.

Static definitions of the customer's context are of little value. These are profoundly judgmental and inherently confining. For tomorrow's organizations, the customer is an open system – one that cannot be defined, and one whose future definition must undoubtedly include surprise. Identification of the developmental factors – the factors that can and will contribute to the extension of customer boundaries – is what is important. Tomorrow's organizations are already going beyond the use of the concepts and methods of customer behaviour analysis – they confine the organization to tracking and responding to the customer's behaviours. They are beginning to redefine their ability to be concerned co-definers and co-producers of customer lifestyle visions. Being positioned as concerned co-definers and co-producers, enables the organization to work with the customer in real-time to create their futures. Prejudice and guesswork cannot be part of the process – they will limit the customer by confining him or her to their past, or limit the organization by its blatant lack of concern.

Of course, the customer cannot be described or understood definitively. Any understanding of customer behaviour should only be relative to what the customer wants the organization to know. Understanding the customer is not about voyeurism, although that in some form is important. It is about dialogue with customers, and in particular, the mutual search for a definition of what is valuable. As such it – value – is a moving target. As anyone who has built one will know, customer databases are hazardous. Increasing the understanding of the customer is not a case of increasing how much customer data is stored, it much more about how to change views of how the customer can and should be perceived and understood. It is also much less a case of attempting to define the absolutes demanded by most current computer systems, and more a case of identifying cues, pointers and indicators which can lead to a human-centred dialogue about how to help the customer create his or her future.

ACCUMULATING VALUE

For tomorrow's organizations, value is accumulated through a designing relationship which evolves along with evolving customer lifestyle boundaries. The business process – the means by which world class resources are brought together to assemble and integrate a unique customer experience – is not the product. The designing capabilities of the organization applied in the direction of redefining customer boundaries, are where value is created. The forward-oriented development and application of those designing capabilities determines the value accumulated over the longer term. The business process, to the extent that it does not operate flawlessly, can only diminish the quality of the experience anticipated during the designing process.

Product quality is a reflection of the extent to which what is delivered meets the design specification. Process quality reflects the ability of the process to produce products which meet the design specification. An obsession with these technical definitions of quality is important, but technical assessments of quality only reflect the extent to which delivery meets specification. Increasingly, the ability to produce precisely to specification is a hygiene factor – it does not create value but its absence can destroy it. The ability to produce precisely to specification is increasingly a minimum entry requirement for being in business. For tomorrow's organizations, the first important issue is the one of design validity – the extent to which the design meets the customer's actual rather than inferred needs. The second important issue is design vitality – the extent to which the organization's designing capacity plays a living role in the furtherance of the customer's lifestyle over the longer term.

For the customer relationship to be vital and alive, each customer encounter must be seen as an opportunity to gain a new insight into how to apply designing skills to further develop the mutual attraction between the organization and the customer. The need for a holistic perspective on the customer and his or her lifestyle requires the organization's designing capacity to be its point of contact with the customer. The task is not the one of bringing the different and often narrow R&D, marketing, production, sales, distribution and service perspectives together, the task is to find a way of putting the organization's various sensory capacities at the disposal of the front-line and/or directly at the disposal of the customer during design-centred encounters. The 'value chain' shifts from being a sequence of events or steps, to being a number of inputs, resources or tools available to those engaged in the co-design of customer experiences.

EXPRESSING INTELLIGENCE

Tomorrow's organizations are not primarily characterized by what they know – though this is profoundly important. They are primarily characterized by how they go about developing shared understandings of what makes sense for customers. Their emphasis is not on predicting customer behaviour, it is on being in touch with actual behaviour. Tomorrow's organization uses its designing behaviour to engage the customer, and this is the way in which it stays in touch with the real world. The organization's intelligence is therefore not what it knows, it is how it is seen to behave – and this is primarily in terms of its social behaviour. As primarily a social animal, its primary social behaviour is that of concerned and informed one-to-one conversation about possibilities, and how the customer might best be empowered to realize them.

Behaving in a human way and not in an industrial way, is essential if the space for human-centred possibilities is to be created. The low-touch high-impact industrial model can only prevent the organization from establishing a rapport with increasingly intangible-seeking customers. For the organization, the issue is increasingly one of the rate at which it is able to increase its abilities to work with the customer to develop a mutual understanding of the customer's requirements and how best to fulfil them. Unless it is able to maintain a mutual attraction with its customers, they will spot its irrelevance before it does. Unless it can offer a response which is relevant to fast-changing customers, it is immobilized. For the customer, the intelligence of an organization is a simple reflection of whether or not the organization, in a holistic sense, is in touch and able to make a difference. If how the organization goes about things makes a meaningful and relevant contribution to the immediate developmental needs of the customer, or helps intelligently to create the conditions where the future is more likely to evolve in a fulfilling way, then that organization will be seen as 'knowing what it is doing'.

Organizational intelligence is therefore not the result of a process of massive data gathering – though this can be useful. It is a reflection of the organization's learning orientation, and one which has its foundation not in the accumulation of knowledge, but in its ability to redefine what it can do in the light of newly discovered insights into the customer's requirement.

Tomorrow's organization develops its capabilities to express three aspects of intelligent behaviour. The first is that it develops its designing abilities as a means of engaging the customer in active inquiry and discovery. The second is that it uses its resources and capabilities as tools in a co-simulation of what could and can be realized to meet the customer's requirement. Thirdly, it designs and develops its business processes to enable the flawless expression of the agreed design. By doing all three and appearing intelligent, far-sighted and helpful, tomorrow's organizations can be in a position to generate value through the creation of a powerful mutual attraction (see Figure 2.3).

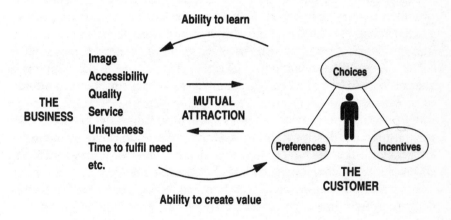

Figure 2.3 *Creating value through mutual attraction*

CATCHING THE MOMENT

The trend reflected in companies re-engineering business processes to reduce the time it takes to deliver the product or service, and the dead time between production and delivery, is less to do with being able to do things faster. Viewed fundamentally, it is about developing the capabilities required to change what is done whenever and wherever required. Unless attention is focused on developing the instincts and abilities required to identify changing customer needs, and developing the ability to transform to fulfil them, the organization will do no more than change once. When what is required is the ability to change rapidly and continuously, the once-off change will be seen as the last gasp of a dying organization. The ability to continuously change has less to do with tools and techniques. It has perhaps more to do with observation, sensitivity, concern, awareness and nimbleness than with techniques like business process re-engineering.

Catching the moment is about the predisposition to change. Clearly, changes in the organization's perceptions of its customers must precede any change in what the organization does and how it does it in the future. However, if the time it takes to deliver the product or service is glacial, and the dead time between production and delivery is soporific, then the organization will at best be seen as well-intentioned but clumsy and insensitive. Good timing in a fast changing world must be accompanied by a predisposition for change. Fast reflexes tuned to do one thing only may be suited to very simple high volume products, but will not be effective when dealing with the prevailing complex conditions and with the creation of powerful relationships with customer values. Catching the moment is for the most part an adaptive response, that is, one which requires a change for it to be produced. The change may be structural or procedural, or to organization or resource configurations, or involve roles, assumptions, attitudes and relationships – whatever it takes to enable the organization to do something differently than it was able to before it encountered the customer and their need. Ideally, it must also be accompanied by changes which make it easier to change next time round.

The predisposition to change is reflected in the ability to catch ever-decreasing windows of opportunity. What exists today must not determine what may exist tomorrow. There must be a recognition that much of what exists today must inevitably be irrelevant to the needs of tomorrow. There must also be the ability to reconfigure what exists today, incorporate the new and discard the old if the organization is to remain connected to the fast-moving wave of what works today and tomorrow. In this process of adaptation, perhaps the human aspects of change are the most important of all. We cannot change easily unless we are aware of what connects us to the past and present, and what blinds us to new perspectives and horizons. A priority is the constant review and transformation of the organizational learning process reflected in policies, procedures, processes, attitudes and assumptions. For the future-oriented organization, this organizational transformation is not just a process of challenging the old and championing the new, it is about developing the capabilities of the organization to recognize what is inhibiting progress towards a dynamic state or condition in tune with a surprising high energy world.

All organizations inhabit the narrow space between what no longer works and makes sense, and what meets the needs of customers who aspire to realize their futures. Occupying that space requires the instincts of the surfer – keenly and holistically tuned to fast moving currents and constantly seeking to be propelled by their energy. Tomorrow's organization develops its sense of the energies of tomorrow's relevances. In the past, you could be content with catching the spirit of the age. Now, catching the moment is the key.

LEARNING LOOPS

Traditional one-way 'communication' directed at the customer, or simple two-way communication involving the exchange of scant detail, is obsolete in a world where organizations can no longer tell people what they want – and where organizations that don't listen don't get to hear what they do. In tomorrow's organizations, the use of communication is giving way to a process of learning-oriented inquiry. Learning and exploration is replacing telling and selling. Tomorrow's organization wants to enable its customers to change in ways they see as bringing about a better future. Its customers are those committed to extending their boundaries in a positive and informed way. They are fast-changing. The connection between the organization and its customers is the mutual positive-sum learning that results from their relationship. As the customer learns so must the organization. And, as learning becomes part of the organization/customer relationship, fast-learning becomes a fundamental part of the process of continuously seeking out what customers will value, however much these needs change, and of the process of changing to reflect what needs to be done to meet those needs.

Faster feedback increases the effect what is heard will have. Faster feedback makes it more likely that what is heard will seem to be real and meaningful. It also makes it possible to learn faster, try more things out and thereby create more opportunity to get 'it' right. In tomorrow's organization, the marketing, design and product development cycle is more a process of inquiry and definitely not a process of one-way, 'source to sink' communication. The cycle is increasingly becoming a joint one, involving the customer as a co-designer, as faster organizational feedback speeds to the level of human conversation.

As satisfying customers with one-off products and services tailored to meet their individual needs becomes more important, it becomes a primary responsibility of everyone throughout the organization – not only those in sales and marketing who deal with customers every day – to identify customers' individual needs, to find ways to meet them better and to do so in full knowledge of what the competition can do. Few assumptions can be made about the customer or about what will satisfy their needs. Each encounter has to be a forum for mutual exploration of how to extend the boundary of the possible, and how to find the means to bring into existence that which did not exist before the encounter. Information technology is rapidly making it possible for organizations of all sizes to build convincing profiles of customers and their behaviours. Bringing an intimate sense of the customer and what is likely to satisfy them next time round, increases the necessity of direct involvement of everyone in the process of designing, developing and delivering products or services. It can also make a major contribution to everyone feeling they are co-designers of customer satisfaction.

The need to improve customer orientation from listening to delivery – and in the widest sense – is driving increased management interest in increasing the learning orientation of the organization and its people. This learning orientation is becoming dramatically important. The growing immediacy and organizational breadth of the organization/customer dialogue greatly increases the potential for organizational learning, and the prospects of real customer value arising from customer-knowledge intensive offerings. Importantly, organizations with short customer learning loops can shift their emphasis from one of pushing solutions, to one of enabling its people to engage with their customers in the search for solutions. Shorter learning loops exposes them to new ideas, technologies and practices more frequently, and constantly challenges them to introduce customer-enhancing innovations faster. The shorter learning loops that result from linking inquiry, the perceived need for change and its application, greatly increases the chances of the organization and its people being prepared, getting it right at the right time, and being in the wrong place at the wrong time less often. As getting it right more often at the moment of truth becomes ever more critical to competitive success (see Figure 2.4), constant inquiry-led learning provides the means for continuous re-adjustment of company positioning – and for the constant preparation of the organization to respond to whatever inquiry uncovers. Simple prediction may miss the mark. Simply learning from the customer restricts him or her to what he or she can imagine. The aim of learning loops is to increase the mutual perception of what is possible and will make a meaningful difference – and to encourage the continuous regeneration of the means.

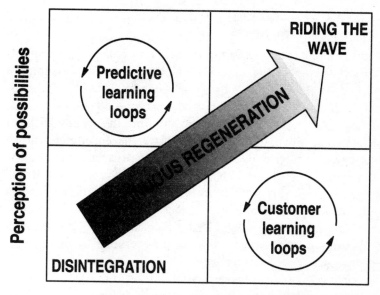

Figure 2.4 *Learning loops*

INDIVIDUATION

Mass markets are exploding into niches that are uniquely defined by the latent and expressed wishes and needs of increasingly individualistic people. Only those companies who can identify and address increasingly smaller niches by constantly pushing, dividing, and redefining current niche boundaries can follow the trend from markets to individual needs.

The ability to address individual customer needs will decide who will succeed and who will fail. Unless the needs of customers as individuals are known, the high costs of the blanket advertising and sales campaigns required to reach 'target markets' will make an increasingly attractive target for any competitor with a keener sense of the individual and unique. The relative costs of serving mass markets versus the costs serving individual unique customers have long been in favour of the former. With the only and ultimate response to the market fast becoming the unique response to the individual, and as the costs of addressing shrinking mass markets increases, the unique response will increasingly become the only cost effective response. As the resources required to deliver the response become increasingly complex, intangible and information intensive, those

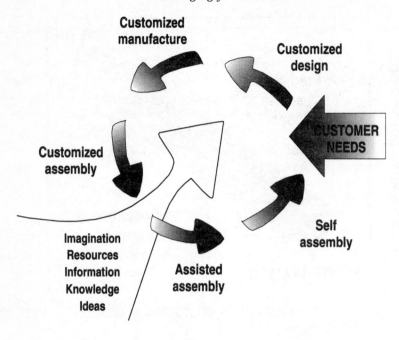

Figure 2.5   *The customization cycle*

who fundamentally redefine the individuation cycle will create the greatest opportunity (see Figure 2.5).

   How do you know what people want when they don't know themselves? After all, there are a lot of customers who only know what they want when they can see it or when they can 'test-drive' it. It is interesting to reflect on why this is easier for the customer to do when buying a car than buying a financial services product. But the problem is widespread. If many people can only relate to what they can see and touch and reflect upon, how do you test market? Knowing exactly what individual customers want means working with them as co-designers to explore needs, simulate possibilities and realize the next step in lifestyle evolution. Real-time designing simulations are already being used to go beyond traditional test marketing techniques. The Japanese consumer electronics industry is already putting the process of exploratory design directly into the hands of the customer. For them there is no such thing as a static design – product design is seen as an evolving real-time, real-life simulation. The latest ideas and features are attached to each generation of the product enabling the customer to 'play' with it and then decide whether it is a good idea or not. Feedback can then be based actual customer responses to the feature in use in the customer's context. And given short product development cycles, the design rapidly be re-expressed in its next form. By investing to have these tight listening feedback loops on what individual customers value and what they do not, design features can be retained, enhanced or removed from the next live simulation. Real-time co-designing intimately links the development of the organization to where the individual customer is going, enabling it to stay in touch with its future.

More fundamentally, real-time exploratory design is one way in which a continuous search for the customer takes place. And specifically it is the search for the product or service design that best meets the customer's needs. This however may still reflect a 'push' view of the world. If it is seen as a process of assisting the customer in his or her search for what they value, then it reflects a 'pull' world. For tomorrow's organization, the definition of 'pull' goes beyond simply being 'customer driven'. It means empowering the customer in his or her search for individual value.

EMPOWERING THE CUSTOMER

The ability of organizations to create customer value will increasingly depend on their ability to enable customers to create unique experiences and lifestyles. Tomorrow's organizations are already shifting rapidly towards expanding the capabilities of the customer to get what they want, or to do what they need to do. A characteristic capability of tomorrow's organization is its ability to deal with the unique and to put the unique within the grasp of all.

Creation of the unique depends on being able to identify and bring together a unique combination of tangible and intangible resources that together enable the customer to meet his or her unique needs. All organizations will increasingly depend on their abilities as lifestyle integrators – those able to enhance the whole from any one part. The only, and apparent, differences between organizations and industries will be the kinds and scope of lifestyle engineering they choose to specialize in.

Airlines and travel companies are two current examples of lifestyle integrators. In these cases, the trend is towards customers taking the lead in the design of their own lifestyles – the organization's mission is to reduce the boundaries of the lifestyles that may be created. The plane is merely the support infrastructure – or stage – and an increasing range of possibilities are provided from which the customer can choose and create his or her own lifestyle for the time period in question – increasingly intangible lifestyles are increasingly disposable. In the airline industry, the range of things the customer can use to shape his or her experience has already been extended to include to space, comfort, personal attention, time, nutrition, stimulation, art, work, information and communication – vast technological achievements have already been 'relegated' to the role of a lens capable of focusing the best of human achievements, and all the known wonders of space and time, in unique combination onto one individual 35,000 feet above the earth's surface. And still we complain. Travel companies do the same thing as airlines, but extend the boundaries to include being able to experience the sunshine, get wet in the rain, breathe the air and meet the people.

All of tomorrow's organizations specialize in making the integration of things, ideas, philosophies and concepts into customer lifestyles possible – and in the enhancement and creation of new lifestyles. In the social and organizational contexts, integrating new ideas, assumptions, practices, processes and relationships into individual or corporate lifestyles can be a very complex process – but unless organizations can do it, they are dumping the problem of integration on the customer. All organizations live in a complex world. One where the customer is only empowered when his or her lifestyle is extended or redefined in a positive way by encountering the organization directly through the use of its products.

Whatever the industry, the ability to design – and/or the ability to facilitate the realization of design – is becoming the front line and the value-added dimension of business. The creation of meaningful products and services increasingly depends on the creation of a complex, and one-off configurations of ever more diverse resources, which in unique combination meet the specific needs of the customer. This is an area in which organizations can and must distinguish themselves. To have any meaning, the ability to create the unique customer specification must be matched to the delivery capability. The operations, manufacturing, distribution and whatever other capabilities of the organization make sense, must be in a position to provide access to whatever resources are required to realize the customer's individual design at the instant the design is recognized and agreed. Tomorrow's organization has two primary capabilities – the ability to co-design lifestyle enhancements with informed customers, and the ability to enable the customer to synthesize that design from the necessary tangible and intangible resources wherever they are located. In a real sense, the customer must be able to self-realize the design.

As designers and integrators, tomorrow's organizations have to be boundary-less. In effect, they create value by providing the customer with gateways to the best information, knowledge, products, services, arts and experiences in the world, and by their ability to apply design and integrative skills to enable the customer to achieve the required customer-specific lifestyle enhancement. The role of the customer is fast shifting from passive and uniformed recipient of whatever is on offer from the organization. Increasingly, customers have many gateways to the best and will, before long, have increasingly powerful tools at their disposal to enable them to reach for what they want and need. As the sophistication of software tools extends their conceptual skills and boundaries, they will expect more of what used to be at the disposal of organizations to be at their disposal. A key to creating value in a future of highly informed, capable and empowered customers, lies not in holding capabilities behind the organizational walls, but in enlarging the capabilities in the hands of the customer. The key skills become those of making the best in the world integratable and in offering the tools – software agents, knowledge, experience, ideas and concepts – which allow the customer to self-integrate unique solutions and experiences in a boundless multi-integratable world. Design and the designing experience are no longer peripheral to the customer and to business. The unique experience is the customer-empowered design and integration of the best of human achievement.

THE RELATIONSHIP IS THE PRODUCT

Design and integration organizations operating in customer lifestyle enhancing ways, are in the business of providing gateways, tools and skills that enable the customer to extend his or her capabilities and lifestyle boundaries. As the value of what organizations do and how they do it becomes increasingly the product of their ability to create possibilities for the customer, organizations which do not extend boundaries will be seen as limiting them. The customers of organizations which reduce net lifestyle value – and there are many – will represent attractive targets for organizations committed to lifestyle enhancement. As organizations move from and through the 'push' and 'pull' phases of business evolution, those that become the best enablers of lifestyle value creation, rather than the simple producer of products or services with no concern with where they fit, will become highly valued co-creators of customer value.

As the perceived quality of the organization and what it can do depends on the quality of the individual customer's experience of his or her interaction with the business, the role of products and services is shifting to that of a catalyst in the many complex interactions between producer and the customer. To effectively co-design and integrate organizational expertise with the individual customer's needs and lifestyle, the organization must be able to identify and respond to the uniqueness of the customer's ideals and lifestyle patterns. As the organization becomes a co-designer, so must the customer be increasingly considered as the primary creator of the product or service. In other words, the ability of the organization to enable the customer to realize his or her dreams, determines the relationship the organization has with what is valuable to the customer.

Co-creation requires a 'place' where the customer and the organization can interact. These shared spaces or virtual markets are replacing marketplaces. Markets, if they ever were, are no longer physical targets for goods or services. Nor are they, as Stan Davis pointed out, physical places, but shared environments in which customers' needs can be identified and in which a valuable experience can be created.

The customer relationship becomes the market niche defined by a unique contribution to the evolution of customer's ideals and lifestyles. The perceived quality of the relationship depends on the customer perceiving that the organization is the best, and highly attuned to what it takes to make a real difference to the customer. If the organization and the customer are on the same wavelength, then and only then will the customer invite the organization to show what it can do. These wavelength-defined markets place high demands on the organization's outlooks and attitudes – the ability of the business to bring together all the resources required to design and integrate a high quality customer experience is becoming technically straightforward all the time. The increasingly intangible nature of these wavelength-defined marketspaces makes the human dimension in business far more important than the technical one. As the technology becomes more powerful and easier to use, the intangible resources – such as knowledge, trust, creativity, skills and integrity – play the lead role in holding the marketspace together.

Marketspaces, and the human and technical requirements for holding them together, therefore define the business. Increasingly, staying in touch with what it takes to enhance the customer's lifestyle requires sensing, design and integration skills to be in the front-line of a network which accesses the world's best. The growing need to deal with experience design and its creation in real-time, requires that the growing importance of the human element is integrated with the ability to bring together intangibles and tangibles in real-time, to ensure that products and services and experiences can be designed, produced, and delivered to exacting customer requirements – as and when required. As the product falls from centre stage, the human agenda in organizations must be revisited and revised. How can the sensing, designing and integrative skills be amplified, and how can they have the best in the world put at their disposal? How do management and business processes need to be redefined to enable customers and people to work together, using their imaginations to manipulate tangibles and intangibles towards the enhancement of the customer's lifestyle?

Tomorrow's organizations are in the business of bringing the best in the world to the customer's actual or electronic doorstep. They are also in the business of providing the expertise and tools which enable the customer to design and realize lifestyle enhancements. Its economic reward, as ever, lies in what the customer will pay. The important message is that they never pay for the product, but for what it can do for them. The distinctive change in their lifestyle is what they pay for.

Market niches which are defined by the complex and changing characteristics of customer ideals and lifestyles, depend on the ability to identify what is unique, and on the ability to create the unique in a way which enhances the overall effect. Designing and integrating the unique is a dynamic process where increasingly it must be the customer who is control. As each customer's understanding of what they need and their ability to create it is at a different stage – and evolving continuously over time – what the organization can offer and in what way, depends on it being acknowledged as having recognized and respected the situation. For tomorrow's organization to increase the spaces within which it can utilize its talents and abilities, it must be constantly redefining them. Markets are no longer even remotely static definitions or classifications – they are the dynamic spaces in which the organization and customer can meet to develop a shared understanding and co-create a unique experience. The concept of distribution, or its equivalent, shifts from being a way of getting to a niche, to a way of bringing the world to a niche. The impending explosion of customer on-demand electronic channels – low-cost personal computer systems integrated with home-based broadband multimedia – will provide an explosion in the access the customer has to the best in the world. It will also, in a few decades, extend the number of accessible marketspaces in which customers and suppliers can interact to the 7–10 billion people that will be around at that time. Marketspaces will become the dynamic excellence-populated environments in which customers can design and extend lifestyle boundaries.

EMPOWERING THE FRONT LINE

With so much hinging on meeting the unique with the unique – and with intangibles being used to create the intangibles of customer value – organizations need to be able to bring the best of the world's capabilities and its intangible and tangible resources to bear at the moment of customer contact. In the customer's eyes, tomorrow's organization is the gateway to the best in the world. The person at the point of contact with the customer is its human interface – he or she is seen as what the organization can do for the customer. The impressions gained during that period of contact, however short of long it may be, set the tone and expectation, not so much about what the organization can do, but more about what the experience of doing it will be like. At that point, the customer does not see the individual as only one cog in a giant and impressive machine which has vast wealth and technology at its disposal. What the customer sees is what he or she will be getting for his or her money.

The front-line is the organization's point of contact with the world. The front-line of the organization is the only place that an informed learning-oriented dialogue can take place. There are several requirements for the dialogue to result in the organization being able to create excellence for the customer by assembling its best possible response. The point of

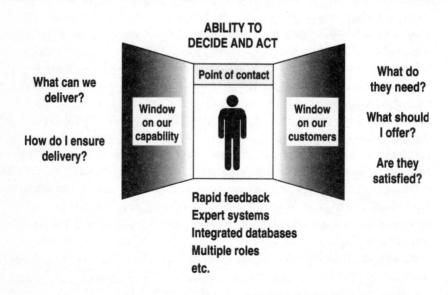

Figure 2.6 *Empowering the front line*

contact must be empowered to decide on how best to meet the customer's needs and to invoke the organization to respond in the best way (see Figure 2.6).

All barriers to open dialogue with the customer must be eliminated. All internal barriers must be replaced with the means of enabling the instant response. Every possible point of contact with the customer – not just the formal ones of marketing – is being recognized as a primary source of dialogue with what is happening in the marketplace and with customers. The front-line's importance as a two-way organization/customer dialogue channel is now paramount as organizations recognize that their futures depend on their abilities to: express what it can bring to enhance the customer's individual lifestyle, express what it can uniquely contribute to the design and integration of lifestyle enhancement, and to ensure that what the organization knows tracks fast changing customer circumstances. Real-time front-line dialogue is increasingly recognized as the source of the real-world connections that will ensure the continuous reshaping of what the organization knows and can do in the service of the customer.

Dialogue with customers and their fast-changing realities is a vital role of the front-line. The front-line shifts from being a passive product-shifting or information-gathering conduit, to an active element in the organization's continuous value-seeking dialogue with the customer. Transforming the front-line from conduit to rapport-developer becomes vital. The right place for the most comprehensively skilled people is no longer somewhere 'flying a desk', it is in the front-line. The front-line is where the rubber hits the road. It is only there that the organization's values and abilities can make a difference. Putting everything in the front-line turns organizations upside-down and inside-out. Organizations can no longer afford to hoard their best behind the castle walls, they have to have them out where they can reshape the world. If everything the company can bring to bear is not in the front-line it is playing with at least one hand tied behind its back. Putting the best people, backed up by the best possible expertise, technologies, business processes and intra and extra-organizational networks, into the front-line, is now a basic entry-level requirement if an organization really is to be able to bring the best to the customer's doorstep. Unless the best intelligence and experience is available to the organization, and instantly available to the front-line, the company will look stupid in comparison to its knowledge-intensive, rapid-learning competitors.

Information technologies have the potential to be an important enabler of the transformation of organizations into networked front-lines. If used as the means of expression of organizational values and integrity – and not as a substitute for them – they can empower both the front-line and customers alike. They can amplify what the organization really cares about and amplify the customer's ability to get what he or she needs. Before long, the capabilities of the new technologies of information will mean that organizations will only have front-lines. Tomorrow's organization is one that lives in the front-line – only there can it experience the world as it is, and only there can it decide on what it needs to be.

Transforming organizations into networked front-lines is more a state of mind than a product of using the latest technology. Organizations which deprive people of even basic authority and decision making, which confine them to narrow boxes, and which make resources and expertise the stuff of territorial warfare, are at best seeking comfort in the slow-moving environments of the past. Only by engaging the individual with what the customer needs, and making it possible for the individual to do something very significant about it, can the organization even appear to be remotely connected with the customer's purposes. When organizations disconnect their people from the meaningful realities of customers and their needs – and what the competition can and are doing – they disconnect themselves in the minds of the customer from those who have something excellent to offer.

The individual, sensitive to the customer, aware of what the organization is capable of, and empowered to deliver, is the dynamic boundary of tomorrow's organization. The human dimension is key and the dynamic allocation of tangible and intangible resources to customer purposes is key. Organizational structures, assumptions and practices which get in the way of the dynamic allocation of what is required, put too much time and distance between the customer's needs and the organization's ability to fulfil them. Competitors operating without the baggage of old paradigm constructs find it easy to appear to be on the ball. Dynamic re-allocation creates the space for customer-centred and customer-unique design and integration. The value-added of managers is increasingly the contribution they can make to reducing the barriers to rapid allocation and re-allocation of the best to meet the customer's needs. Managers working in this way enable the front-line to operate on the same wavelength as the customer – not on the wavelength determined by an institution designed to preserve the past and to tie the customer to it.

Customer orientation is highly dispersed capability – not a specific capability located in one place. It is a capability that can be uniquely brought together and concentrated as and when required. In tomorrow's organizations, capability results from the additive effects of dynamically combining every input required to meet a customer's unique needs. The structures of tomorrow's organization are not static, they are defined by events. These are not the events which result from the annual reorganization, but the events which occur unpredictably with each customer encounter. Every allocation of resources is dynamic, and no pattern of allocation is repeated twice. Every allocation of resources has to take place as near to instantaneously as possible. This requires effective co-operation rather than formal control structures. The only recognizable structures of the organization are its resource enabling structures – the means by which the best resources can be identified and allocated to the unpredictable interactions the organization has with each customer. The ability to make new connects between resources and capabilities within and beyond the organization is fast replacing the tendency to find permanence by restricting the uses to which things can be put. For tomorrow's organization, its permanence entirely depends on its permanent ability to bring whatever is required to wherever and whenever it is required. Its permanence does not depend on its ability to consistently bring one thing to the customer, but on its ability to consistently bring different things and experiences to the customer all the time.

The dramatic improvements in the capabilities and costs of information technologies will soon mean that there will be no limit to the dynamic reconnections that can be made between people, resources and others part of global alliance networks. Indeed, the concept of spans of control, whether or not they do increase to spans of twenty, fifty or a hundred, is already being rendered redundant by the new technologies of information. The competitive issue is fast becoming the ability to dynamically reconfigure according to customer needs. This requires not just an organizational reconfiguration, but a transformation in views about what it takes to manage and be managed. Information technologies will soon offer the realistic potential for not just unlimited 'spans of control' based on customer-oriented self-directed control, they will enable the auto-reconfiguration of human and other resources according to customer need.

Tomorrow's organization will not look to management to be information relays, controllers of resources, creators and preservers of structures, and inhabitants of hierarchies. The only static structures that will have a place are monuments to the past and reminders of a history which is there to prevent us from making the same mistakes twice. The role of management is already being redefined, as those who have experienced delayering will know. The reduction or elimination of the hierarchical layers between those that have the information or skills, and those that need them at the point of customer contact, is only in part about eliminating time delays. It is more to do with making it possible to have different combinations of those that have the information or skills to meet different customer needs. The value-added of 'management', lies less in them being controllers, decision makers and order givers, and more in their ability to make it possible for skilled and motivated people to bring their best – and to integrate the best – in the service of the customer. Their value lies in their ability to provide the organizational infrastructure within which good people can do great things – and do different great things in different ways time after time. As organizations require to continuously regenerate what they do and how they do it, shoring up the past becomes less important than building bridges to the future. In tomorrow's organization, no one in a management position will be judged on what they control or 'own'. They will be judged on the basis of what they made it possible for their people to achieve.

Empowering the organizational front-line requires a recognition that organizations only have front-lines, and that what they do there and how they do it, depends on constantly redefining the end and the means. Transforming an organization in such a way, requires the focus of management to be less on maintaining yesterday's winning formula, and more on creating the conditions for the dynamic regeneration of the organization. The challenge for managers is to fundamentally reconceive what their organization's fundamental capabilities are, and to build the capabilities to ensure that each encounter with the customer extends the boundaries of the customer's lifestyle.

BEATING IN TIME

Organizational dynamics are moving from the institutional to the human scale. Customers live life in real-time and they increasingly insist that organizations respond in the same way. Organizations that put the customer's life on hold while they do what they do, are not only wasting the customer's time, they are declaring a supreme indifference to customer's dignity and lifestyle agenda. Minimizing the time required to fulfil a customer's need is already assuming great importance on the agenda of many organizations. Organizations everywhere are working to eliminate waiting and queuing times and to increase the speed of their responses to customers. Everywhere, services are being offered as close to instantly as is currently possible. However, more fundamentally, this universal rush to reduce time-lags is about passing ownership and control to the customer. In the past, business, and other institutions set the tempo of life and felt free to squander the customer's time in their own interests. Now, the 'sin' is to not to be on the same wavelength as the customer.

Few customers will tolerate having their time wasted. Only the desperate will tolerate having their time wasted to meet the ends of an institution which thinks it exists primarily to serve its own priorities. All customers are becoming sensitive to having their use of time dictated by organizations. Organizations that do not deliver on time are dictating how the customer should use his or her time. Organizations that assume they can waste customer's time in queues, long procedural processes, or by manipulating customers to run through sales and marketing mazes to get what they want, get condemned as time-wasters and substituted at the first opportunity with more time-respecting suppliers. Not wasting customer's time is an important route to customer loyalty because it signals respect for the customer's agenda and lifestyle. Respect for the customer's agenda and lifestyle is the platform for doing business in ways which enhance the customer's lifestyle. The losers in the future will be those that compromise the customer's dignity or lifestyle. The ability to design and integrate in ways which enhance rather than diminish customer lifestyles is the difference between being a time-waster going nowhere, and being a time-enhancer creating the opportunities and possibilities for increasing customer value. The true measure of being able to meet the needs of customers who see their time as their own time, can be realized when customers who value their time willingly give that time to you.

Customers only give their time to organizations if they know it will not be wasted. Process re-engineering approaches frequently tend to look at reducing the time required to complete business processes end-to-end. The value however, is not in the internal time saved. Increasing the speed of product design and development or service delivery gives the customer more time to use the solution and brings the customer's future forward. Identifying a customer's unique needs, designing a unique solution and delivering it in real-time, means that customers have to live for less time with a solution designed for someone else – the mythical average man. Real-time responses designed to ensure availability and delivery to a customer of the product whenever it is required, result in the customer's lifestyle being on-hold for less time. What organizations are doing when they reduce the time they require to do something, is to enable customers to do more with their time. Those organizations that enable customers to do more with their time create more value.

The customer not only sets the tempo, the customer determines the value of time. On the mechanistic level, beating in time with the customer requires a greater emphasis on understanding the elapsed time for each interaction with the customer. The internal mechanistic approach focuses attention on ensuring that all aspects of the business process can respond to each area where the customer is time sensitive. The touchstone however is the time the customer takes to feel that his or her need has been recognized, and the time customer the customer feels he or she is in suspended animation while the product, service, experience or satisfaction is created and delivered. The customer's judgement, however, will not be on what you do with your time, it will be on what you do with the customer's time.

Beating in time does not mean frenetic activity. It means doing things with the customer's time but not in his or her time. Tomorrow's organization sees time as a resource, not something to be minimized. A goal is to put more into and get more out of time. Those who can, will have more of this valuable customer-owned resource given to them.

GETTING IT RIGHT

The quality of the product or service is becoming increasingly defined in terms of its ability to extend the boundaries of the customer's lifestyle. Extending lifestyle boundaries depends on knowing exactly what the current boundaries are. This can only be understood if the customer is part of the process of designing the solution and how it can best be integrated into the customer's lifestyle.

Virtual reality computer systems are already being used to provide the customer with direct experience of the product or service before it is created. For example, complex real-time simulations can be used to elicit the design requirement and to test it out – not just analytically, but in terms of how it will be experienced when delivered. Good design is rapidly being redefined as a process which assists and enables the customer to understand and reflect upon needs and the best way of fulfilling them. The trend towards simulating the requirement and its solution in real-time, and with the customer in the driving seat, is already accelerating. It is already realistic to explore the future in real-time.

The customer's experience is increasingly the product of the entire organizational process. The customer's experience is increasingly determined by what the organization can bring to bear to enable the customer to simulate and ultimately realize the desired experience. The ability to simulate and create experiences is becoming less the result of the traditional forward planning approaches to product and service design, and more a function of the planning and thought that has gone into the design and realization of the organizational processes required to enable the real-time design and creation of experiences. Simulation and realization has to be the entire organization in action. The customer's experience cannot be separated into product and process. As the customer's experience increasingly becomes a function of the total organizational capability at work, high standards cannot be achieved by organizations which are less than the sum of their functional parts. In tomorrow's organization, the product and the process are the same thing, and the process is the organization. Creating exceptional experiences and lifestyle enhancements depends on an organization which is on song and which can strike the right chord with the customer (see Figure 2.7).

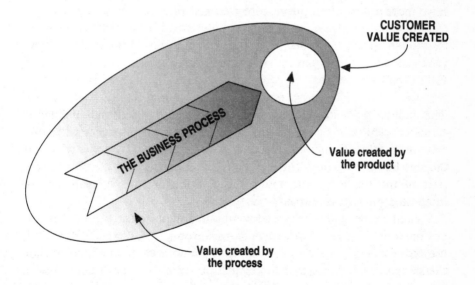

Figure 2.7 *Getting it right*

Getting it right is about getting it together. Customers see organizations in a total sense – they are either seen as knowing what they are doing or they are not. Those who don't know what they are doing will not be sought out by customers seeking partners with whom to co-produce a unique experience.

ELECTRIC WEBS

Embracing the customer is a complex process. Not only do organizations need to bring the best of everything in the world to the customer, they need to be able bring it together in unique combination to deliver a unique response. This increasingly means identifying the need, designing the solution, producing and integrating the solution into a complex lifestyle in real-time. Every activity and resource of the organization is now in the front-line – everyone and everything are now what the customer sees reflected in what the organization does and how it does it. The point of contact with the customer is no longer merely the point of sale – the end of a sometimes long, lumbering supply chain. The point of sale used to be a specialized and limited form of encounter with the customer. Now it is the opportunity to establish true contact with the customer. Directly or indirectly, every aspect and dimension of the organization is in contact with the customer, and every aspect and dimension is critical to the organization being in a position to create unique customer value. In the past, distance from the customer was determined by structural, physical, technological and cultural factors. Geographic distance no longer distances what the organization can do from the customer. Computer technologies increasingly mean that anything or anyone need not be separated in time. The functional divides that caused design, development, production, delivery and service to be remote in time, are being demolished of necessity as the time it takes for the company to configure resources and ideas on demand to meet customer specific needs is now at the centre of organizational relevance. Perhaps more importantly, transformations in organizational and management philosophies are beginning to combine to enable organizations to reduce the psychological distance between themselves and ideal-pursuing customers.

The entire world of organizations is being transformed and their responses and reflexes electrified. Instantaneous access from the front-line to the world's best requires immediate event-coordinated and simultaneous action throughout the entire organizational network. The ability of the company to bring its resources and the resources of others to dynamically achieve customer value, requires seamless integrations which transcend all boundaries. Bringing this about increasingly requires instant technology-enabled communication to integrate knowledge, experience, capability and resources throughout and from beyond the organization, and the ability to make the all important human element of dynamic multifunctional teamwork the centrepiece of the performance. Both together are required to create the impression that meeting the customer's unique needs is the organization's basic instinct.

Tomorrow's organizations require any point in the organization to be able to initiate a unique organization configuration in response to any customer encounter. Direct unintermediated communications are key for each point in the organization's internal and external network to know what it needs to do to play its part in the fulfilment of customer's needs. Each point in the network – a person – must be able to mobilize and make their contributions available quickly without the time-lags that characterize traditional organization optimized only for the routine and the predicted. The ability to be able to make what is required available when and where it is required, is a basic requirement for participation in the customer experience-generating network of tomorrow. A commitment to the predetermined routine, unquestioned historical precedent, or to imaginary boundaries, is a request for self-exclusion. Equally important is the ability to co-operate, interrelate and recombine in whatever ways are required. High levels of human versatility, innovation, creativity and resourcefulness are therefore required if the organization is to pursue the path of customer-led transformation.

Rapid developments in information technology are enabling dynamic reconfigurations of tangible and intangible resources inside and outside the organization's network. It is enabling the instant and optimal combinations of tangible and intangible resources to be configured as required by individual customers and changing circumstances. This electrification of the organizational network and its capabilities is vital to organizations determined to meet the needs of fast-changing once-only markets. By enabling the creation of an infinite variety of customer-specific experiences, organizations can reduce the time between what could be achieved and what can be achieved. By so doing, organizations can participate in the extension of customers' lifestyle boundaries and accelerate the arrival of future life-enhancing possibilities.

PROFILE OF THE NEW PARADIGM

The characteristics of organizations that embrace their customer and those that don't can be summarized as follows:

Old paradigm		New paradigm
Responses to the market	$\longrightarrow$	Co-creation of lifestyles
It's all in the product	$\longrightarrow$	The product is part of the package
The product determines the customer's lifestyle	$\longrightarrow$	The product extends the lifestyle
Distinctive products	$\longrightarrow$	Distinctive relationships with customer values
Service as an adjunct	$\longrightarrow$	Service is the business
Multiple points of contact	$\longrightarrow$	Single (apparent) point of contact
Power in the hierarchy	$\longrightarrow$	Empowered points of contact
'Don't blame me'	$\longrightarrow$	'The buck stops here'
'I don't think we've met'	$\longrightarrow$	'We know who you are'
We define the business	$\longrightarrow$	Customer defines the business
Value at the end of the chain	$\longrightarrow$	The chain co-creates value
The business sets the tempo	$\longrightarrow$	Customer living in real-time
Customer life cycles	$\longrightarrow$	Moments of truth
Quality equals low deviations from the specification	$\longrightarrow$	Quality equals getting the specification right

3 Delivering the Right Response at the Right Time

'In the future sustainable competitive advantage will depend more on new process technologies and less on new product technologies.' (Lester Thurow)

A WHOLE NEW BALL GAME

Markets are becoming unique sequences of unconfigured possibilities. Co-creation of unique value is replacing control and domination as the primary characteristic of the customer/producer relationship. High-touch replaces market assaults as intangible-seeking customers need only those things they can live without. Not only are these customers becoming less dependent on the organizations and institutions which got them where they are today, their needs are shifting to the more complex ones required to further their lifestyle ideals and unique circumstances. Organizations now face customers with complex requirements they don't need fulfilled. As the whole ball game shifts, design and integration become the value-adding capabilities. Expression of these design and integration capabilities requires the customer to be centre stage in the production performance.

The competitive high-ground is shifting to the creation of new possibilities. New organizational approaches are combining with new technology to bring new possibilities within reach of everyone. As demand for specific products becomes increasingly transitory, only capabilities that can deliver new possibilities quickly can avoid being rapidly superseded by unpredictable shifts in customer tastes, and by increasingly lifestyle-specific needs. Zeroing product development cycle time becomes of increasing importance in determining if customer satisfactions can be delivered while they are still useful to the customer. The time it takes to do things must be constantly reduced if an organization is to be able to fit with the customer's schedule – not its own self-optimizing one.

The arrival of customers intent on living their lives in real-time – not in institutional time – is precipitating the end of the traditional organization. As the predictability of customers with limited choice goes, market windows shorten and become harder to meet. As the one-customer once-off niche increasingly becomes the norm, the simple and long cycles associated with slow-moving mass markets are being transformed into diverse, complex and highly individual blips. The organization accustomed to operating in a world when the future was a far-off place, is having to do or die in a world in which the future can come and go without the organization knowing it. This all is coinciding with advances in technology, and challenging innovations in organization, management and business process design which together have the potential to enable the dramatic shortening of product life cycles.

The world of the blip has many important implications and shifts the basic requirement for creating and sustaining a presence from one of the activity of territorial competitive advantages, to a constant process of business reinvention. The right response is no longer the one-way-only-for-always response of the mass production era. The right response is now increasingly the design and creation of customer-specific products and services, once and once only. The time and cost required to get unique products and services to ever more discerning customers is fast becoming the competitive high ground. The ability to respond rapidly to changing market conditions increasingly requires instantly redefinable products created by processes designed for the rapid design, integration and experiencing of what ever it takes to extend lifestyle boundaries at the right cost. The era of organizational processes designed to optimally produce only one product is passing as fast changing conditions require unique upward moving responses in fast succession.

Responding to change is a major challenge when production processes and organizational mindsets have been engineered over generations for life in a monochromatic never-changing world. Organizations locked into yesterday's models of success will frequently go belly-up long before they will admit that no formula is a winner for all time. Organizations that thought it was enough to learn and encapsulate one thing for the next 3–5 years, now find they are unable to meet the needs of fast moving micro-markets which require many things but seldom the same thing twice. Organizations which have perfected the art of meeting the needs of the masses at a price which the masses can afford, find they have done so at the cost of eliminating the abilities and imaginations required to meet the needs of individual at a price the organization can afford.

Any way of doing things, if done more than a few times, becomes easier to repeat and therefore harder to change. Any way of doing things that insists there is only one right way, will not only resist change, it will have eliminated the ability to change. The nature of the old industrial paradigm is that it unwittingly assumed it had the one winning formula – the only issue was how long it would take to perfect it and whether technology could be used to perfect it some more. A flaw in its approach to perfection was that the new only made sense if it fitted within the existing definition of perfection. Management techniques and technical principles emphasized the goal of improving the efficiency and quality of the model and its ability to one thing well. For economic and technical reasons, extending the life cycles of existing products is a dominant consideration in the old paradigm, and the rate at which new products can be introduced is extended to intervals of years as the constraint and challenge becomes one of justifying throwing away everything that it took years to build. Indeed, the very feasibility of introducing new products is called into question when the entire organization and its production process needs to be uprooted, redesigned and replaced every time product requirements change.

A notable characteristic of the old production paradigm is that it achieved production for the masses at the cost of driving out diversity and the ability to produce variety in small volumes. With the arrival of a highly individual world of transient needs, organizations conceived in the foundations of the mass production paradigm have painted themselves and their people into the shrinking corners of marginal markets – markets where the needs, behaviours and expectations of customers have not yet locked into the tempo of more advanced markets. The longer the organization is locked into serving the shrinking low expectation markets of yesterday, the more that fast moving competitors will lock it out of the individualistic markets of the future. The organizational costs of change can only increase as they are postponed. As the inability to recognize the needs of the individual exposes the organization to the growing numbers of those capable of dealing with the needs of the growing virtual economy, their only prospect is to crumble with the crumbling markets they serve.

The production paradigm of yesterday is a diversity-free zone. Having achieved its low unit costs through the division, standardization and simplification of each factor in the production process, diversity is its enemy. The principle was extended to people. Seen as dangerous sources of diversity and variability, they and their contributions too had to be reduced to the performance of simple, repeatable roles which could and perhaps should wherever possible be replaced with machines – whenever the production economics made sense. People as sources of flexibility, change and organizational learning were suppressed in the quest for reduced unit costs based on large scale standardized production. Consequently, the old paradigm adds the costs and uncertainties of culture change to its many costs of change.

Despite a growing realization of the potentials of information technology, there are few examples of its potentials having been realized. With a few exceptions, information technology has been incorporated into the old paradigm rather than being used as the means of its transformation. In most cases, the result has been to increase the long-term costs of unwinding the old. Vast billions of investment made to little effect. But perhaps a necessary learning curve has been climbed.

The assumptions underlying the business process, its design, organization and management, are now being questioned from every direction. A combination of process, market, technology and product turbulence has placed the transformation of the entire organization at the centre of a heated management debate. New capabilities – not simple extensions of the old – are being sought to make it possible to provide unique solutions to transient and increasingly intangible customer needs (see Figure 3.1). The emerging paradigm is one whose operating philosophy puts the human back at its centre and which makes the unique its standard

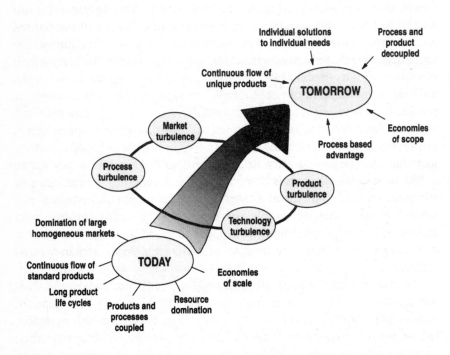

Figure 3.1 *A whole new ball game*

product. It is designed to create the unique, and to do so in a world where little can or should be predicted. It rests on the principles that the customer sets the tempo, that customer time is valuable, and that the challenge of production is to enhance and extend the boundaries of the customer's lifestyle. The speed with which things can be done is key. The ability to do them once and still make money is key. The ability to provide access to the best from what ever source and enable the customer to achieve complex integrations of them into fast evolving lifestyles is key. The new paradigm achieves its scale not through monotony, but through continuous variation.

Alvin Toffler coined the term 'mass customization' to describe what he saw as the essence of the new paradigm of production – its capacity to meet the individual needs of masses of individuals at similar economics to those of mass production.

As currently articulated, the principle of mass customization has its basis in the assembly of uniform parts to create unique products, and not on the production of uniform products from uniform parts. It is widely argued that its central feature is its ability to rapidly and dynamically assemble many components into a large variety of different products each designed to meet individual customer needs. Its production process is not seen as being integrated in the traditional sense of being rigidly configured to assemble resources in one way for a long time. Instead it is coordinative and integrative. That is, its essential feature is the node of assembly which has the ability to quickly bring together many other nodes of assembly, whether or not these are located within the organization, and in whatever combination is required to meet individual customer needs. However, and perhaps more profoundly, the distinctive feature of the new paradigm is not that it is enabled by some form of rapid assembly capability, but the fact that the human capacity for, and urge to design, and is now being thrust to centre stage, and is being released from the production cages of the past. The fact that the ability to dynamically combine resources is a source of the capacity to live with change, is important but only incidental. The new paradigm of production – whatever it is called – is providing a platform for the creation of design-expressing human-centred futures.

The ability to enable individual customers to enhance and extend their boundaries, and to put more life-enhancing possibilities at their disposal, is a central feature of tomorrow's organization. It achieves this by multi-factor customer-specific design connected to multi-factor dynamic sourcing of the best of everything in the world. It turns this into distinctive value by having the ability to rapidly integrate extraordinary amounts of diversity successfully into customer lifestyle designs. Its foundations are not the determinisms of the past, but the indeterminisms of the future. Its foundations are human, its processes and its outputs are life-enhancing.

FASHIONIZATION AND FRAGMENTATION

The right response at the right time is the one that hits the mark despite no-warning unpredictability and instability. One of the factors that guarantees that what is being done today is one of the last times it will make sense to do it, is the phenomenon of fashionization – the condition where product life cycles are unpredictably shortened by customers whose definitions of value are volatile, short-lived and not determined by predictable survival needs. Fashionization is already a feature of virtually every industry and market – there is almost no product that is not now being wrapped for consumption in volatile and intangible lifestyle imagery. As every marketplace becomes redefined as mind-share, the stuff of product is increasingly mental and intangible. The speed at which markets can be redefined is the speed at which a teenager can change his or her mind. As fashionization means that what is seen as the product is in fact a mental creation, and one which may rapidly and unpredictably become obsolete, the need for the capability to introduce new products on demand becomes an essential survival requirement.

Time to market becomes one key measure of organizational capability. One relevant definition of this capability is the ability to identify new needs, and to design, produce, and integrate changes to the customer's lifestyle. Capability therefore is systemic – it depends on all aspects of the organization acting in concert – rather than being a reflection of what the individual parts can do on their own. The capability index of an organization whose production process is geared to making one product in one way for a long time is low – it may not go out of business but its margins will decrease. The capability index of organizations who can in practice create unique customer experiences in real-time is high. The interesting by-product of the capabilities required to operate in transitory markets, is that they ultimately take the ownership of technology, capital and resources out of the equation and put the access to ideas, customer-specific know-how, and the creative capabilities of customer-oriented people to the fore. The new paradigm is turning industry from a technologically dominated past to a technology enabled, customer-controlled and human values-centred future – where the capability index is everything.

The effects of fashionization and fragmentation have already dramatically reshaped the behaviours of organizations in every industry and made the customer's lifestyle the product. These effects are combining with rapidly evolving technology and telecommunications to redefine every industry.

The consumer electronics industry once positioned its products as furniture around which nations and empires could assemble. Now, high-technology user-directed multi-media capabilities are combining with powerful communications to make it possible for the entire world and the best it can offer to revolve around the individual in real-time. In the broadcasting and entertainments industries, broadcasting is not only giving way to narrowcasting, it is giving way to video-on-demand. As video-on-demand soon becomes the norm, even the schedulers of narrowcasting will be under threat from programme and entertainment schedules designed entirely by the volatile tastes of each individual customer.

The communications industry is being transformed as its ability to dominate the barriers of time and space has been eliminated in the face of rapid technological advances which allow the individual to transcend them. The industry has already moved from forcing the user to operate in one configuration of time, space, medium and message – the real-time connection of the voice of one person to the ear of one person at one place and one point in time. Cellphones, mobile faxes and tiny modems dissolve the physical barriers that in the past made the individual revolve around the physical structures of the communications network. The network and its capabilities now revolve around the individual customer – readily accessible software now enables the user to self-configure temporary virtual networks enabling many to talk to many wherever they are located. Time-shifting technologies such as the many varieties of voice messaging, extend the scope of human contact from real-time only to across time, enabling the customer to configure his or her own use of time. Revolutions in video technology, are rapidly extending the visual domain enabling the customer to personalize human contact and to re-assume control of his or her own visual experience. Information services are proliferating exponentially – services such as Internet, already offer access to a bewildering variety of information sources spanning virtually everything that is known about news, travel, products and academic research. And the point at which virtual networks with 'intelligent software agents' will enable everyone to custom configure that information into personalized newspapers, magazines, entertainments and 'books' – and to configure out the middle man – is not far off.

The customer increasingly determines the configuration of products on display in shops, stores and supermarkets. Retailers, already stocking many thousands of items, are using information technology to enable the dynamic recombination of what is made available to their customers in order to stay in tune with the changing preferences of their preferred customers. The attractiveness of every product is continually monitored in real-time – every product is in constant real-time test marketing, and any low performers instantly removed to be replaced by the next live market simulation.

The financial services industry, once dominated by massive companies with one or two products offered as a privilege, is being challenged by those adopting the philosophy of 'tell us what you want' – most anything can be had in any combination, anytime and delivered electronically. The virtual financial services company has already arrived – organizations which sell the intangibles of time and space-independent access. The information technology revolution is rapidly moving the industry towards being independent of space and time, being able to operate on and with intangible resources, and being able to achieve customer satisfaction through information and the elimination of tangible barriers. Time and space independence is already becoming well developed and will increase as information superhighways proliferate, and as low-cost intelligent domestic multi-media become the norm. As these developments combine with customer empowering software such as personal broking 'intelligent agents', the need for massive distribution and sales networks and the vast transaction and customer shuffling bureaucracies that comprise most of most financial institutions today, may well dissolve entirely away.

The car industry is already responding to the trend towards the unique by moving towards production to customer concept. Going beyond the simple incorporation of customer-determined variations, virtual reality technologies are already being actively tested out and their realization may not be too far away – the industry may soon offer as many unique cars are there are people who want to own them.

The dramatic shift from 'you can have anything we do (and that's not much)' to the 'we can do anything that you want (and you name it)' – and the speed with which it has occurred – is nothing short of breath-taking. The entire business process is already reflecting this shift in control from the producer to the customer, and it must be a basic feature of the design of tomorrow's organization that it is able to ascertain and fulfil the individual needs of its customers wherever and whenever they arise.

OUT WITH THE OLD

Attempts to create stability by taking instability out of the market have always stifled the real-time dynamics of real life. Fortunately, control has now shifted from the producer to the customer, and from the simple relationship of producer to market to the complex and unstable relationships of many producers to masses of individuals. The stage has now been reached where any attempt to eliminate real-time dynamics by lock-in tactics will be seen by customers as an infringement of their humanity and integrity, and rejected by them.

The massiveness, rigidities and long cycle times of the old paradigm and its variety-eliminating assumptions, meant that its economics depended on eliminating any unpredictability which might upset the precarious equation. Elimination of the unpredictable was achieved through building dominant shares of mass markets, ownership of resources, capital, and employees, lock-in strategies involving suppliers, intermediaries and customers, and many and varied lock-out strategies for the competition. Lengthening the window of the predictable – the period in which nothing changed and nothing new was required – was essential to make the economics of rigidity apparently viable.

Extending the past into the present by attempting to control the future, is to ensure that when change becomes inevitable, it is both massive and brings with it the threat of destruction. Competitors without old paradigm assumptions are steering clear of static configurations of resources. The time and cost of change is becoming a determining factor in the new competitive equation. The creation of complex and static organizational, cultural and process configurations increases the costs of change – the costs of discarding massive investments in the past tends to argue for its preservation. When it is the overall costs of changing business structures constructed to 'stand the test of time' that immobilize many companies, the new competition see minimizing the costs of change as an essential part of a necessary high speed adaptive business strategy.

Low-cost rapid reconfiguration requires a low-inertia organization. Creating unique experiences in real-time cannot be accomplished through organizational and business processes applying production concepts and techniques designed to do one thing. The reconfiguration costs of old paradigm production rule out the creation of the unique and rule the organization out of tomorrow's markets. High reconfiguration costs increase the organization inertia to the point where, if the organization can respond at all, it can only do so after the customer has gone elsewhere. Reducing organizational inertia requires the organizational system to be changed. Business processes must be able to design, assemble and integrate unique lifestyle enhancing products and services to meet unique once-off customer needs. The ability to effortlessly reconfigure business processes, resources, suppliers, intermediaries, capital and skills and roles to identify and create the unique becomes a key requirement. To achieve costs of change which must tend to zero, tomorrow's organization must work with very low levels of inertia. Anything that compels the organization to do what history not the customer dictates – for example, stock, obsolete skills and knowledge, obsolete attitudes, assumptions, culture and processes – will consign the organization to history.

Low inertia requires the absence of static interconnections. Skills tend to be specific combinations of knowledge. Processes tend to be static combinations of assumptions about how work and resources should be organized. Cultures tend to be expressions of relatively static assumptions about how we should behave to achieve apparent organizational purposes. Old paradigm thinking tends to prefer supplier and customer relationships to be locked-in and static. For low inertia to be a reality, the issue is one of how to avoid the comfort zone of the static conformation, how to increase the potential for alternative combination, and how to increase the predisposition to recombine. To achieve low inertia, tomorrow's organization sees its continuous transformation as a continuing priority.

A NEW PRINCIPLE OF PRODUCTION

The new paradigm of production is not about static control, it is about operating at high levels of dynamic instability. It is not about insulating the organization from a rapidly changing world, but about fundamentally rethinking concepts of organization and production to maintain a viable way forward when all around is in flux. The new approach is already clearly in evidence. As we have seen, the new paradigm is not about producing standardized products or services for mass markets or indeed 'simply' about delivering individual solutions to individual customer needs. It is about building the ability to achieve life-enhancing purposes through design-expressing change.

The need to be able to pursue purposes through dynamic instability means the end of organizations whose anchor is stability and who are drifting on the legacies of glorious pasts. It means the ascendancy of those organizations whose assumptions are of continuous change, who welcome continuous change and who are geared up, (if gearing is the right metaphor) to read the signs and steer a course through a world in a state of discontinuous change.

The structures of tomorrow's organization are not intended to be permanent. Its aim is to provide a vehicle for the energies, imaginations and creativities of people rather to freeze itself around one idea, or to constrain the energies of today by the structures, processes or products of the past. Its appearances are therefore transitory and its essence is virtual not massive. Its appearances are expressions of its ability to design whatever structures, processes and products may be required to meet customer needs. As these change, so must the organization's appearances. Tomorrow's organization is a vehicle for expressing design – not an expression of a particular design and its production requirements. Its source of energy is the spirit of design. It designs its structures, processes and relationships to facilitate the expression of customer-specific and customer-conceived design solutions through the rapid sourcing and integration of whatever ideas, resources and skills are required. The effective organizations of tomorrow will be those whose designs always express the best ideas as possible, and whose expressions are realized from the best tangible and intangible resources in the world.

Organizations with the capability for the rapid realization of individual lifestyle designs will thrive in intangible fragmenting markets and will be in a position to redefine the competitive high ground away from those whose vision is restricted to confining the future to the past. By excelling at customer-specific design and extending the organization's network to enable integration of the best to ensure that every customer gets exactly what they want, the competition can be left looking like a relic from the past and out of touch with the customer. The organization that can design, develop, integrate and deliver satisfactions uniquely to meet unique needs will be in a position to attract the customers with most to offer, and most able to pull the organization's capabilities forward fastest. Tomorrow's organizations need to be in those markets where they can learn most – and where they have to learn fast to stay in them.

The continuous delivery of intangible satisfactions to volatile customers with complex and exacting requirements, requires an organizational capability which is fast, flexible, highly integrative, human focused and in tune with changing circumstances. The organization of the future can be described as a virtual system with no mass, based on the creative mental capacities of customer-oriented future-creating people. Its ability to reconfigure means that its abilities and resources are not preconfigured – they self-configure for each unique performance and release themselves at its end. The ability to rapidly reconfigure requires every aspect of the organization's potential to be capable of rapidly assuming new relationships – and the rapid regeneration of its embedded know-how, knowledge, skills, capabilities and assumptions.

Dynamic instability requires short response times, and these in turn require the very short feedback loops of an organization in close synch with its future. In a world in which past-confining stability and change-resisting control no longer make sense, a key feature of the new paradigm is its ability to support continuous approximation – a dynamic stability (see Figure 3.2) borne out of having ideas, resources, people, energy and vision which continue to meet the needs of today and tomorrow, and out of the ability to discard them as soon as their usefulness diminishes. Tomorrow's organization therefore maintains its relevance to changing tastes through its ability to create the unique to meet the changing customer requirements as they arise. It responds to uncertainty and its apparent threats by using its forward looking capabilities to generate and realize the new possibilities of an emerging future.

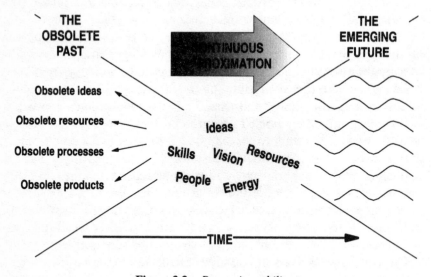

Figure 3.2 *Dynamic stability*

THE PROCESS IS KING

In the old paradigm, each individual product had its own production process designed and configured to meet the product's particular needs.

Now, it is the ability of the organizational process as a whole to generate unique products all the time that has become important. The ability of the organizational process to design and integrate endless unique experiences, is what determines the ability of tomorrow's organizations to forge ahead in fast-moving intangible markets.

Tomorrow's organizations are not concerned with the design of business processes that are optimized to a one-way-only predictable world, but to the needs of a dynamically evolving environment. There are no sure bets in an unpredictable world. And there is no long term place for the one trick player. Individual products are less important than the ability to re-invent them. Organizational capabilities become the platform from which a stream of new ideas, designs and customer-specific solutions can arise. Process and product life cycles used to be the fascination, and they both were of the same duration. Now the requirement is to make the organizational capability independent of the product life cycles of which it is the source rather than the consequence. Durable organizational capabilities which are independent of product-life cycles are an expression of the organization's total ability to bring everything it needs to bear on the individual customer's requirement time after time. Organizational capabilities which are a reflection of individual products, carry all the risks of an all-or-nothing and once-for-all commitment. Long-life organizational capabilities reduce the commitment to one outcome, increase the ability to address many possible outcomes, and make today's turbulent environments interesting rather than death-defying places to be.

Systemic organizational capabilities provide the basis for adaptability and the only basis for future stability – always being in the right place at the right time. The ability to produce and deliver the unique into unique customer lifestyles, increases the chances of getting it right when needed, and being able to respond effectively to competitor actions. Systemic organizational capabilities not only provide the means to satisfy the customer once, but the opportunity to be there when the next need arises – and to be the first to satisfy it.

Tomorrow's organizations are sources of infinite possibility. Availability, re-usability, diversity and versatility are among the primary characteristics of its assets and resources. Ease of use and reuse in different ways as situations require, is a source of flexibility and responsiveness. Versatility is the expression of the ability of resources to be used across a range of unique circumstances. Versatility extends the range of possibilities resources can be involved in. In a discontinuous world, extending the range of possibilities to which resources can be turned makes it possible to predict the return on investment in them. The stabilities of tomorrow's organizations arise from the extended capacity of its resources to flow into an ever-changing configurations of products and services over an extended period of time. Tomorrow's organization depends on its ability to use assets and resources in many different ways, and on its ability to enable them to make their contributions in many different ways. Nothing is forever, so tomorrow's organization is not designed for one possibility. It is designed for the possibilities it can create, not for the immediate solutions it can offer. It is designed not to have to be redesigned to meet the needs of each new customer requirement.

Lester Thurow of MIT in his recent book *Head to Head*, reinforced the fact that in the new system of production, processes are more important than products. He wrote:

> . . . *In the twenty first century sustainable competitive advantage will come much more out of new process technologies and much less out of new product technologies . . . New products can be easily reproduced. What used to be primary (inventing new products) becomes secondary, and what used to be secondary (inventing and perfecting new processes) becomes primary.*

The issue however, is not one of the application of computer technologies to make it feasible to produce the unique on demand – however sophisticated virtual reality might become – the issue is one of how to design organizations which do not need to be uprooted when they need to change shape on demand.

In the old paradigm, the particular shape of the production process was a source of instability in a fast-changing world. The requirement now is to reshape the process as the source of stability. This requires tomorrow's organization to create organizational capabilities which have been specifically designed as a means of expressing a continuous stream of unique possibilities. Tomorrow's organizations need capabilities which make change a natural reflex and the well-spring of future stability in an unstable world.

NEW ECONOMICS AND DYNAMICS

Economies of scope rather than the traditional ones of scale, characterize tomorrow's organizations. The need for economies of scale derives from the need to produce enough of something to justify the capital costs of assets that could only produce one thing. Long production runs culminating in large aggregate production volumes were required. As product life cycles diminish, long runs cannot be sustained and investments in production processes relying on them are increasingly difficult to justify. In contrast, economies of scope derive from the aggregate uses to which assets can be deployed. A long run of any particular product or service is not required so long as the assets can be rapidly reconfigured to meet the production needs of another product or service. The scope of the process in terms of its ability to generate possibilities provides the volumes of unique customer satisfactions which justify its capital cost. The apparent paradox of low-cost uniqueness is achieved through high possibility versatility.

Me-too equals so-what in a marketplace consisting of an aggregation of demand for unique products. Sources of revenue are becoming increasingly volatile and require the ability to meet the unique with the unique. The ability to produce the unique is the means of staying close to the source of real customer value. Continuous regeneration is required to pursue ever changing definitions of customer value, and to pursue ever shortening blips of demand. Investing in the capabilities required to produce ever more uniqueness is perhaps the only route to future revenue streams. Investing in these capabilities is perhaps the only economically viable way the organization can continually regenerate itself.

The economics of tomorrow's organization depend on its dynamic capabilities. Its ability to attract profitable revenue depends on its ability to address multiple fast-changing unique customer requirements. While the economics of any given niche are volatile and its potential as a source of high-margin revenue short-lived, the ability of the company to stay closely in touch with and fulfil changing customer needs creates a stable and profitable demand for the company's capabilities. Demand for capabilities is the dynamic basis for the economics of tomorrow's organization.

The dynamics of change determines the economics of the new production paradigm. The more time it takes to change processes and products to meet new needs, the more it costs to change and the less able the company is to stay in touch with fast changing markets and competitors. The longer and more costly it is to change, the longer the change must apply – longer production runs may be required to justify the consequences of slow change. The company is in a downward spiral. Where change can be accomplished at low or perhaps no incremental cost, the organization can respond quickly or instantaneously and be able to produce greater possibilities at much lower costs. The costs of generating revenue when customer needs are changing rapidly and demand is uncertain, are lowered and the prospect of uniqueness which has no cost penalty to the customer or the organization becomes real. When the cost of change is low or zero, uncertainty and unpredictability no longer have pejorative implications. They become the stuff of opportunity and new possibilities.

The new paradigm is human in its scale and its dynamics. In its outward sense it is judged on its ability to makes things happen on a human rather than institutional or glacial scale. Its success depends on its concern with the tempos of lives than with the regulation of social patterns on the grand scale. Quality ceases to be a technical or arbitrary abstraction – its definition is value to the customer, enhancement of the customer's lifestyle, and the absence of constraint on other possibilities for the customer. The notion of quality as a cost of production gives way to the notion of quality as the purpose of production. In its inward sense, the new production paradigm puts people back at the centre of the production process rather than relegating them to the margins or eliminating them altogether. The business process becomes a possibility-creating vehicle for the expression of what humans do best – imagine, create and hope. Tools, technologies and machines are put at the disposal of people rather than vice-versa. Engaging people in the purposes of the organization is seen as the source of its future. Whereas in the past the future was an extension of yesterday, tomorrow's organization looks to creative destruction as the guarantor of the future. The creative process is profoundly human, and the human dimension in the design of tomorrow's organization is the force that creates tomorrow. When the capabilities of the future are being constantly created today, the costs of change tend to zero. When the future is left to take care of itself – to be the concern of another generation – the cost of taking the future on board is the cost of tackling, shifting and managing a massive past legacy plus the costs of capital required to support a business that is not making any money.

ELECTRIFYING THE PROCESS

New technologies are bringing 'soft-logic' to the processes and operations of companies in all industries. Processes in the past had 'hard-wired' configurations determined by technologies, practices and procedures. Flexibility was reduced or effectively eliminated. Processes in manufacturing and elsewhere are now increasing under the control of the ultimate general purpose machine – the computer. This (in theory at least) allows everything to be reconfigured to meet new needs. Computer-configured processes can in principle enable flexible organizational approaches and thereby allow a wide range of possibilities and outcomes to be created in accord with the needs of changing market conditions. Properly used, the new technologies can enable the soft configuration of processes, ultimately allowing organizations to adapt instantly as circumstances evolve.

This ability to adapt is being passed on from process to product as products increasingly become productive systems in their own right. Microprocessor technologies are being routinely embedded in a wide array of products from domestic goods, entertainment goods, cars and perhaps increasingly dramatically to TV and video. Increasingly adaptable products are being put in the hands of the customer, and product intelligence is also emerging allowing products to self-adapt to circumstances. As product intelligence continues to grow, the role of products as tools will increasingly give way to their roles as intelligent companions.

The new technologies bring the speed of light as a tool. Instant responses to changes in demand are possible. Networks of resources, designers, production and assembly sites, distribution and services companies can be instantly brought together to co-operate in the fast creation and delivery of customer value. The rapid identification, development and translation of product ideas can be enabled by the various forms of computer-aided design (CAD). Computer-aided design can allow ideas to be immediately translated into specifications and immediately tested for fit with customer needs. Computer-aided engineering (CAE) can enable the design of the product to be evaluated in real-time for technical and economic feasibility, and can be used to design the production processes required to assemble the product or service. Linked to computer-aided manufacturing (CAM) in its various forms and disguises, the resources and raw materials required by the product or service can be transformed on demand into the necessary components for assembly. Computer-aided assembly (CAA) can instantly assemble the parts into the product, service or experience itself. In manufacturing, the integrative framework that holds the whole thing together is often called computer-integrated manufacturing (CIM) (see Figure 3.3). In other areas, the ability to dynamically reconfigure the productive network to translate ideas and needs into assembled solutions might be called co-operative processing, simultaneous engineering or the spreadsheet organization.

Most attempts at transforming business processes using the new technologies of information have failed. They have failed largely because organizations believed that merely substituting various parts of the

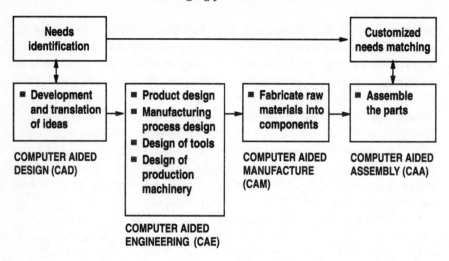

Figure 3.3 *Computer integrated manufacture*

existing process with their 'automated' or computerized counterparts would result in step-changes automatically occurring. Existing configurations of structures, processes, management approaches and supplier relationships were left in place. The potential soft-logic flexibility of the new technologies was lost when they were used to shore up yesterday's production architectures. By applying the new technologies within the confines of the old, the potential benefits were limited to the inherent boundaries of a process designed for a world that had already passed. The new technologies were used as a magic wand, and with similar effect.

The new paradigm operates on the assumption that what it is doing today is unlikely to be what it is required to do tomorrow. The design aim of the new paradigm is to create the capability to produce unique responses in the least time to meet exacting customer expectations. The entire process from unique needs identification to a unique solution to them, is seen as a fast loop operating on the assumption that its purpose is an adaptive and integrative one – pulling in whatever resources are required, and channelling them in unique combinations towards the fulfilment of customer's unique needs.

The new production paradigm is integrative. It depends on its ability to dynamically allocate resources from whatever source within increasingly global networks of world class companies each committed to playing its role in the creation and integration of end-customer value. As the information-based costs of co-ordinating resources and activities trends towards zero, so do the historical barriers to organizations accessing the best to produce the best. The new technologies of information are already being used to free organizations from the constraints of their own limitations, and to extend access to those who can overcome them. Information technology, applied to enable the realization of the new paradigm, extends the boundaries of an organization's capabilities, enabling it to redefine and transform them by combining them with others. By enabling instant interconnections between demand and the best means of fulfilling it, instant and temporary coalitions can be created to create an electrifying world class response to a unique customer requirement.

MULTIFACTOR INNOVATION

Delivering the right response at the right time is not a technological problem – it may, but need not, rely on high concentrations of information technology. At its essence is a transformation in what the organization does and how it does. And people are at the centre.

Tomorrow's organization is an expression of what its people can do which is different, creative and daring. The many process-centred debates bound up in concepts such as lean manufacturing, concurrent engineering, mass customization, and business process re-engineering, are in essence debates about how to find better ways for expressing the essentially human characteristics of creativity, design, flexibility, innovation and sensitivity to customers. None of these techniques can in any way substitute for or be the source of these characteristics. Correctly applied, the many tools and techniques of process management can provide the means for expressing the human. Incorrectly applied, they cannot substitute for the human, and can only eliminate the human from the proceedings. Effective management is no longer about substituting people with technology – any more than it is now about preserving the legacies of the past – it is about using technology to amplify what people can do, and to increase the levels of uncertainty and instability at which people can operate.

The introduction of new technologies is not the source of new organizational capacities. The capacity of organizations to deliver the right response at the right time is a complex process of changing how the organization deals with its changing environment. At the present stage in technological evolution, only people can deal with a changing world. The process and organizational design issue is one of how to create the necessary conditions. Process and organizational designs which eliminate the human, eliminate the ability of the organization to deal creatively with change. The issue is not one of increasing the capacity of people to respond to change, the issue is one of finding process and organizational designs that do not eliminate the ability of people to find expression for their inherent ability to change. Most organizational and process designs seen to date have not made it possible for most people to make anything other than the minimal contribution – and frequently the contribution the organizational design has allowed them to make is only a sub-human one, and one which is ultimately soul destroying. It is the ability to increase the human-expressing capacity of the organization – not its technological capacity – that determines its resourcefulness, flexibility and innovativeness. Extending the range of the human factors that can be expressed by the organizational and process design is what makes sustained advantage a possibility.

Perhaps one of the most important human factors of all is that recognized and emphasized by Peter Drucker about 40 years ago – knowledge is the only resource a business has – the business process is the way that the company's knowledge is translated into value. However, knowledge is not an abstraction, it is the ability of confident, innovative knowledge workers – all people – to combine with new organizational, process and management approaches to invent and deliver fast responses to unique fast changing markets.

The success of tomorrow's organization will be determined by its ability to bring about management and processes which can be enabled by technology to give expression to the highest qualities of people (see Figure 3.4). Whatever the name given to the new process paradigm, it must be capable of achieving multiple outcomes from the widest range of possible inputs – and doing so fast. Whatever the fate and role of management, they must be adept at creating the conditions wherein innovation becomes the norm and where human energies can find useful expression. Whatever the vogue name is, technology must give expression to the designing impulses of people, it must provide information which enables them to self-direct, and it must enable them to work with others to achieve staggering results.

The new paradigm is anchored in the ability of the organization to bring as many human factors as possible into the productive equation. As such, tomorrow's organization and its processes have their foundation in the creative abilities of people – its capabilities must be at the disposal of people, not the other way round. The purpose of management becomes one of creating a management, technology and process environment within which the creative abilities of people can be expressed. Technology

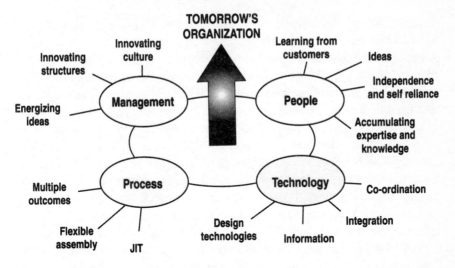

Figure 3.4 *Multifactor production*

and processes are the enablers – but ultimately the technology and the process is neutral. The competitive game becomes, and can only ever be, a contest of innovative future-creating minds.

TELESCOPING THE BUSINESS PROCESS

Responsiveness to fast changing customer needs requires that everything required is brought together quickly and their integration brought close to simultaneity. End-to-end process time is important, but with a widening range of knowledge, resources, and experience being required at the point of customer contact, the organization is required to operate more in parallel than in sequence. Time-sapping functional, physical, procedural and attitudinal barriers to movement of tangible and intangible resources must be eliminated if the customer solution is to be designed and integrated as and when required at the right cost. A key management challenge is to ensure that the 'big picture' and the total implications of the customer requirement prevail over the apparent needs of the parts. As the organization increasingly needs to operate in parallel, systems thinking and holistic perspectives become basic management tools. As access to resources, not their control, becomes the priority, the whole

thinking behind functions and processes, and what they are and what they
need to be, requires to be redefined as well.

Increasingly where the competitive challenge is to be in a position to
respond quickly to the unique with a unique response, the predetermined
response – most business processes and most approaches to management
and organization – is becoming less useful less often. The full implications
of a customer requirement can no longer be anticipated – they need to be
responded to as they are encountered. The implication for the business
process, and for organizational designers and managers, is that there can
be no predetermined sequence for satisfying the customer. The need to
satisfy the customer is the goal, not the need to deliver the pre-
programmed sequence. The issue is one of developing the means of
effecting co-ordination of resources and people, not the one of preserving
historical demarcations of role. Business is now moving so fast, that all the
functions and people must play their part when the need arises, and all
must share responsibility for the process of turning identified need and
unique capabilities into distinctive customer satisfaction.

The horizontal flows put forward by the proponents of 'business
process re-engineering', are a valued element in telescoping the business
process. However, where networks of ideas, resources, knowledge workers
and capabilities are required to deliver unique value once-off, more broad-
based and innovative organizational transformations may be required to
ensure that everything required – whether tangible or intangible – is
telescoped to focus onto the moving ball of customer satisfaction.

UNBUNDLING

Static configurations of resources which cannot be unbundled to form
new configurations are useless in a world of constant variation. The future
is constrained to the combinations of the past, and the costs of production
soar as new assets need to be acquired to replace inflexible combinations.
The product development time required to produce new designs increases
as static configurations need time consuming re-engineering or replacement. In a world of unique responses, resources which can only be used in
one way will increasingly only ever be used once and then discarded. For
people this can only be a disaster, for organizations the capital costs
would be prohibitive. For the life of resources – human and otherwise – to
be extended, they have to be capable of being used in many ways. Their
value depends not on their ability to do one thing countless times, but on
their ability to do countless things once.

Unbundling is not the simple breaking apart of resources from their current configurations – this would not equip them to assume any configuration beyond the one they have just left. Unbundling is not simple disassembly, it is the redefinition of the parts to play multiple roles, and the redefinition of the whole to make use of versatile parts – using them in many ways to achieve unique outcomes which achieve the required result for the customer. The aim is to increase the possibilities the organization has, and to increase the possibilities for utilizing the parts in as many different ways as possible. This creates interesting and developmental possibilities for people and reduces the costs of change for the organization.

Few supply chains are now of the massively horizontal or vertically integrated kind. Flexibility is now more highly prized than the illusory benefits of deeply inflexible lock-ins. Increasingly, flexibility is seen as having its major source in dynamic arrangements of suppliers, subcontractors, channels and commercial affiliates which are able to combine to meet a particular need (see Figure 3.5). The aim for the 'core company' – the company with the primary relationship with customer values – is to find particular partners who can provide access to the best and who can ensure its integration with the customer's lifestyle.

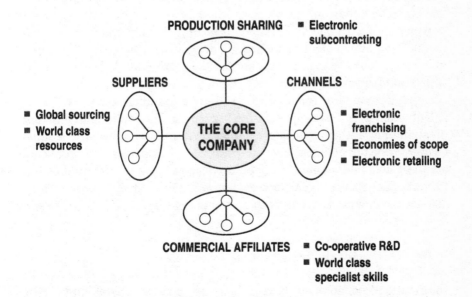

Figure 3.5 *Unbundling*

This unbundling of the supply chain avoids the all-or-nothing risks of one-way-only, and the risks of being left behind that accompany my-way-only, while enabling the required levels of scale to be achieved – organizations can deploy their capabilities in many ways with a variety of other organizations. Instead of doing things in the one way dictated by a seemingly one-way-only supply chain, organizations can have access to many ways of doing it better. By being able to find wider markets for better ways of doing things, they are incentivized to progress rather than to seek the 'secure' niche within an eternal monolith. By only having markets for excellence, they become better placed to earn a place in the future scheme of things than those who may be tempted to grow sleepily within an integrated corporate umbrella or supply chain cartel.

The consulting industry, is an interesting example of a transformation from the previous arrangement where managers, professionals and technical specialists were almost always securely employed for the long term within the boundaries of one industrial organization. The rise of the profession illustrates industrial unbundling. Even very large industrial organizations are no longer big enough to have all the skills they require, or big enough to need them all the time, or fast enough to develop them in time. Independent consulting companies are 'hired' to provide a wide range of services from strategy development, brand development, management of the introduction of new information systems through to the transformation of production processes. The consulting teams provided will exist in the required form only for the duration of each unique client assignment. Sometimes, a consulting company will be hired to act as 'prime contractor' contracting the services of large numbers of specialized organizations such as computer and software companies – in effect contracting out the need to configure unbundled resources.

Unbundling is a way of creating the space for continuous different possibilities. Rather than developing relationships to guard against change, new possibilities must be possible if companies and industries are to be able to dynamically adapt to constant surprise. Unbundling is a formula that makes dynamic reconfigurations possible, and one which enables the new to be embraced and the past to be let go.

LOW TECH, HIGH TECH

Information technologies have a part to play in enabling the new disaggregated paradigm but they are not a substitute for it. Those flexible applications of technology that do exist, only make sense within the context of new management approaches and practices and when combined with the inherent flexibility of people. The rapid development and production of new products and services that meet individual customer needs, can be achieved and have been achieved without the extensive use of information technology – the formula typical of many major western companies.

Information has more often than not been applied to addressing business problems that should not have arisen in the first place. Rather than using information technology in an attempt to integrate the business around the limitations of functional and bureaucratic structures, it is now recognized that the limitations must be reduced first and before information technology is applied. Rather than using information technology to track and schedule all the parts involved in making a complex product, the emphasis is now on making the product easier to make in the first place. Rather than designing information systems to handle complex inventory, inventories are being eliminated in favour of just-in-time techniques. Rather than having purchasing systems that can handle countless suppliers and using the capability to trade them off against each other, strategic alliances are being forged with fewer suppliers to arrive at a situation where both the supplier and purchaser can benefit from a long-term partnership towards a common goal.

The belief that ever more technology equals competitive advantage has taken a battering in the early nineties. The monolithic mainframe-based data centres are increasingly seen as burdensome legacies. 'Big-iron' is seen as dead weight, and companies in search of flexibility and adaptability are resorting to so-called 'client-server' architectures – small centres of localized computing able to meet local needs while co-operating with the larger company as required. Integration, a watch-word only a short while ago, is being replaced by the now more politically correct 'inter-operability'. Whatever the merits of this shift, the clear message for tomorrow's organization is that information technology is neutral – it can only amplify the management assumptions in operation at the time. Just as apparently disaggregated computing in the form of client-server approaches will not disaggregate the business process, and 'open' computing systems will not of themselves enable the dynamic reconfiguration of information and resources, so personal computing does not automatically empower the individual or create effective teams. Whether in big lumps or small, throwing iron at the sinking ship only brings the inevitable sooner.

Fundamentally reconceiving all aspects of business organization is the key to having a place in the world. All the technologies currently and soon to be available are powerless to make any impact at all if used to automate existing ways of doing things. Technology for technology's sake is a fetish. The assumption that low tech is bad tech is at best a reflection of the same fact. The application of new, emerging and future technologies without radical forethought is to consign the organization to repeat the mistakes of the past – and to a business world that no longer exists.

CONTINUOUS APPROXIMATION

Tomorrow's organizations are engaged in the continuous search for what makes sense in a changing world. Its engine or core capability is its ability to identify and assemble the best ideas, concepts, resources, skills and components that will enable it to bring the best to its customers before the competition. Equally important is its ability to stay ahead of the fast advancing front of what no longer works by the continuous disposal of obsolete knowledge, assumptions, processes and practices. This carries with it the benefits of reducing the inertia arising from the costs of carrying the past, and ensures that the organization is more likely to always be in a position to deliver economically what makes sense to the customer. The ability to continuously reconfigure resources to produce the new combinations required for value to be delivered to the individual customer, is a way of not letting the past take hold and of opening the door on possibilities for the future. Reducing the time it takes to set-up and produce new combinations of ideas, information and resources enables the organization to shift from producing to guesswork or historical patterns – to forecast – to producing to and on demand. Compressing the time between events and a response to them enables the organization to explore its experiences in real-time. By so doing it can continuously explore the emerging frontiers of customer value and make its approximations ever closer to the mark.

Stan Davis, in his book *Future Perfect*, said, 'The general message is, the more a company can deliver customized goods on a mass basis, relative to their competition, the greater is their competitive advantage.' For tomorrow's organization the trend towards individual solutions to individual needs is a trend towards enhancing the unique lifestyles of unique customers. The production requirement is the requirement inherent in the customer's unique circumstances, and the means is the ability to generate a wide range of possibilities. For tomorrow's organization, the new production paradigm has its essence in the creation of an organization which is designed to progress through a process of generating possibilities – a process whereby the organization steers by a keen sense of what no longer works towards what may or will work (see Figure 3.6). Its ability to create greater possibilities more quickly is not inherently virtuous. It is the fact that the ability to create possibilities enables the organization to continuously approximate – to continuously search for what is valuable – that is important. Delivering the right response at the right time is its ambition. The ability to create infinite possibilities is the means. Its will to chart a course to the future is its guiding light.

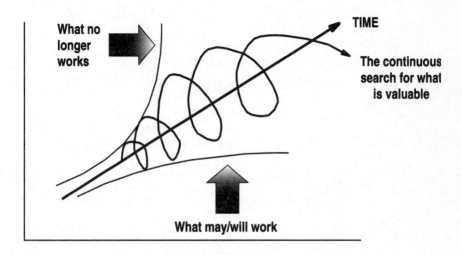

Figure 3.6 *Continuous approximation*

PROFILE OF THE NEW PARADIGM

The old production paradigm can be contrasted with the old in the following way:

Old paradigm		**New paradigm**
Mass markets	$\longrightarrow$	Markets of one
Long product cycles ('instability')	$\longrightarrow$	Short product cycles ('stability')
Long process life cycles	$\longrightarrow$	Real-time dynamics
High volume, low price	$\longrightarrow$	High variety, low cost

High volume, low variety	$\longrightarrow$	Low volume, high variety
Product determines the process	$\longrightarrow$	Process enables many products
Product is king	$\longrightarrow$	Process is king
Produces standard products	$\longrightarrow$	Assembles standard components
Economies of scale	$\longrightarrow$	Economies of scope
We sell what we make	$\longrightarrow$	We sell what the customer tells us to make
Produces to forecast	$\longrightarrow$	Produces to demand
High inertia	$\longrightarrow$	Is just-in-time
Frozen around one idea	$\longrightarrow$	Expresses imagination

4 Creating Entrepreneurial Structures

'A bureaucracy can be defined as a business that exists to carry out an organization.' (Stanley M. Davis)

THE VIRTUAL ORGANIZATION

Markets can no longer be secured through domination – they can only be continuously re-created through the distinctive satisfaction of fleeting customer needs. Any organization that is limited to less than the best, and to less of the best than is needed to bring distinctive satisfaction to each unique customer, is no longer in the position to transport itself beyond the boundaries of yesterday's fast-receding markets. As intangible assets such as customer orientation, knowledge, adaptability and innovativeness are coming to the fore in the quest for a sustainable presence in the scheme of things, future-creating dynamic behaviours are becoming more important than the past-preserving static positions and structures of the past. As organizations are required to continually transform what they do and how they do it, massiveness, a limited repertoire and a fascination with form and structure – once the stuff of substance – are increasingly being seen as the stuff of nonsense. As companies seek to develop the mobile and versatile capabilities required to thrive in the turbulent nineties, they are required to reduce their mass and inertia. To do so, they are throwing out yesterday's structures, configurations and relationships to be sure they have the ability to continually bring distinctions to their customers.

In a world where what makes sense seldom makes sense twice, the future of organizations increasingly depends on not being confined to what made sense the last time. Tomorrow's organization is not a static structure – it is a virtual means of expressing as many configurations of the world's physical, intangible and human resources as possible to produce the unique result required by each individual customer (see Figure 4.1). The issue is not the extent of its repertoire. The issue is the variety of the means it has available to express its creative capabilities. The world and all it has to offer is increasingly at the disposal of those with the ability to turn it into the means of extending the boundaries of customer's lifestyles. In a world where the value of resources depends on their ability

81

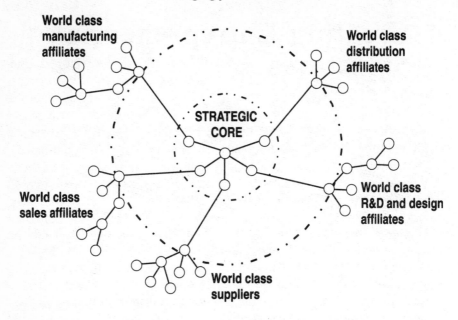

Figure 4.1 *The virtual organization*

to be incorporated into that which will make sense tomorrow, each new encounter with the customer redefines their value. The issue for tomorrow's organization is not the fast-becoming-simple one of access to the world's best – that is already possible – the issue is fast becoming the one of how to enhance and find expression for the art of customer-enhancing design using the most appropriate media available at the time. Tomorrow's organizations are not structures designed to give limited expression to limited resources. Instead they are conceived to give continuous unique expressions to unlimited resources whose value they multiply in the process.

Giving continuous unique expression to unlimited resources is not possible for those organizations who place greater value on the baggage they can carry than on the value they can create. Increasingly, no organization will create a place for itself if it has to carry its past everywhere it goes. No organization will create a place for itself if it has to carry around everything that might one day come in useful. To carry the baggage of activities that confer no distinction is to invite destruction by those who can perform quicker, more effectively, and at lower cost by not having to carry it around. In a fast-moving world, yesterday's baggage can only ever be a tribute to past success. Where the need is for the means of expressing the human spirit in new distinctive ways, the past can never secure a place in tomorrow's scheme of things.

Management techniques, attitudes and mindsets developed and venerated over generations, are challenged as tomorrow's organization requires the continuous redefinition of tangible and intangible boundaries if it is to stay focused on the customer's rather than its own needs. Management skills that were designed to increase stability by reducing and resisting change, have already become irrelevant and ultimately destructive. The dynamics of organizations are shifting in favour of those managers who have the skills and aptitudes to be excellent facilitators of the actions of those employed because of the excellent possibilities they can create. They are also shifting in favour of those not conditioned to managing within a narrow organizational space, and who are able to multiply possibilities by redefining resources and the uses to which they can be put.

Tomorrow's organization multiplies and exploits possibilities in real-time. Time-lags resulting from decision making which is distant from the tempo of the market are already being reduced by empowering those in touch with the market realities to make most of the possibilities they create. Massive functional and bureaucratic structures are being broken apart to get the past-preserving bureaucratic process out of the way of organizations that need to be in a hurry to get anywhere at all. Managers everywhere are being asked to rethink their roles in ways that gets them out of the loop between need and fast action. Business units are being floated-off to give them the chance to deal with the realities of their markets without being second-guessed by a parent organization who cannot possibly know as much about what is actually happening as those in the front-line.

Perhaps most significant of all is the trend towards increasing possibilities by abandoning resources, cultures, technologies, practices, knowledge and skills which lock the organization into previously learned patterns of behaviour. The drive is on to ensure that the organization can respond quickly to changes in the environment – those confined by the dead weight of past experience can only look on as the world passes by. The drive is on to continually refresh and replace resources, and to shift to resources which are disposable and easily replaceable with more appropriate resources whenever required. The limits to possibilities resulting from the baggage of being tied to particular resources, processes, technologies and people, is giving way to alliances and relationships with third parties who can supply whatever know-how and technologies are required. Not being burdened by means which can only do one thing in a world where variety and versatility are increasingly important, increases the possibilities for all.

Dynamic rather than static configurations are being pursued. No-one knows what intra and inter-business and industry combinations will make sense in the future. The organizations and 'industries' of tomorrow are marketplaces for freely available capabilities – capabilities that are free to join together in whatever way makes sense and which ensure that they have the opportunity to make their fullest possible contribution. Capabilities that can multiply their options and possibilities by temporarily combining with others to achieve greater individual and common purposes, are replacing the static configurations of the past. Dynamic recombination is replacing the lifetime combinations of the past – meeting the challenges of the day and the foreseeable future increasingly depends on not having sacrificed capability in the service of a future-confining past. The trend is towards virtual organizations consisting of dynamic and transitory combinations of world-class resources, temporarily combining to create the world-class capabilities required to meet increasingly transient customer needs.

With the growing recognition that survival and growth utterly depend on having distinctive capabilities, and in working with others to maintain them in circumstances that can remove their distinctiveness overnight, a great many organizations are already rapidly transforming themselves to become virtual organizations. The emergence of virtual organizations is reflected in the many disaggregations and dynamic recombinations going on all around the world. The focus of the virtual organization is the moving ball of customer lifestyle-enhancing value – not the particular means of producing it at a particular point in time. Its capabilities are not the static concentrations of the slower-paced past. Its capabilities are what it is able to dynamically concentrate to meet transient needs.

Tomorrow's organization moves with fast-moving times because, rather than being full of dead weight, it has no weight. Its capabilities are those which can find expression for the best, and by so doing create possibilities for the future. Its energies are directed to the search for whatever is required in whatever combination to express customer lifestyle-enhancing designs. Its sense of identity is its purpose rather than its substance.

ORGANIZATION IN FLUX

Organizations pursuing the change-resisting strategies of monoculture, impermeable boundaries, and domination of markets and resources, are being swept aside by a rapidly changing world that requires continuous reconfigurations to meet new definitions of customer value. To seek to create stability by denying and defying instability, is to seek to squeeze the life out of the customer.

For tomorrow's organizations, the rigidities of the structures of the past are serious obstacles to flexibility, adaptability and fast responses. Instead of enabling the organization to maintain a dynamic orientation to the customer, the structures of the past confine it and its people to the diminishing groups of customers who have not yet moved on. The structures and cultures of the past and their obsessive and impermeable inward-looking tendencies, isolate the organization and its people from the dynamics and immediacies of a fast-changing world which otherwise would compel them to engage in rapid and continuous learning. Their not-invented-here attitudes preclude the formation of the many alliances and relationships required to ensure access to the best resources in the world. Their fascinations with form and formality merely embroider organizational baggage – actions which can only increase inertia and distract attention from the need to move rapidly and positively ahead.

Organizational structures are snap-shot configurations of human assumptions about how best to achieve business goals at an instant in time. When time was apparently moving more slowly, each snap-shot looked much like the next. The transformation of large organizations and their layered hierarchies that we all see, is not the breaking apart of functional and bureaucratic structures and their once massive and rigid supply chains – with all their negative connotations – it is their rapid evolution from undifferentiated monolith to dynamic polymorph. The de-layering of middle management reflects a shift in the need from those who plan, predict and control the future, to those who can make it happen. The fascination with stability, fixed assets and the static is giving way to being in touch with the dynamics of things.

The dynamics of things are determining what organizations or configurations of resources, ideas, assumptions and technologies make sense. From being a cage for those resources, ideas, assumptions, skills and technologies that had been captured or entrapped, organizational forms are being reconceived as platforms for the expression of their possibilities (see Figure 4.2). The emerging new forms of organizations such as 'virtual organizations' are characterized by their lack of predetermined form and by their ability to take on any form. The virtual organization is an organization without time-spanning structure. It is a way of approaching things which allows any possible configuration of resource including culture, beliefs, management and operational assumptions to take place quickly as needs and purposes require. It also allows any prior configuration of things to be rapidly disassembled when its usefulness has passed. Its virtue is its ability to behave in ways appropriate to circumstances – not in the gothic elegance of its structures. Virtual organizations are about the dynamics of possibility-creating instability and the capabilities required to participate in creating the future. Being a part of one is as different as being part of the architecture is from being the architect. (See Figure 4.2.)

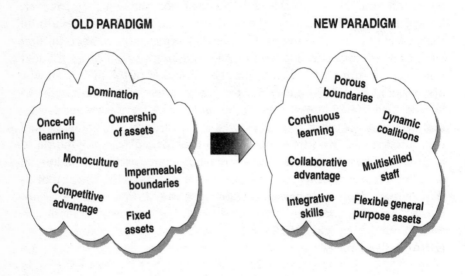

Figure 4.2 *Organization in flux*

DEMASSIFICATION

Massiveness is about being burdened with the legacies of the past and being excluded by them from participating in the future. Culture, beliefs, processes, technology, and management and operational assumptions that permit only limited possibilities, are legacies not assets when the imperative is to create as many new possibilities as quickly as possible.

Transforming processes, technology, skills, structures and management practices is not the whole story. As Peter Senge and others have made plain, perhaps the central issue is how organizations and their people see the world, and about how they are changed by what they see. The inability of organizations to learn is perhaps the biggest source of organizational sloth. The continuous transformation of assumptions and know-how is central to the ability of an organization to demassify, and therefore to its consistent ability to stage whatever customer-enhancing performance is necessary wherever and whenever.

As it becomes clear that leveraging and utilizing the collective knowledge of the organization's people provides the only sustainable advantage, knowledge which is inaccessible or tied up increases the inertia of the organization. The amount of knowledge that is built into most organizations is vast, and their learning capacities – the ability to regenerate and apply knowledge – is also potentially vast. However, knowledge that is bound up in the productive, organizational and cultural legacies of the past is useless. Productive, organizational and cultural legacies which are inflexible, confine the organization to what it thought was true in the past. These legacies also stifle the ability of the organization to learn by making it impossible to apply new organizational learning fast enough for it to still be useful. Only by having access to new know-how and capabilities as and when required, and by not constraining what the organization knows and can do to a particular configuration of process, technical, organizational and management assumptions of the past, can the organization have the potential to operate with zero mass – the ability to express its changing know-how in real-time.

DISAGGREGATION

Tomorrow's organization is light-weight and fast on its feet. Its structures, processes and practices are not designed to be past-preserving and to limit the range of its possible futures. Its dynamically shifting forms are determined by the unique needs of each customer. The particular forms it assumes from time to time reflect the particular combinations of resources required to create the capability needed to meet customer demands. Its allocations of resources instead of being determined by hoarded, slow and concentrated decision making approaches, are directly in contact with and influenced by the customer. The aim is to ensure that the organization can respond more closely to the customer by changing what the organization does to meet customer-defined criteria for success – not by preserving its past assumptions and past configurations.

Tomorrow's organization is determined to go about increasing its organizational surface area and by so doing making the market realities the organizational realities. By being intimately connected to the market realities, it is easier and faster for organizations to acknowledge them as real and as primary determinants of survival and growth. Most organizations that get left behind got left behind because they did not know they were being left behind. In the past this process may have taken some time. Now, in a fast moving and instant information global world where there are no quiet backwaters and no safe hiding places, that which is not competitive with the world's best rapidly becomes common knowledge. And in a world of increasingly direct global sourcing, those who are not continually stretched by being connected to the market realities being continually redefined by the best, will be configured out of the commercial equation. Disaggregation allows for alternative configurations of organizational resources and capabilities, and by multiplying the connections the organization can have with the wider world – disaggregation multiplies the possible configurations the organization can have. As the time it takes to turn new possibilities into action needs to decrease, disaggregation can increase the speed with which new configurations can be created.

Disaggregation, reflected in the current waves of 'downsizing' and 'rightsizing', can free management from the massive task of maintaining the organization and its legacies, and allow them to focus on the realities of creating value in a fast-changing world. The results that are relevant to creating customer value, and the standards required to outpace the competition, become the sole reason for the existence of any part of a disaggregated organization – what needs to be focused on for results to be achieved becomes clear and self-defining – no part has anywhere to hide and no part has any tied customers. As the value of management increasingly becomes defined in terms of their ability to create the future, disaggregation releases them from being the prisoners or custodians of the past.

As the clear emerging pattern is not one of the static concentration of resources, skills and management expertise to produce the strategic capabilities of the organization, but the diversified access to the best of key capabilities such as design, manufacturing, sales and distribution wherever they are located, disaggregation opens the organization to accessing and working with world class providers of products and services to create powerful new and dynamic capabilities. As a key management requirement is an uncompromising insistence on sourcing and combining the best, disaggregation empowers managers by increasing the possible ways in which they can deploy resources within the organization and in conjunction with others outside. Disaggregation provides managers with more scope to dynamically design and realize their customer-centred visions in ways that add distinctive value in the marketplace.

It used to be that global companies needed global mass markets in order to compete. An important consequence of disaggregation is that it allows organizations to combine with others to create that which clearly stands out in terms of building a future in global markets. The dynamic combinations that disaggregation makes possible, extends the ability of all committed to excellence to add clear value individually and to amplify their contributions in concert with others. The multiple possibilities that disaggregation enables, allows global behaviour from organizations which otherwise would be confined within the limitations of a one-product niche.

PARTICIPATION

World-class capabilities are increasingly the result of dynamic relationships between those who are best at what they do. The ability to bring the best to the most demanding customers increasingly requires access to the best in the world – and the ability to intelligently and dynamically recombine them to meet unique once-off customer needs.

Access to the best, and the ability to contribute to the best, are key issues in tomorrow's transient world. The basic entry standard for being part of the dynamic world of expressing excellence in unique ways, is to be the best at what you do. The increasingly intelligent information infrastructures spreading rapidly within and between organizations and cities make it possible for everyone, wherever they are, to accept nothing less than the best. International, industry and technical standards are proliferating in the rush to extend the scope of markets for world-class niche capabilities, and in the rush to be part of the customer's complex individual or organizational lifestyle formula. As intelligent information infrastructures proliferate, the need for entirely new organizational behaviours and operating patterns is thrust to the forefront. The physical and visible organizations of the past and present, and the industrial infrastructures that are cities become irrelevant, as virtual organizations operating globally but from nowhere in particular, increasingly inhabit a global anything-anywhere-anytime intelligent info-sphere.

The ability to be part of tomorrow can be influenced by factors other than technical standards, for example, language and culture. But increasingly the only constraint is not having something distinctive to offer – anything-anywhere-anytime intelligent information infrastructures are rapidly eliminating barriers and enabling access to distinction. No organization or country is big enough to excel at everything or single-handedly dominate the competitive high ground. As it is the customer that increasingly determines what is distinctive, no organization can limit itself to playing in the game with anything less than the best – wherever it is located. Tomorrow's organization is about amplifying the best to provide distinctive customer value beyond that which could be provided by any one organization alone. The success of tomorrow's organization is about the advantages borne of amplification not the frequently negative-sum games of competitive advantage.

DYNAMIC COALITIONS

As markets rush towards once-off occurrences of the unique, and as the complexities of customer lifestyles and the requirements for enhancing them increase, it cannot be assumed that the relatively static supply chain relationships that worked in the past will meet future needs. The continuous shifts in expertise, resources and process configurations required to meet each new situation, make permanent configurations increasingly unrealistic. The need to meet opportunities as they arise, makes it increasingly important for organizations to gain rapid access to whatever capabilities they require to meet the newly encountered customer need.

Dynamic coalitions enable organizations to assume as many configurations of resources and resource providers as may be required. Dynamic coalitions transform organizations from static combinations whose classifications stand the test of time, to that indefinable something that makes a difference in the world. As the static characteristics of products become less and less important, the value organizations can create becomes increasingly defined in terms of their design-intensive relationships with evolving customer lifestyles. Everyone is in the customer satisfaction industry and the only issue is what dynamic and changing configurations of the best are needed to deliver satisfactions to the customer.

Tomorrow's organizations are vehicles for participation in a world of uncertainty whose only certainties are dramatically compressing cycle times, ever more transitory market conditions, and customer-specific configurations of resource and capabilities. They cannot operate effectively unless they have the ability to respond quickly on their own and in concert with how ever many others need to be involved to deliver the required response. The more time-critical the conditions for success, the more that organizations have to transcend inter-organizational

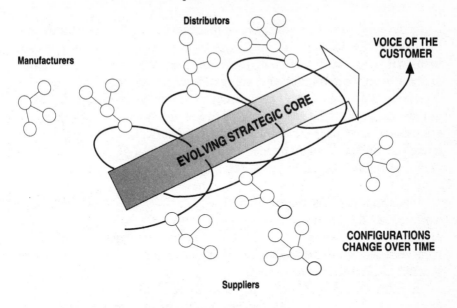

Figure 4.3 *Dynamic coalitions*

boundaries. The aim is not merely to achieve end-to-end process integration – that is no less static than what was possible before. The aim is to enable dynamic behaviours – to extend the range of the possible ways in which the organization can interact with its evolving customers, co-producers, suppliers and customers. Extending the range of organizational behaviours requires a fundamental rethink of processes, structures, cultures, systems, skills, rewards, management practices – and adversarial attitudes to those who are not self. The dynamic behaviours required by the organizations of tomorrow are founded in a radical rethink of organizational capabilities and what it takes to produce them.

CO-OPERATIVE ADVANTAGE

In today's world where no organization is an island and where only the best is good enough, competitive advantage is giving way to co-operative advantage – the ability to amplify the best.

The need for tomorrow's organizations to be able to amplify the best is reflected in organizations all across the world demassifying and disaggregating. Functions, skills and resources which no longer contribute directly and necessarily to organizational distinction, and the ability of the organization to maintain a distinction in the face of fierce competition, are being shed rapidly and universally. As the energy-sapping baggage of industrial age structures is being dissolved away, highly focused, versatile and distinctive capabilities and competencies are taking their place. As excellence and total quality become a basic requirement to have any place in the commercial scheme of things, it is the ability to apply excellence in unique ways that can form the only basis for distinction. As the economics of distinction increasingly depend on the application of excellence across multiple global niches, only those that can amplify their distinctive capabilities across the world will survive to become tomorrow's organizations. As satisfying customers with complex lifestyle requirements depends on the integration of a diverse array of products, services and resources, few organizations will be able to develop, sustain and exploit their unique capabilities without close collaborations with those who themselves are the best at what they do.

Co-operative approaches are increasingly required for any world class response to take place. Co-operative approaches depend on every organization aiming to have a future by increasing its ability to take advantage of, and work with, differing capabilities. Organizations and individuals who are limited by conditioning, culture, attitudes, skill or language to working with a few, will not be able to amplify their contributions to the scale required to make a difference. Having a future depends on being in a position to amplify the potentials and benefits of the best.

Individual organizations increasingly depend on customers seeing them as being the sum of themselves and their collaborative relationships. Organizations positioned in this way to take advantage of the best in the world improve their competitive capabilities. They can bring much more to any situation than they alone could. They might not be large themselves but they can mobilize large possibilities. Likewise they can be brought into the frame by others committed to bringing the best to their customers – their market access is extended by the needs of others who cannot stage the best performance without them.

Being in a position to amplify the potentials of others, transforms the role and outlooks of organizations. Instead of thinking within the limitations of the present roles, boundaries and niches, the basic instinct becomes one making them bigger and different. Rather than being there to channel and manage what is currently available, the outlook becomes one of finding new possibilities for what is available, and by finding new possibilities, to redefine what we thought we had available. In the old paradigm, most organization spend most of their time managing weaknesses. Managing weakness is an unwelcome distraction from the central task of realizing the potentials of that with most to offer.

Co-operative advantage is about converging with the best to form future-creating outcomes which are an expression of the best in the world (see Figure 4.4). Access to world-class suppliers ensures world-class inputs and offers the potential to do the best with only the best. Access to world-class design houses offers the potential to increase the rate at which designs evolve to track advancing customer expectations. Access to a proliferation of physical and electronic distribution media transforms the local into the global. Access to specialist producers makes it possible to do things in small volumes, and to do different things every time – individual once-off niches can become the natural market for world-class capabilities. The economics of business are transformed as business processes – previously designed to defend boundaries and to manage weakness and limitation – are re-engineered to eliminate the many costs of producing for markets that do not exist, and to eliminate the need for the many duplications that arise from lack of information, trust and common purpose. Perhaps most important of all, by co-operating with others committed to excellence, the organization can extend the range of

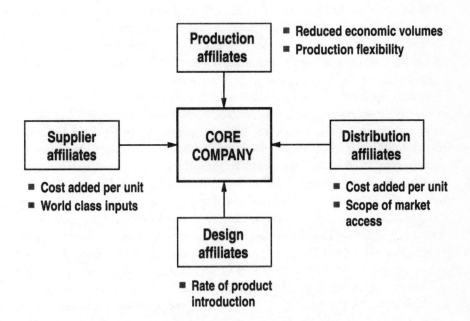

Figure 4.4 *Co-operative advantage*

possibilities it can be part of – its whole becomes the sum of its capabilities and their relationships.

As globalization accelerates, boundary-less global participation and collaboration will become essential. The prize of mastering the dynamics of working as and when required with the best in the world will be the opportunity to amplify special contributions across global markets.

NETWORKING SKILLS

The only skill of value in tomorrow's organization, is the ability to make a difference – however big or small. Those who have been conditioned by having a fixed job to do within the confines of a corporate machine seldom know more than how to keep the existing machine turning. Tomorrow's organizations depend on those conditioned only to making things happen, and on those conditioned to building the future with or without the past.

Participation in the organizations of tomorrow depends entirely on having something unique to offer and being able to market it successfully to those working to extend customer lifestyle boundaries. This depends on more than 'technical' and 'professional' skills – although these are essential requirements – it depends on people being complete, well-rounded and concerned for the totality and consequences of things. As Buckminster Fuller pointed out, 'specialization has bred feelings of isolation, futility, and confusion in individuals. It has also resulted in the individual's leaving responsibility for thinking and social action to others.' The skills required to operate effectively in tomorrow's organizations are designing: integrative and creative. They are sensing and intuitive. For these essentially human attributes to find expression – these attributes will be the only things in demand – they must be backed up by a wide range of 'professional' and 'technical' skills. In tomorrow's organizations, 'professional' and 'technical' skills will be of no value unless they are the means by which the person can make a designing, integrative and creative contribution. It is these contributions that are vital. 'Professional' and 'technical' skills as they exist and are understood at any point time are only the current tools that complete people have at their disposal.

For anyone to have a place in a value and versatility-demanding future, the sole concern must be with the totality of what it takes to find the shortest route to customer value. This makes the difference between those who create opportunities and those who are content to shore up past positions.

MANAGING WITHOUT BOUNDARIES

Organizational boundaries once defined by the need to channel and interpret information, are being dissolved by electronic media which do it better. Middlemen – be they middle managers or intermediaries – are being replaced by electronic markets able to instantly connect those who know and those who need to know. Computer-enabled integration shortens the distance between intra and inter-organizational processes. Information technology is making the entire organization, and the value network of which it is a part, transparent – visible in its entirety from any position and by anybody. The transparent boundaries increasingly characteristic of organizations and industries, change the manager's role dramatically. Instead of managing within known confines and with direct control of the required resources, the only confines are the results which must be achieved with whatever resources from wherever that can be brought together to achieve the desired outcome better and faster than the competition.

When only the best can create the best, it is short-sighted and limiting to confine the organization only to those resources which are owned by it. Increasingly few organizations have all the resources they need to do the job within the narrow confines of organizational boundaries – however large the organization. When definitions of the 'best' vary with every customer requirement, it is difficult to ensure that the most appropriate designers, manufacturers, suppliers and distributors are accessible wherever and whenever they are required. When access to the best and most appropriate resources are the minimum requirement for the delivery excellence to the customer, the management horizon must not be artificially limited to obsolete territorial concepts such as ownership and organizational boundaries. The management issue is not one of making do with what is available. The management issue is finding the best and creating markets for the best.

Managing without boundaries is a commitment to creating markets for the best. It is a profoundly entrepreneurial management mandate. The territorial and feudal inclinations of many managers are just as constraining as failures of leadership, vision and imagination. Managing without boundaries means managing without the structural and psychological boundaries of the past – and without putting boundaries on the inevitably surprising possibilities of the future.

The vital endeavour of management in tomorrow's organizations is to learn how to make better use of the best, how to multiply the possibilities the best can bring to the customer – and how to create the future. The organizational learning that results is not knowledge. It is the capacity to find new ways to transcend the physical and mental boundaries of the past. The vital role of tomorrow's managers is not to maintain structures and boundaries – that is to guarantee the past – but to actively redefine them. Managing without boundaries is a commitment to adaptive and discontinuous learning, where the driver is an uncompromising commitment to bring the best to customers intent on furthering their own ideals.

THE ESSENTIAL RESOURCE

Tomorrow's organization depends for its success on its abilities to apply its specialist capabilities and expertise to a wide range of collaborative possibilities.

In a world where effectiveness in markets depends on the creative, designing, entrepreneurial and architecting skills of people, confining them within the rigid structures of past processes and management practices is a sure way of restricting rather than enhancing the capabilities of the organization. Where fixed competitive positions restrict movement they are more likely to result in competitive disadvantage than advantage. Massive organizational structures may give a sense of comfort but increasingly only the comfort of not being alone in distress. Where processes, technologies and systems can be copied or obtained in the market, any advantages they once offered can be quickly eliminated.

Only effective managers and innovative people can be the source of the designing and architecting skills, and the dynamism and entrepreneurial flair that are the essential resources of tomorrow's dynamic organizations. Individual organizations may require fewer people than in the past – certainly fewer drones – but its key assets are increasingly and absolutely its people. Not just any people however – there can be no right of belonging, or salaried sinecures, and only less demand for those content to simply trade labour for wages. A commitment to lifetime learning and to the creation of distinctiveness for the organizations they are associated with, will be the basis from which people will become valued and sought after resources. Those who are readily able to perform many roles will be a valued source of flexibility. The sustainability of organizations in the future will depend on the abilities of their managers and people to understand and apply world-class practices in the pursuit of world-class customer-enhancing capabilities. Only those individuals who are committed to being lifetime learners will be given continuing learning opportunities.

A continued place in the scheme of things depends on developing the capabilities that are continually pulled ahead by fast growing people. Massive organizations designed to preserve positions rather than to continually develop new capabilities and extend the boundary of the possible, will not attract, develop or retain the people who can be its only source of future success.

MANAGING INTERDEPENDENCE

The organization of tomorrow can only satisfy its customers if it is able to bring the best of everything from a changing portfolio of resource providers and alliance partners around the world. The customer and his or her need is the common space in which the best in the world must converge. The issue in bringing the best together is less one of the speed with which the best can be brought together to behave as one system, it is more one of making it possible for all to act with one thought – how to extend the boundaries of what is the best in the world.

Competitive conditions increasingly require the ability to enable the best in the globe to focus their capabilities onto local opportunities wherever they occur on the globe. Competitive conditions are fast shifting to the point where all organizations – whether local or not – have to deal with the movements of global competition intent on bringing the best to whatever they do wherever they do it. When increasingly all issues, opportunities or threats are global, individual organizations need the ability to converge with others to form whatever capabilities are required, and to be in a position to bring their unique contributions to extend the boundaries of what otherwise would have possible. At a time when real value can only be created when the needs of fast-changing individual niches are fulfilled, all organizations must be able to pour themselves into local niches. When the global market is increasingly a sea of individually unique niches, organizational destiny depends on being better than the best global competition in focusing the best in the world onto the widest range of unique local opportunities. Under these conditions, interdependence is not a structural, systems or procedural problem, it is about enabling the best to converge to bring the best in world to their individual customers wherever they are located.

In an important sense tomorrow's organizations are lenses which depend for their success on their ability to amplify and focus the capabilities of others. Amplifying capabilities results from leveraging them across multiple global niches. It depends on the best being able to bring their best to the right place at the right time. It depends on the best knowing fully what they have to do to play their part in meeting the challenge laid down by the customer. The voice of the customer must be clear to all and the best means must be available to all. Unless the best in the world is available and is usable, individual companies will invariably do their own thing to meet their local challenges. The customer will get less than the best and certainly will get no more than the best of one small organization.

Unless all the resources and capabilities of organizations can behave as one, there can be no recognition that what may be happening in one market may not be local but the result of a global initiative from another global player – and one which will be coming to other markets soon. Unless the resources and capabilities of organizations can behave as one, little can happen in local markets – without the global to back it up, the local may not be enough. For the right people and resources to be identified and brought together to deliver the best response, there can be only one view of the organization and that is the global view. With the global view, whatever a global competitor is doing in a local market, the organization has the entire world at its disposal – and it can ensure a response that does everyone justice.

Competing in the global marketplace depends on all providers of resources and capabilities being able to converge to meet a common need or goal whenever required. The only structure that makes sense is the one-off combination of resources and capabilities required to meet the once-off customer need. Elimination of internal and external boundaries is not the issue – though they do need to be reconceived. The issue is primarily one of freeing up resources to be able to perform multiple roles, and putting them in a position to respond to the voice of the customer.

The inhabitants of tomorrow's organizations depend entirely on their ability to respond to the call of the customer. They need to be attuned to the customer's needs and be willing and able to contribute in whatever way to ensure that excellence is delivered to the customer. Managing interdependence is not about management process, it is about ensuring that each part of the organization has no obstacles to seeing and hearing the customer, and what needs to be done to satisfy his or her needs. The customer must also to be able to see the organization in terms of its total capability – not in terms of the limitations of the part with which he or she has come in contact. The customer must only be aware of the excellence the organization as a whole can deliver – not of the difficulties a lumbering bureaucracy may have in doing the most elementary of tasks.

Fast-changing customers demand the best, and fast-moving global competitors are only too keen to bring it to them. Organizations now need to be able to dynamically reshape what they do and with whom, to bring the best in the world in as many ways as possible. When only the best is enough, only those without physical and intangible boundaries can deliver.

PROFILE OF THE NEW PARADIGM

The characteristics of old organizations and their new entrepreneurial counterparts can be summarized as follows:

Old paradigm		New paradigm
Integrated/high inertia	$\longrightarrow$	Autonomous/low inertia
High fixed assets	$\longrightarrow$	Low fixed assets
Single-purpose assets	$\longrightarrow$	Multipurpose assets
Nobody does it better	$\longrightarrow$	Extensive outsourcing
Combative	$\longrightarrow$	Collaborative
Functional managers	$\longrightarrow$	Network managers
Clear boundaries	$\longrightarrow$	Fuzzy boundaries
Rigid relationships	$\longrightarrow$	Dynamic coalitions
Resource led	$\longrightarrow$	Capability led
Independent parts	$\longrightarrow$	Interdependent parts
Ownership of all processes	$\longrightarrow$	Subcontracting and alliances
Arm's-length relationships	$\longrightarrow$	Linked by one thought
Undifferentiated monolith	$\longrightarrow$	Dynamic polymorph

5 Change-Seeking Culture

'Every creative act involves . . . a new innocence of perception, liberated from the cataract of accepted belief.' (Arthur Koestler)

ADAPT OR DIE

An essential characteristic of tomorrow's organization is its ability to adapt the changing criteria for success into a behavioural repertoire that ensures its continued survival, growth, and development. In other words, tomorrow's organization needs to excel in the translation of new priorities into new organizational behaviours.

Organizations have a strong tendency to preserve what they have learned in the past. They have a strong tendency to preserve legacy assumptions about people, and the nature of work, in the institutions of management. They preserve their assumptions about what value is and how it is created in legacy business processes and procedures. They tend to assume that the preservation of past success is more important than the creation of tomorrow's success. The challenge is a complex one. Almost by definition how we see the world determines how we interpret the world, and how we 'choose' to behave in it. The basic values and assumptions of an organization absolutely determine how it perceives the world and unless challenged, can only lead to actions designed for that perception of the world. If the organization cannot see the world as it is, but as it was, it cannot adapt to it – and it cannot survive for long in it. A culture that reinforces behaviours not relevant to the organization's current or future business environment can only confine the organization to an increasingly irrelevant past.

Adaptation requires changing expectations and letting go of the past. It requires the continued redefinition of what makes sense and of the behaviours consistent with success. This is difficult to achieve and painful. Despite the obvious benefits of anticipating future problems when things are still going well, it is usually only when an organization is clearly sinking into deep trouble that the obvious need for change becomes generally recognized. Even then, change is not easy. Changing the winning formula of the past, the expectations and assumptions that go with it, and replacing old ways of doing things with something unfamiliar, will always be difficult and challenging. Changing the winning formula of the past challenges those associated with it and who have chosen the permanence of a monument, to the permanence of being up with the times.

Turbulent times require the ability to adapt processes, structures, assumptions, and models of past success quickly. The ability to adapt requires the processes, structures, assumptions, and models of past success to be challenged, discarded where necessary, and rapidly reconfigured to produce behaviour consistent with the requirements of where the business needs to be. A challenge to managers is to become the catalysts, not just of change, but of the redefinition of organizational culture. Rather than seeing themselves as overseers of a static feudal estate, they must become the guidance and renewal system of a fast moving body (see Figure 5.1).

The adaptability requirements of tomorrow's organization require that managers are able to deal with the tensions inherent in challenging the past, discarding it where required and regenerating the capabilities required to deliver new excellence at low cost. As the organization's guidance system, managers will need to increase the capacity of their organizations to continuously renew themselves. Rather than being the custodians of the past, tomorrow's managers need to be at the centre of transforming new requirements and old assumptions into new values and new ways of doing things.

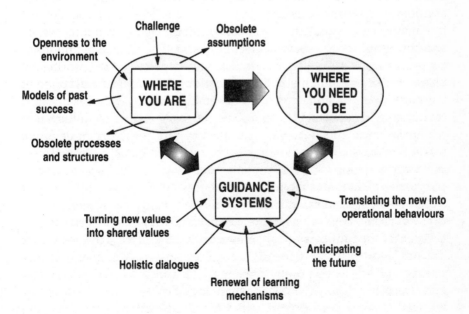

Figure 5.1 *A model of adaptation*

For those who aspire to become the managers of tomorrow's organizations, the key issues are how to transform their cultures into dynamic systems attuned to fast-evolving customer needs, and how to turn new cultural assumptions into new adaptive behaviours.

STAYING IN TUNE

Change-seeking organizations are those that are capable of maintaining their forward viability however circumstances change. They are in tune with their times – change is welcome and continuous and the natural companion of evolving circumstances. They see the future coming and have less to do to adapt to it than those for whom each change is a surprise.

Change is always a surprise for those who succumb to the inclination to use what has proven itself to be useful in the past as the judge and jury of the present and the future. To have any chance of staying in tune with the future, the values, beliefs, and meanings that influence and determine how and why things get done today, must be understood – and made explicit, examined and evaluated – before the merits and usefulness of new values, beliefs and meanings can become tomorrow's source of relevant, consistent and adaptive behaviour.

Tomorrow's organization is change-seeking. Its assumptions, beliefs and values are seen as resources like any other, not some ancestral totem whose influence is for all time. Its assumptions, beliefs and practices are resources like any other in that they are merely part of the necessary logic of transforming raw materials into something useful to customers. If it was a computer system's job to receive, interpret, and translate signals in the environment to ensure that the company was not flying blind, and it was not doing so, it would be dispassionately and quickly replaced. For tomorrow's organization assumptions, beliefs and practices serve the same purpose and are evaluated in the same terms.

Tomorrow's organization sees culture as a resource that will increase or decrease its ability to behave effectively in turbulent times. Its priority is to ensure that the cultural resource is useful in that it increase its chances for survival, growth, and success. It recognizes that everything it does is a product of its assumptions, and that its strategies and tactics for effectiveness and growth will be determined by them. The cultural link between required performance and what will be achieved is clear. The management priority is to ensure that the tendencies of the organization are not the result of historical pre-programming, but the result of a management process designed to ensure that basic beliefs, values and assumptions are continuously transformed to maintain their relevance.

The change-seeking organizations of tomorrow are committed to ensuring they evolve the distinctive capabilities required to create meaningful futures for themselves and for their customers. They require an outlook which is centred in the desire to change the world for the better. They require the ability to respond in ways which will ensure that the organization and its people can indeed meet the challenge of redefining the future – when that is what its competition will also be trying to do (see Figure 5.2). Whether the organization ends up as a bystander or worse, depends on the capacity to reconfigure whatever assumptions, values, behaviours, structures and processes are required to enable the organization to see its challenges clearly and respond quickly and confidently to them. Tomorrow's organization must therefore become the master of complex adaptation – able to continually change structures, processes, products and skills in a way that ensures its future. These changes are unlikely to happen unless its basic beliefs, values and assumptions are in tune with what is required. The capacity to adapt

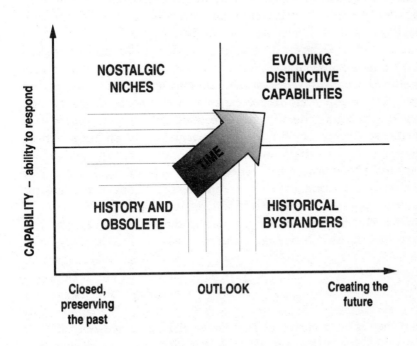

Figure 5.2 *Staying in tune*

therefore has its foundations in a future-creating outlook, and its expression in adaptive capabilities.

Culture and capabilities are not two different things. They are both expressions of the same thing – assumptions about what it takes to grow and survive in an apparently hostile world. However forward looking a culture, and however intent its people are on making a positive difference, without structures, processes, resources and practices that can be changed to stay in tune with events, the organization cannot realize its future-creating mission. If the organization's structures and processes are immovable, the will to adapt may fade, and along with it the organization's future. The question of what it takes to stay in tune with events, requires a holistic discussion of the assumptions, beliefs, values, structures, practices and processes required to enable the organization to behave in the required way. A major rethink of the cultures and capabilities together is required to ensure survival.

Tomorrow's organization must have a culture which is open to change, and which is capable of being changed. This does not happen by chance. Developing the capabilities required to ensure survival is predicated on uncovering cultural assumptions, exposing them to challenge and having the ability to replace them with others with greater potential for success. Management's critical role becomes the process of continuously redefining, replacing and reconfiguring cultural assumptions in such a way as they enable the organization to stay in tune with the turbulent worlds of today and tomorrow. Developing the capabilities required to ensure survival also depends on the simultaneous reshaping of the organization's structures, processes, skills, resources, assets and practices to enable new assumptions to be expressed in the form of the behaviours required by a fast-changing world. To ensure responsiveness to a changing world, management has a vital responsibility to continually refresh the organization's assumptions and beliefs about what will work and ensure that practices, structures, processes, skills, resources and assets change in an adaptive way. When the need is for organizational forms capable of continuous transformation, tomorrow's managers must become the primary catalysts of holistic organizational renewal.

OPENNESS

There is no comprehensive and provable theory of business and no cookbook solution which if copied will guarantee success. All organizations are operating on the boundary between success and failure, and the boundary is a moving target. In a very real sense each organization is engaged in exploring what will work and how best to turn what has the potential to work into practice within its own individual and unique context. In that sense, organizations are vehicles of discovery engaged at the edge of current boundaries and charged with pushing them forward. For managers who see themselves in that way, the fact that the future has no track record and that the current boundaries of business are moving faster than the theories which seek to explain what is happening, holds no fear. There is now no option but for each manager to invent the future. This means generating theories and attempting to turn theories into practice (current practice being almost certainly obsolete), and turning experience into the next theory. The only issue is how quickly this regenerative learning loop can be made to operate – practice is the way we learn and theory is the way we make sense of what we learn.

For tomorrow's organization, its 'guidance' system is the rate at which it can learn. The closed organizations of yesterday tend not to learn – they tend to preserve the past. They tend to seek the imagined comfort of remaining fixed to yesterday's wavefront, trading complacently on past success. The open organizations of tomorrow are less concerned with preserving knowledge and experience than with refreshing it. They have no time for the bureaucratic and political structures that create defensive walls and water-tight compartments around everything, and which make it difficult for the organization to learn. Organizational learning is vital and this requires change and adaptation. This does not occur if what is known and assumed cannot be challenged and changed. Organizational learning is about creating a close interchange between what the customer needs and the required configurations of organizational capabilities – and using that intimate interchange to fuel continuous transformation.

Tomorrow's organizations are profoundly concerned with being connected intimately to the future as it unfolds. Staying on track with the future requires everyone to understand how they and their organizations are connected to the conditions for future success. Everyone needs to be able to see and experience the vital connection between their own interest in the future, their assumptions about it, and the personal transformations they must accomplish. Staying on track with the future is profoundly behavioural – it requires every individual to be connected with the future. Staying on track also means that as behaviours are transformed so must their means of expression also be transformed. The organization must not only be able to be changed by the future, it must be able to create it. Its knowledge, processes and its wider capabilities must be undergoing continuous transformation so that the energies and resourcefulness arising from people's vital connection with the future can be amplified and expressed in future-creating ways. Staying on track with the future requires the organization to constantly be pulled forward as part of a strategic feedback loop connecting the customer to the evolving resources and energies of the organization (see Figure 5.3).

In an important sense every organization exists on the boundary between what works now, what no longer works, and what will work in the future. And this boundary is not static, it is moving and moving in such a way that results in the organization always being poised between relevance and irrelevance. What keeps an organization relevant is its ability to learn about and respond effectively to what will create tomorrow's customer satisfaction. In tomorrow's organizations everyone, not just those few concerned with specialist aspects of planning, has to be concerned with what will bring tomorrow's success – and how opportunities and new ideas can be used to change the way the organization works. Tomorrow's organization can only succeed if the future is everyone's concern.

For the change-seeking organizations of tomorrow, the basic requirement is for everyone to be actively seeking what is needed to keep the organization relevant. The goal is to transcend the present and the past

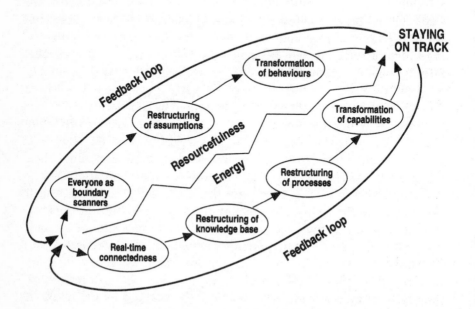

Figure 5.3 *Strategic feedback loops*

with a commitment to creating new futures and the capabilities required to bring them about.

SHORTENING THE LOOP

The rate at which new responses can be learned and applied is on the critical path to the future. Shortening the loop between significant events and them being registered, puts organizations in touch with real-time. Closing the loop between significant events and a world-class response enables them to operate in real-time. Shortening the loop between local innovation and wider innovation determines the effective intelligence of the organization.

How quickly new practices, ideas and innovations can be made available to and applied around the organization, determines whether the organization has any effective scale. For tomorrow's organizations scale means intelligence and the ability to express it, not mass. An organization which cannot transfer new insights and new means of achieving future-creating responses up, down, across and around the organization, may have size but little effective intelligence. The cultural and attitudinal dimensions of shortening the organizational learning loop are key. Communications infrastructures – however advanced – will have little effect unless the organization puts building the future ahead of preserving the past. Organizations that put mutual respect before mutual respect for the future, are at best making the future walk on glass. Cultures where certain functions reign supreme, or specialists presume they have superior know-how, or where imposition, self-concern or exploitation are the management strategies of first resort – have chosen limitation over the extension and redefinition of today's boundaries. They will find that innovation – however fine – will not travel. Without a high value being placed on amplifying the best – rather than hoarding it or confining it – the chances of the organization acting with its collective intelligence to solve problems, and acting with its collective capability to create the future, are near to effective zero.

PLASTICITY

Organization is the persistence of memory. However, what worked today is less likely than ever to work tomorrow. Tomorrow's organization needs the capacity to change every aspect of its culture, structures, processes, products, skills and management practices. It needs the capacity to transform, reorganize, and move off in new directions. This ability to change shape to meet new challenges is central to the ability to express whatever behaviours are consistent with whatever is required by a changing environment. Whereas bureaucracies confine the organization to yesterday's possibilities, tomorrow's organization needs to respond to tomorrow's possibilities. A task of management is to develop this capacity in ways that ensure the organization can redefine what it can do and how it does it, as fast as its fastest moving customers.

Tomorrow's organization cannot afford outlooks and means which confine it in space and time. No boundary – technical, professional, cultural or mental – can afford to be fixed. Particular configurations of ideas and means must exist to meet a purpose, but no configuration has any merit beyond that which it contributes to enhancing the customer's lifestyle. In a world of continuous change, tomorrow's organizations need to be capable of endless reconfigurations.

The persistence of an irrelevant past can only limit the scope for creating the future. The persistence of the past is fine as long as it works. Changing and adapting to meet the changing demands of markets, competitors or technological possibilities means being able to erase and reprogramme the organizational memory. It means recognizing that what we know is all we know at the time. Organizations and the individuals in them are not slaves to what is known. What is known is a tool – and only so as long as it is useful. When what is known is no longer useful, what is known needs to be redefined.

PARADOXES OF CHANGE

Culture has a powerful influence on what the organization can do and how it can do it. Where the groundrules are clear and reinforced by the rituals of procedure, processes and management practices, an organization can move quickly and easily – it does not have to waste time thinking or making up the rules each time it does anything. A powerful culture affords everyone the comfort of following well-trodden paths, and makes management the relatively easy task of ensuring that the values and purposes of the organization are routinely expressed and monitored and their expression controlled. Bureaucratic processes embodying the organization's view of the right way to do things, can be a powerful way of ensuring that what gets done is done the way it is supposed to be done.

It is part of the nature of things for the powerful influences of culture to tend to sink to the unconscious level. When this happens, cultures tend to become static. A culture which reinforces and mandates an operating ethos which is out of touch with what is required, becomes a major liability, and one which is perhaps the most difficult of all to shed. The unconscious influences of culture make it very difficult for the organization to change. In fast-changing times, the inability to change, or to change rapidly enough, makes it virtually impossible for the organization to survive or succeed.

Bureaucracy is culture in its frozen state. It is a visible form of clinging to the past. When culture has been frozen, preserving the creations of bureaucracy – past-fixing routines, change-resisting controls, and present-confining processes and procedures – becomes the reason for having the organization. When the ability of the organization to pursue its purposes as a means of creating the future has been sacrificed to the past, the sole purpose of the organization becomes one of preserving itself in its historical form. As such, its fabric gradually becomes more important than its vital commitments to the future. Perhaps worse still, it tends to insist that commitment to current organizational practices is more important than commitment to a different future.

Organizations need a culture which can change and adapt and keep its eye on the ball at the same time. The ball is the ability to respond to customers with increasing choice, increasing expectations and fast-shifting needs. This means that if the organization and what it does is not world-class, then it can forget any idea of having a place in the future scheme of things. The status of world-class is not achieved without a tremendous single-minded focus on what it takes to deliver consistently to high standards. The big issue is not the preservation of a particular form of excellence achieved at one instant in time. The big issue is how to preserve the means of expressing it at any time. In tomorrow's organizations, what is done today – practices and processes – is no more than today's means to an end. The processes and structures-of-the-day only have as much significance as their ability to be of service to the customer. In tomorrow's organizations the disciplines which are insisted upon are not those required to preserve the past, but those which are inherent in building the future through pursuit of customer values. The inherent, not the inherited, discipline prevails.

For tomorrow's organization, the ability to focus and the ability to change are the same thing. Preservation is in change. The disciplines of tomorrow's organization are those which are inherent in transforming customer's lifestyle boundaries. Achieving any goal requires its inherent disciplines to be submitted to for the sake of the goal. The issue for tomorrow's organization is one of whether its disciplines – its structures, groundrules and ethos – are consistent with what matters in terms of creating the future. Bureaucratic structures, groundrules or an ethos which insist on themselves, tend to do so by excluding everything else. The more powerfully they are enforced, the more powerfully they exclude the future. For tomorrow's organization, creating the future is not about doing the same thing all the time – it is about doing a different thing every time.

Cultures have a strong tendency to be inherently preserving – by so doing they enable people to get on with life. For tomorrow's organizations, there is no paradox in the apparent opposites of preservation and destruction – the means of success must be preserved. The issue in turbulent times is that the means of success are different for every organizational performance. What must therefore be avoided, is the tendency of cultures to preserve the particular expressions of the means – the winning product or service. What also must be avoided is the tendency of cultures to associate the ends with the particular means – the winning idea, process or procedure. By advocating adherence to a particular means, the organization eliminates the ability to adopt new means of success. In turbulent times, where any means and their particular expression are likely to have a limited timespan, a culture designed to preserve the means rather than to transform them, will confine the organization to the past. Change may come, but late, and perhaps too late and after the most able, flexible and innovative have already moved on.

The tendency to preserve and the ability to change must become the same thing. What must be preserved is the ability to deliver tomorrow when the requirements for success will undoubtedly be different – not what brought success yesterday. This may sound like changing the organizational wheels while the vehicle is still in motion, but clinging to the past has little to offer in the face of obsolescence-creating reality. The means of continuous transformation are what must be preserved.

RENEWING CULTURE

Organizations see and do what their implicit, or less likely explicit, assumptions or theories allow them to see and do. Only organizations with the capacity to see and do things differently will survive, grow and develop. Unless actively managed and renewed, the hidden and explicit assumptions will soon limit the ability of the organization to adapt and change. The difficulty is one of recognizing and dealing with the powerful influences of assumptions which have never been made explicit.

Being human, we tend to attribute our success to ourselves and our failure to circumstances. When an organization has known success for a long time, or spectacular success for a short time, the assumption is that success will continue just because of who we are. Success tends to suppress any tendency to question whether what has brought success about will bring success in the future – to question success is to question ourselves. Cultures and the structures they spawn become the unquestioned means of preserving success and a way of putting the organization onto an automatically piloted course. The organization's destiny is placed in the hands of some dimly understood assumptions which imply that the past guarantees the future and that the future is much like the past. As the underlying assumptions which are shaping the business remain hidden, the pro-active management of the future becomes impossible.

The continuous renewal of culture depends on the organization's people being closely in touch with the assumptions and beliefs that are determining how they see the world and how they respond to it. Renewal of culture requires the management process to be one of the continuous examination of assumptions about how the world operates, and how it should best be approached. When an organization's assumptions are no longer in touch with the world as it is, only a deep-felt sense of the need to change can jolt it back onto course. Organizational change programmes can have a part to play in helping with the management of change. But unless they enable each person to touch his or her operating assumptions – the need for change needs to be experienced at a gut-felt level – any organizational changes that result will be of the changing the deck chairs on the Titanic kind. A change programme that is not the result of a personally discovered deep-felt sense of a need to see things differently, will have little effect beyond that which can be attributed to the short term effects of novelty – the Hawthorne effect. It unlikely to lead to a fundamental transformation of the organization's capability, or of its ability to stay connected to the real world.

INVOLVEMENT

Tomorrow's organization believes that involvement in the purposes of the organization is essential if it and its people are to have a future. However, it believes that involvement cannot and should not be imposed – whatever the circumstances. Tomorrow's organization does believe that it has an obligation to provide the means of involvement but that no single way of achieving involvement will ever be enough to achieve more than the limited involvement and the limited contributions of the few. Formal and informal forms of involvement are both seen as having a part to play. There may be multiple ways in which involvement can take place – but none of which is mandatory. Organizations which make any of the formal and informal forms of involvement mandatory are announcing that they have lost their way – and that the emperor has no clothes. The procedures of involvement are not the end in itself. Tomorrow's organization passionately believes that involvement is about the individual being connected with his or her future, and the ability of the organization to create the space for this connection through its own uncompromising commitment to creating the future. As long as there is this connection, there will be no way of limiting the only involvement that matters – the personal commitment to making a difference to tomorrow.

Any involvement system that is an end in itself brings an end to the connection between the human spirit and its future-creating possibilities. What is the only route to stretching the organization forward is whatever means enable every individual to grow and to take the organization forward in the process. The formal mechanisms of involvement – doing a job which enables the processes of the business to be carried out efficiently – are an essential feature. However, the tendency for formal mechanisms to be used as coercive sources of involvement should be avoided. Sources of involvement are the ways of enabling involvement of individuals who are willing to give their energies and the best of their abilities. Tomorrow's organization needs these people – not those who are dependent or who have been coerced into compliance.

Coercive involvement can take many forms. Up-or-out, and up-or-nowhere internal promotion systems coerce by making one's existence intensely precarious and dependent on the utmost conformity to the prevailing organizational norms. As long as the organization only needs what has gone before it will have a highly focused capability. Where the conditions for success change as they are in the current transition from mass stable markets to dynamic unstable micro-niches, the organization that continues to aggressively create the illusion that involvement depends on climbing up the hierarchy will be detaching itself and its people from the reality that involvement – and the ability to earn a living anywhere – depends on having the ability to make a unique contribution to the creation of distinctive value.

Non-coercive involvement borne out of being stretched by one's own high standards, and the opportunity to make a difference to tomorrow, announces that the future depends on things that have not been done before. It announces that all good ideas have not already been thought of, that the source of good ideas is not restricted to the good ideas already discovered by the few, and that a good idea is not something to be preserved like a hunting trophy – good ideas are things with a very limited shelf-life. It also announces that what encourages involvement is what ensures a place in the future – something for which all are responsible.

In tomorrow's organization, involvement does not rely on coercive means. Involvement is seen as having its roots in the creation of opportunities for people to create their futures and the futures of the organizations with which they are associated.

SHARED VISION

The purpose of vision is not to dictate action or to predict or paint the future. It is to stretch the organization forward in time, release it from the cages of the present, and release the human energies that will make the future possible. Tomorrow's organization believes that self-directed behaviour is the primary source of the energy it will require. Vision attracts the energies of the individual towards building the future. The purpose of shared vision is not to insist that there is one view of the future – nor is it a stick with which to beat independent people. The purpose of shared vision is to ensure that everyone is more concerned about the future than the ever-pressing concerns of the present.

A shared vision provides a reference point from which everyone can take bearings and decide how best to make their contribution. A vision is not a set of concrete features and narrow objectives. Rather it is an ongoing attempt to evoke personal identity with how the organization might look, feel and function in the future, the things the organization will need to be capable of, and the values it will need to espouse. The key thing about a vision is that it brings the future into the present and enables people to deal with building the future day-to-day. In tomorrow's organization, a vision is not the end-point – something to be nailed to the wall and pursued. The 'end-point' is everyday initiative, innovation and energy – not a dart-board. Envisioning, more than the vision, is what is important, and envisioning is a continuous process involving all, and one that ensures that all individuals can bring their initiative through their own choices guided by a growing sense of what will bring success in the future.

The vision of tomorrow's organization is an evolving one – one that evolves out of the abilities and desires of its people to create the future. The future is not handed down or entrapped, it is created. The rules of its creation are not to be found in the past, but in the disciplines inherent in the challenges presented by eager fast-moving competition, demanding customers, increasing standards of excellence, and the need individuals have to pursue their dreams.

STRATEGIC LEARNING

Change-seeking organizations are organizations that are able to keep pace with fast-evolving customer needs, and that are always in a position to contribute to their further evolution. They see progress in terms of shortening the loop between the new and their ability to do it routinely. They see the structural, spatial and cultural separations of thinking and doing as major obstacles, and anything that gets in the way of incorporating the new and discarding the old, as obstacles to the rapid learning required to stay in the game.

For tomorrow's organization, the processes of regenerating its ability to prosper in the world as it is unfolding is key. Transforming assumptions about reality and regenerating the means of responding to fast-changing reality effectively assumes a central position. Strategic progress becomes the consequence of collective learning (see Figure 5.4) and this has its foundations in individuals exploring new realities, their consequences and the opportunities for advancement these present. The progress of tomorrow's organization is energized by individuals reflecting on the issues, the opportunities and what can be done and developed into shared purpose through dialogue with others.

A priority for strategic learning, is to ensure that the capabilities of the organization expand as expressions of the growing capacities of its people. This depends on people who are growing and developing rapidly, and on the organization working on the assumption that what it can do in the longer term is an expression of the unexpected things that people can become. Organizations that insist – overtly or otherwise – that people grow and are grown to fit the received models of the past, are insisting that people give up their responsibility for the future, and are insisting on reducing the organizational gene pool of future possibilities.

Developing the strategic learning capacity of the organization is not the simple equivalent of participative policy-making. Participative policy-making is frequently a procedural checklist-like device that ensures that

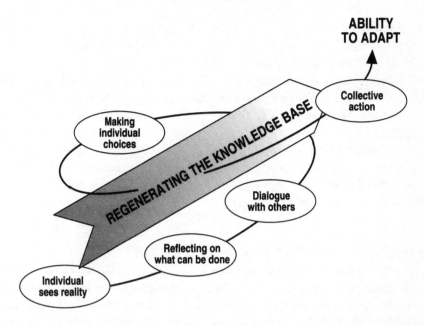

Figure 5.4 *Collective learning*

people have been informed and have had their opportunity to pass comment. Developing the strategic learning capacity of the organization however, is about developing people so that they can be active participants all the time – not just at the organizational set-pieces. It is about encouraging and enabling people to explore, examine and initiate changes in how they see the future and how work is done. Managers are required to make sure that the need for organizational changes is self-evident rather than a surprise. They are required to ensure that their people are always prepared – not through fear, uncertainty and doubt – but through their own recognition of the requirements of future success – and their pride in being prepared for it. Planning is neither short nor long term, eastern or western in outlook, or separated from doing. It is continuous and the active concern of all. Planning is a way of preparing for the future through continuous simulation. It is less to do with building bridges to the future than to do with making the journey attractive and worthwhile.

Strategy development is a process of continuous dialogue between those who have an interest in the future. Tomorrow's organization depends on everyone having an interest in the future. The grand plan developed by specialists behind closed doors cannot have the understanding and informed self-chosen commitment required by those who alone can make it happen. This is not to say that it will be a possible lack of consensus that will cause the plan to probably fail, or to take far too long to be implemented, it is that people will not have had the chance to identify with its aims, its relevance and significance to them, and their roles in making it happen.

For tomorrow's organization, strategy is an organization in continuous reflection. Its immediate experiences gained in practice and from the practices of others are the food of thought, and practice is the continuous expression of digested experience.

REGENERATING THE KNOWLEDGE BASE

The continuous regeneration of the organization's knowledge base is required if it is to always have a distinctive understanding of customer value, and if it is to always have the ability to fulfil identified customer values distinctively. In the increasingly intangible world of customer values – where the physical product is less important than its symbolic value – the relevance of the organization's knowledge base increasingly determines whether it is a position to create value or not.

In an important sense, distinctive knowledge and the ability to express it in the service of the customer determine the economic prospects of the organization. This means that increasing the knowledge base is not the same as accumulating the ability to create value. What is important is the increased ability to behave intelligently. It is learning ability not knowledge accumulation that is important – where learning is defined as the ability to transform behaviour through continuous change in the assumptions, structures and capacities of the organization to create distinctive value.

Learning fast enough to survive is becoming an essential requirement for success. This requires the organization to be in a position to change its products and productive processes to reflect what is learned. As knowledge workers become more and more important, the central challenge becomes not to make them more productive – though that is important – but the ability of the organization to change what it does and how it does it to reflect the potentials of new knowledge. Keeping up-to-date is becoming more important all the time, and is as much to do with shedding the old as it is with accumulating the new. But as rapid change changes the relevance of structures, processes and practices, organizations unable to change what they do and how they do it fast enough, have a learning disability – however up to date their knowledge may be. Those that are not able to 'learn', are in great danger of obsolescence. The rate at which individuals and organizations can replace and reconfigure their assumptions and practices, determines the rate at which they can learn. The rate of learning – the rate at which the past is shed and the new incorporated – is quickly becoming a primary basis for organizational survival.

High rates of reconfiguration and regeneration are characteristic of learning organizations. Sustaining them requires the organization to accelerate the rate at which it learns to a level which will enable continued distinctiveness in the face of fierce competition. Transforming the organization into a learning organization is becoming a major priority. Organizational learning has two parts – making the current self-evidently obsolescent (where this is so or soon to be so), and transforming the ability of the organization to reconfigure to apply new assumptions and knowledge quickly.

Increasing the direct experience of obsolescence-creating reality requires an increase in the exposure the organization and its individuals have to what is new. 'Planning' processes which involve more people in a wider range of situations expose more people to different perspectives and new points of view. Close links with suppliers, customers and strategic partners increases the volume and variety of information transferred, and to a point way beyond that constrained within the confines of the traditional business transaction. Broad-based training increases the possibilities for increased and more complete exposure to the realities faced by the organization. The continuous benchmarking of competitive best practices directly exposes the organization to what the best in the world are doing. The introduction of strategic thinking tools to managers and others enhances the ability of people to understand their organizational experiences and accelerate their ability to deal creatively with the situations they face, and the consequent changes their organizations must make.

The continuous and aggressive refreshment of the many assumptions and knowledges encoded into management practices, business processes and working procedures, makes possible new organizational behaviours. Approaches such as business process re-engineering, total quality management, and systems thinking are ways of confronting the fact that tomorrow is different – the issue of how best to do things to meet new conditions, and to how enable the organization to express its constantly refreshed distinctive knowledge about the customer.

Tomorrow's organization – a learning organization – is committed to enabling its people to learn and to turning what has been learned to good effect in the market. Not only are new ideas, practices and successful initiatives made available to others, the organization continuously develops its ability to turn them into practice. The organization assumes that new ideas and practices can arise from anywhere and they can only arise from what individuals have learned. The assumption that only the organization knows best, that it has learned everything its people will need to know, or that it is the only judge of what is relevant, cannot be any part of an organization committed to learning. The purpose of the organization is to learn and learn fast. It depends on its ability to transfer learning from individual to individual and from its individuals to its group purposes and practices.

Tomorrow's organization depends on the rate at which its people develop their capacities to take the organization forward. It also depends on being associated with the external sources of capability, ideas and challenge that will call its own assumptions and practices into question. The growth and development of tomorrow's organization depend on it being open to the best, and on the abilities and energies of its people applied to its continuous transformation.

INDIVIDUAL LEARNING

Change-seeking organizations have their basis in people who have the motivation and ability to challenge the status quo and to replace it with the new. They depend on the unique talents, experiences and abilities of people. Instead of the profligate and dehumanizing waste of energy, initiative and ability that frequently arises from the Industrial Age model, tomorrow's organization aims to find expression for talent.

The future depends on initiative. It depends on its people taking action, reflecting on the consequences, and finding ways of doing it better next time. Rather than being confined to a task, people need to be confined only to the boundaries of what it takes to get things done, and to get them done better than before. The primary role of people is to create the future and the primary role of machines is to deal with the routines of the present. Tomorrow's organization creates the space for people to show initiative in deciding what to do and where and how to do it. It sees giving its people the tools and training to see the organization, its goals and the issues it faces in a broader sense as a primary responsibility. Only in this way can individuals be expected to apply their initiative to find a way in which they can make their own best contributions.

Tomorrow's organizations believe that self-direction is essential if people are to have a large degree of responsibility for their future and for the future of the organizations they are associated with. Self-direction means assuming the responsibility for one's own destiny, finding ways of realizing one's own potentials, and finding ways for their expression which ensure a better future for all. Just as it means creating the scope for success, so too must it create the scope for failure – responsible risk-taking is part of the package. The development of individuals in a self-directed organization cannot be directed, only facilitated and resourced. Its reward is self-confident people with the abilities to push things forward. Its consequence is the unexpected applied in the creation of distinction in the marketplace.

FORMATIVE SYSTEMS

Most management information systems describe some of what resulted from past action. Few track what brought about those results, and fewer track the ability of the organization to produce results in a different tomorrow. The management system in tomorrow's organization is a means of ensuring that the organization stays in touch with a fast moving world. It is not forward or backward looking. Its purpose is to enable the organization to steer a course in real-time.

Put another way, the success or failure of an organization ultimately depends on its ability to be in touch with the world in real-time. Being in touch is reflected in the ability of the organization to behave in ways which are consistent with the rapidly changing conditions for success defined by a fast-moving real-time world. Accurate perceptions of what capabilities and standards of performance are required to succeed in a real-time world, determine if the organization is capable of finding a suitable direction for its energies and talents. Arresting insights into how well the organization compares with what the high performers are doing in that environment, determines if the organization has and will maintain the required abilities, and if it will express them in ways required for the voyage. The ability to understand the factors which are determining its actual performance determines whether the organization has its steering mechanism connected to the right levers.

The management system of tomorrow's change-seeking organization has the role of ensuring that the organization can adjust to a fast-changing world in real-time, and that its abilities are continuously up to the task of staying in touch with the needs of the environment. Steering by looking backwards to financial abstractions of the business and its performance, is perhaps little better than guesswork. Approaches which see the future as a simple extension of the past make little sense in a world where the past and the future have little in common. Planning approaches which attempt to predict the future are little better – they tend to set the organization on the assumption that the prediction is correct and tend to compel the organization to pursue a course of action for far too long. That is not to say that the long term is not important and that only the present is relevant. What is important are approaches that enable people to challenge their assumptions and explore different ways of looking at their world – rather than being confined to what they already know and think they can see. Change readiness, capability and learning assessments are required if an organization is to assess the ability of its culture to change as circumstances inevitability change. The tools of strategic learning and thinking are now becoming available and need to be universally applied if organizations are to steer a course to the future. In the past the steering system of the organization was its culture. Now the steering mechanism is the levers which shape and determine culture – in all its aspects and behavioural expressions.

PROFILE OF THE NEW PARADIGM

The characteristics of the new cultural paradigm can be contrasted with the old in the following way:

Old paradigm		New paradigm
Adopts few new ideas	⟶	Adopts many new ideas
No common ground	⟶	Envisioning
Clings to the past	⟶	Learns and adapts
Isolated/insular	⟶	Open to the external world
Commitment based on formal controls	⟶	Self-directed future-creating
Complacent	⟶	Searches for new ideas
Parochial perspectives	⟶	Holistic perspectives
Low capacity for change	⟶	High capacity for change
Consistency or flexibility	⟶	Consistency and flexibility
Only one way to do things	⟶	Any way that works

6 Leveraging the Individual

'A key to self-management is the capacity for self-observation. It is important to realize that self-observation is not the same as over-criticism, judgementalism, paralysis of analysis. It is rather a consistent monitoring of one's performance from a perspective significantly detached to allow for accurate evaluation.' (Charles A. Garfield)

MOBILIZING THE GRASS ROOTS

Companies are becoming increasingly dependent on their ability to amplify what their people can do by putting more of the best at their disposal. The organizations that are going to succeed will be those that make it possible for individuals to make the highest and most creative individual contribution, and who see success as having its foundations in the abilities of confident people to make unique contributions as individuals, and world-class contributions as groups. Only people can generate ideas and turn them into action, and future success is increasingly being determined by the abilities of organizations to express the ideas of its people quickly enough. The organizations that will be populate the 21st century landscape will be those who make it possible for their people to grow and amplify their contributions – those that see the essential human contributions of creativity, innovation and energy as the only source of success.

Structures designed to fit the human into the inhuman confines of the static and routine – the inflexible and narrow roles, standardized procedures and dimmed perspectives – are being replaced as the static high inertia cultures they created look increasingly obsolete when faced with a need for openness, fast responses, and new responses to new challenges (see Figure 6.1). Traditional organizational boundaries designed to keep everything in its place and to the eliminate the need for change, are increasingly seen as standing in the way of the flexibilities and innovations required to create elusive customer value. Increasingly, top-down control which distanced the organization from the immediate realities, is being replaced by guidance systems based on customer-oriented feedback. Information technology, almost always used to de-humanize jobs, is now being used being used to humanize work, putting

121

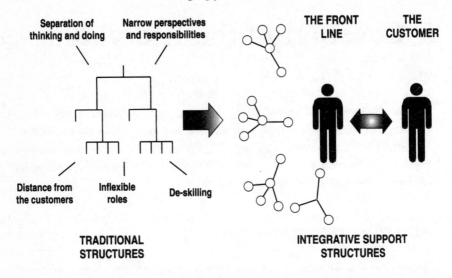

Figure 6.1 *Mobilizing the grass roots*

the human back into the business process and turning it into a vehicle for amplifying the human.

Innovative organizations need people at all levels who have not been conditioned only to expect and deal with the routine. Those that have, find it difficult to accept the fact that change is now the routine and to anticipate new ways of doing new things. The separation of thinking and doing that characterized the Industrial Age, deprived people of the right to participate in their futures and conditioned them to think that their part in it was determined by their ability to passively accept that their futures were in good hands. When the need is as now for change to be a way of life rather than the exception to be faced up to, resisted or avoided, everyone needs to be engaged in building their organizations' futures. This means that everyone needs to be able to combine both thought and action and to be given the authority to take actions in the interests of securing tomorrow's business. This does not conflict with doing the job today, but not doing it conflicts with having a job tomorrow.

Tomorrow's organizations rely on innovation as the force that will ensure that the organization continues to change what it does and how it does it. Only if individuals at all levels are expected and able to innovate, will the organization be able to innovate in its behaviours at the same rate as which it can generate or import new ideas from inside and out. Innovation cannot be a special event or limited to a few periodic stage managed events. Organizations and their people need to be able to see the routine as a sign of the need to bring about the new. Innovation cannot be limited to the few but must be extended to ensure the organization's place in the future.

Traditional functional structures and minuscule organizational compartments immobilize rather than mobilize. Not only is the individual's freedom for action restricted, but the individual develops reflexes limited by the limited experiences provided by the organization's expectations of the role – the organizational world beyond is cut off. The need for co-operation becomes less apparent and the territorial instinct to protect the boundary increases. The organizational fiefdoms increasingly work to their own ends and maximizing personal interest soon exceeds the need to maximize purposes in the market. The highest levels of individual contribution require the scope to contribute. Factors such as respect for the individual, collaboration, flexible roles and dynamic teaming extend the range of possible ways in which an individual can contribute. Roles that are not prescribed in terms of a job but in terms of required outcomes – and which include a mission for moving standards forward – encourage individuals to take initiative and produce more innovative behaviour. Rather than being confined within task boundaries, people are increasingly being given a mission to do what needs to be done to achieve breakthrough results.

In tomorrow's organization, the place for the routine and repetitive will increasingly be the computer. The routine will be put at the disposal of the human – not the other way round. All individuals will have a mission which includes innovation, change and making a difference. Tying people to the present sinks them in the concrete of the past. An organization that gives only the privileged few the right to think, will struggle to extend itself beyond the confines of the unthinking mass.

ENGAGING THE INDIVIDUAL

Getting more out of the individual is about making it possible for them to grow. Amplifying what they can do and giving them the space to grow is key, as is making it possible for them to believe they can do more. For people to be engaged in the purposes of the organization, they must be able to develop the behaviours which will take the organization forward. They must believe they can make a difference, and they must be able to experience that difference first hand. They must see the relevance of making a difference for themselves, and they must see how they can make a difference. In other words, there must be a recognition that people are only engaged when they are engaged in making a difference. If prevented from making a difference by confining jobs, roles which exclude them from directly influencing outcomes, or atmospheres of mistrust and low expectation, the will to create the future dies, and with it the organization's future.

Organizations that welcome people intent on creating a different future, see them as a vital means of creating a powerful connection between their energies and the organization's prospects for success. Individuals are only engaged through their growth in a growing organization. The goal of tomorrow's organization is to grow through the growth of its people and the capabilities they have at their disposal. The management issue is what energizes the individual in the purposes of the organization. Most traditional inducements depend on inducing compliance or dependency. Security in its many guises is offered to those that comply, and exclusion is offered to those who do not. The results are extremely damaging. The organizational game is accepted, rather than being challenged by those who are offered the prospect of hierarchical progress through the ranks of management. For those excluded from the realms of management, and from making decisions which affect personal outcomes or outcomes in the market, the best the organization can hope for is a passive and fatalistic acceptance from people who have given up any expectation of shaping their own futures. In both cases dependency results with the consequence that organizations tend to exclude themselves from the future. By accepting the status quo, managers cease to grow beyond conventional boundaries, and in so doing cease to be engaged in any meaningful way with real sources of having a place in the future – a future which shows little chance of being even remotely like the past. By forcing conformity with the tried and tested formulas, the organization has closed down its engine room. By forcing acceptance of the inevitability of a static position and role among those who deliver the product or service, the organization has disengaged itself from the change-seeking and creative energies of its people.

Engaging the individual does not result from the formal mechanisms of participation. They imply that individuals are inherently purposeless and that they would drift aimlessly without close management, direction and support. The issue is how to avoid crushing natural curiosity. The separation of decision making and action, systematically proclaims that curiosity is the preserve of the few. To avoid this all jobs need to be replaced with personal missions. All people should be employed to make a difference. And the difference should be in the outside world. Exhortations to engage in the purposes of the organization are for the most part meaningless abstractions. A direct sense of personal growth through making a difference in the outside world is perhaps the only reliable way of engaging the individual.

CO-ENACTION

The speed with which change is arising makes it essential that the organization should be continually engaged in developing its abilities to deal with real world conditions as they arise. The sharing or devolution of decision making is not the issue. Preparation, not decision making is the issue. For tomorrow's organization, the future is the shared space created by the growth of its people. Its mission is to amplify the abilities of its people, and by so doing enable them to contribute more than they could on their own. The management challenge is to ensure that the growing capabilities of its people can coincide with and complement the abilities of others to deliver the unique and distinctive contribution to a customer's lifestyle. This coincidence cannot be accomplished by directive or coercion. It cannot be accomplished by resorting to the extensive repertoire of manipulative techniques favoured by old paradigm management. It can only be accomplished by creating the space and finding the means to enable people to explore situations and possibilities, and to draw their own conclusions about what will increase their prospects of inhabiting a better and different future.

The prospects of the individual inhabiting a better and different future, depend on their abilities to engage with others to amplify the outcome – to create the win-win or two-plus-two-equals-five outcome. These outcomes increase the possibilities open to the individual while at the same time creating a sense that amplification depends on the willing participation of others who grow as a result of this participation. It puts the individual at the centre of possibility creation, while simultaneously centring co-creation as the only means of amplifying individual and customer possibilities.

Working with others to extend the boundaries of the present and what is possible, creates the spaces inhabited by tomorrow's organizations. All activity is a search for new possibilities where these will require much more than the individual for their realization. Everything which is done is then a search for better ends and better means – a reaching out for what might come next and for how existing and new resources might be uniquely brought together to make it possible. This requires everyone in tomorrow's organizations to be in the process of continuous simulation of new ends, ways and means.

Simulation must be the natural instinct of all. Short and long horizon simulation are important but neither is a form of prediction. Rather than predicting the future, they aim to prepare better for it. Long term simulation is important because it stretches the boundaries of expectation and what might be possible. It enables the individual and the organization to vault over current concerns and limitations and to see them for what they are – impermanent eddies of the present – not long term inevitabilities. Long term simulation enables the individual to put the future to work today – by having seen what might be possible, the present will never be the same again. Short term simulation is the real-time animation of the future as it unfolds which, if fast enough and routine enough, enables the individual to participate in real-time and to influence how the future actually unfolds. Where short and long term simulation are the routine, the possibility of the future being a shared space increases. Where this possibility increases, the organization has the opportunity to bring more of itself to the future – its powers extend beyond the limited contributions of stunted people with little interest beyond doing what they are told. Its powers extend to the immense beliefs its people have in what they can do beyond where they are today with resources beyond their own.

Co-enacting the future is the way tomorrow's organization creates the space for its own possibilities to be realized, and the way it amplifies and transforms the means it has at its disposal. Co-enacted simulation brings out issues involved in dealing with the future before they are encountered. It increases the chances of being prepared for them when they do arise. Simulation allows the problem and its solution in the real world to be examined safely and at the same time by all those involved. This tends to make problems, opportunities and their solution the stuff of challenge rather than the stuff of fear. The 'selling of decisions' ceases to be an issue. The organization becomes more adept at taking on new challenges. The ethos moves from one of hiding from the future by predicting it, to engaging people as willing co-producers of a better future.

SELF-DIRECTION

Self-direction is replacing decision making as the preserve of management. By emphasizing the outcomes to be aimed for but not specifying the means, thinking and doing are reunited and individuals and teams are enabled to become self-managing. Giving decision making back to the individual creates the space for individuals and teams to take the initiative in determining the best means, and how existing means can be improved. There are many examples where self-directed individuals and teams have the authority to hire and select their own team members, co-opt resources and to treat organizational boundaries as transparent in the quest to achieve their mission.

Creating the future which once lay in the hands of others has become a responsibility of all. Instead of becoming the passive observers of events unfolding before them, people become active participants in the future. Participation in organizations only has meaning if it has meaning in terms of the future – and this requires meaning to an individual with an interest in the future. Only when people feel they are participating in the future will they be actively engaged in its creation. And only when the individual is actively engaged in exploring and finding better ways to the future can the organization really benefit from their energies and capabilities.

A policy of self-direction is about releasing individual energies and finding ways of connecting them with purposes beyond that which the individual could achieve – that is the attraction and the deal for both parties. The organization gives the individual a greater degree of relative independence from the traditional control-oriented and confining approach. At the same time, the individual is given greater responsibility for his or her own destiny. It becomes the individual's responsibility to find ways in which to create synergies between the human and other resources – wherever they are located – and to make things happen. The requirement to make things happen in the service of the customer becomes the basis of interdependence between people and across functions. Creating room for individual initiative while increasing the likelihood that coherent organizational behaviour will result is the management challenge.

The management model becomes one of making it possible for skilled motivated people to make their best possible contribution to the success of the organization. Rather than being the sole centres of decision making and control, a key role of the manager becomes that of organizational facilitators – making it possible for self-directed teams to get quickly to the skills, knowledge and resources they require to achieve their objectives. Managers also assume the roles of valued advisors and counsellors, guardians of organizational values and enablers of the future.

Self-direction is about multiplying the possibilities open to the organization. The source is people able to routinely think beyond their current roles, current ways of doing things – and beyond their current goals. The source is people who see the present not as static, but as a base from which to explore the future. Self-direction is about putting the future in your own hands.

Tomorrow's organizations are dynamic fluid structures where the predominant form is the transitory team formed to address a particular problem or opportunity. They are primarily marketplaces for the skills and abilities of people and sources of opportunity for their development. The individual is given great responsibility for his or her own destiny and has great responsibility for ensuring that their skills, knowledge and experience are marketable within the organization.

Management's role goes beyond rewarding people directly for acquiring skills and abilities. Management's ability to attract the people their organizations need will depend on whether or not they and their organizations can create the opportunities which enable motivated, self-directed people to increase their marketability.

CREATING SPACE

Growth cannot occur if there is no room for it. Where organizations confine people to routines or narrow roles, and where they limit perspectives and interest to the next step in a procedure, people do not grow. This is dangerous when organizations increasingly need flexibility and innovation, and when they depend on growth-oriented people able and willing to look beyond the existing boundaries and practices.

As organizations become less to do with the routine – which is given over to the computer – they become much more to do with the continuous exploration of how they will be able to do business in the future. Creating the space for the continuous pursuit of possibilities requires the structures designed to corral the past to be replaced. Instead of freezing resources into rigid combinations, they need to be accessible by those with the ability to create new possibilities from them. Management instead of being administrators and custodians of the corporate structures become the facilitators of its renewal (see Figure 6.2).

The flattening of traditional hierarchies and the creation of networked structures releases resources from their static allocations. The basis for the political hoarding of expertise is removed enabling resources to be rapidly reallocated to meet changing needs, and to provide the required fast responses to fast moving customers. The information rationing characteristic of traditional organizations is replaced with open availability.

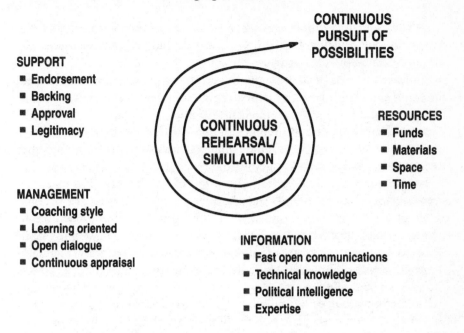

CONTINUOUS PURSUIT OF POSSIBILITIES

SUPPORT
- Endorsement
- Backing
- Approval
- Legitimacy

CONTINUOUS REHEARSAL/ SIMULATION

RESOURCES
- Funds
- Materials
- Space
- Time

MANAGEMENT
- Coaching style
- Learning oriented
- Open dialogue
- Continuous appraisal

INFORMATION
- Fast open communications
- Technical knowledge
- Political intelligence
- Expertise

Figure 6.2 *Creating space for growth*

The elimination of the mind-numbing communications delays inherent in many-tiered formal organizations provides an immediacy of access. The combination of openness and fast access provides the basis for individuals and groups to dynamically reallocate themselves and the resources at their disposal to ensure success in a rapidly changing business environment.

In tomorrow's organization resources are not owned or controlled in the territorial sense, nor is there any reward in their control or ownership. Access to whatever resources are required to produce results is what matters. In a world where ownership of yesterday's resources or of yesterday's configuration of resources is unlikely to yield results today or tomorrow, the finite nature of territorial control limits future possibilities. Access to resources is based on the ability to create results with resources. Success with one configuration earns the right to adopt another. The last thing anyone charged with delivering results tomorrow wishes is to be stuck with yesterday's configuration of resources. Access to the widest possible array of resources, whether owned or not, is what makes possible the realization of unlimited future possibilities. Influence becomes sourced in the ability to produce results by whatever means, not in the control of the means.

Self-direction is about giving all the opportunity to pursue the possibility of creating the future. It is this pursuit that energizes the organization and which provides the source of the intense innovation that will secure distinction in the face of unremitting competition. The success of the organization becomes increasingly dependent on the attractions of the opportunities it can create. Opportunities, not control, provide the means of ensuring the availability of the resources required to achieve results. The ability to contribute as an individual and in teams becomes the means of being invited to contribute.

Self-direction requires the self-allocation of availability. The machine-like control of time allowed organizations to move only to one rhythm. Current and foreseeable conditions require organizations to be able to change tempo quickly and to produce and operate to complex rhythms. Where improvisation becomes more important than monotony, a sense of timing becomes more important than the measurement of time. Unless people can determine to a greater extent how they use their available time, self-direction becomes meaningless. If they are locked into the long-term schedules of others they are not available to participate in different ways. If they are locked in, the dynamic reallocations required to sustain innovative responses become impossible.

MARKETPLACES FOR IDEAS

Tomorrow's organizations are marketplaces for ideas and possibilities. Organizations designed to do one thing for as long as possible can only produce the one reflex action to whatever circumstances require of them. They cannot create possibilities, they can only limit them. Fast changing situations, instability and uncertainty require organizations to be capable of a wide range of possible responses. Resistance to new ideas, or the inability to cope with them, closes the organization off from the future. Organizations must attract those with ideas and it must reward them by enabling them to realize them. By being able to provide the conditions and resources within which ideas can be realized, the organization becomes capable of multiplying its possibilities. The knowledge, expertise and experience of the organization – to the extent that they are not locked into the sclerotic structures of the past – become capable of giving rise to and sustaining the creation of the new. The organization that is dedicated to creating the space for the new will, by attracting those interested in possibilities, creates a space in the future for itself.

Creating the space for the future means increasing the possibilities for new combinations of the old and the new. Where there is no possibility for change, change brings the end. Tomorrow's organizations are not static arrangements – they are in constant pursuit of the best combinations of resources. Information technology is playing a growing role in enabling organizations to bring together resources in whatever way is required to deliver the best result. Where this is so, its primary use is not to control events but to assist in the allocation of resources – whether they are inside or outside the organization. What needs to be allocated are customer needs, available resources and capabilities. The faster these can be reallocated, the faster the organization can adapt to new possibilities.

Tomorrow's organization places a premium on what it might do beyond what is apparently required to meet today's known needs. By rejecting the static and seeking out change and flux, it encourages the view of today as just a stepping stone – not as a monument to past accomplishments. By increasing the ideas it has at its disposal, it aims to crowd out the past by the attraction of the future. By resisting the temptation to see the future as a distraction from the pressures of the present, it does not confine itself to past history. Instead of rejecting the organization's future in favour of the past, the space for potential new contributions is created.

KNOWLEDGE WAREHOUSES

The organizational knowledge base must be continually refreshed and renewed. Continuous organizational learning is vital if the organization is to remain in touch with and responsive to the competitive realities. For the organization and its increasingly self-directed individuals to maintain relevant knowledge and valuable skills, the stimulus of the new must be continually present, as must the means of individuals and groups continuously re-aligning their behaviours and skills. Organizations can only learn if they make a virtue of providing all the information required for individuals to be challenged and self-redirected (see Figure 6.3).

When customer values and needs are constantly changing, and the best means of fulfilling them is shifted by new competitors, new practices and new technologies, organizations will only be able to respond fast enough if their people are predisposed and prepared to change. Insight into the need for change is the magnet that draws people towards the effective and timely response. Yet, traditional organizations are designed to restrict the

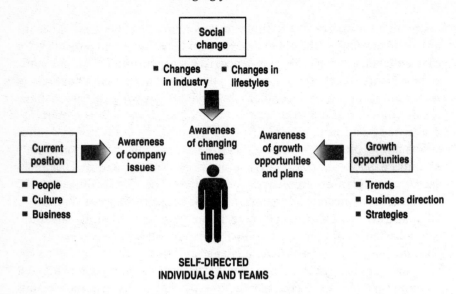

Figure 6.3 *Knowledge warehouses*

required information transfer. Information that *is* transferred is that deemed to be useful by others. The receiver has little or no say in what is received. The impoverished information environment that results provides only ill-defined and confusing images of what is happening – and only on a timescale that makes it of little use. Tomorrow's organization accepts uncertainty and instability as the normal condition. It and its people demand rapid access to the high quality information necessary to ensure survival.

Design of the organizational architecture in such a way as to create the right environment and climate is key. Rapid interchanges of information, thought and practice are essential if organizations are to be able to behave intelligently in a world where the unpredictable is the routine. The intensity of interaction with the outside world – including alliance partners, suppliers, academics and consultants – is being increased. The aim is to accelerate the rate at which new knowledge and capabilities can be created and applied to customer satisfaction.

The hoarding of information is being abandoned in favour of its free transfer within and between organizations. Organizations are making their knowledge, experiences, products, tools and capabilities widely available internally and increasingly to customer, suppliers and partners.

Databases of organizations' skills, expertise and capabilities are being made available to everyone and especially to those in the customer and decision making front lines. As knowledge workers become the primary assets of the organization, the ease with which they can access and use the organization's resources determines their effectiveness and the destiny of the organization. As the information resources to understand what needs to be done combines with access to the tools to deliver a fast or immediate response, the wait-time and dead-time associated with doing the wrong thing long after it is useful is reduced. As people can increasingly see that what they are doing is the right thing – and making a difference – they and their organizations begin to operate with a higher level of energy, purpose and entrepreneurial flair.

OPENNESS TO GROWTH

Growth comes from being challenged. Challenge emerges from the tension arising from a desirable goal, the directly-felt sense of the limitations of the current state, and the sense of being able to do something about it. For individuals to continuously grow and make a fuller contribution, the

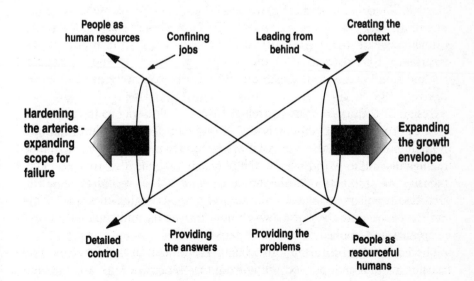

Figure 6.4 *Openness to growth*

organization must create the context for growth (see Figure 6.4). This has many implications. Removing detailed control of individuals and teams and putting resources at their disposal and discretion, creates the space necessary for growth to take place. Removing restrictions that prevent individuals from going across existing territorial, functional and received wisdom boundaries to pursue problems and opportunities, can give them a sense that the organization places more value on moving things ahead than preserving the status quo. Treating individuals as the source of the future and not as the simple means to today's ends, can give them a sense of being part of the future – not its bystanders. Providing people with challenges and problems and not just predigested solutions, opens the door on individual growth. By giving up their directive role and developing a coaching style, managers can foster the belief in people that their destinies are very much in their own hands. Creating the space for growth helps create resourceful people. In a competitive world where resourcefulness, initiative and rapid learning are basic requirements, opening the door on individual growth opens a door on the future.

Deprive the individual of stimulus, space and expectation, and the organization deprives itself of the future. Insist that there is only one right way and the organization can have only one shot at the future – and in a fast changing world one shot is not enough. Confining the individual to the routine, a role, a class, or to the boundaries of lowered expectations, stunts human development and growth and creates either mindless compliance, or an organizational resource pool with no growth or change potential. Both are unacceptable. The former reduces organizational intelligence to the capacities of the few. The latter confines the organization to history.

Openness to growth depends on the possibility of participation in creating the future success of the organization. Being the perpetual bystander to those whose 'responsibility' it is to move things forward creates passivity and ultimately disinterest and decline. The formal and frequently paternalistic or patronizing mechanisms of 'participative management' are of little use if used as smoke-screens behind which to preserve the status quo. Participation is an inside-out phenomenon not an outside-in one. It depends on it being acceptable and welcomed for the individual to seek ways of making a real difference to the organization's prospects for success. It depends on management ensuring that the organizational architecture – its structures, process, systems, culture and management practices – is not one that confines people, but one that makes it everyone's role to redefine the organization's architecture in ways which ensure its continued relevance in changing conditions.

LEADING FROM BEHIND

In tomorrow's organization every individual must be a leader. If an organization cannot create the space for meaningful roles for people – roles in which they can build a sense of mastery and continued growth – it is failing itself and the community to which it belongs. By destroying human capital it is a liability not an asset, however many jobs it may create in the short term. In organizations where everyone is a leader at what they do – or more correctly in how they apply their unique repertoire of capabilities in ever changing ways – the traditional leadership role of management must change.

Leadership is about finding ways of getting out of the way of people who know what they are doing. It is about having the courage to ensure that people find ways of developing their ability to make their fullest contribution. Inspirational and charismatic forms of management are interesting, important at critical junctures and nice to have in others, but in themselves are not the answer – they imply that human motivation is extrinsic rather than the result of individual intrinsic developmental needs. Leadership is about giving people the space and the opportunities to develop the abilities required to choose and meet continuous new challenges.

Leading from behind means managers getting comfortable with a situation where a primary role is to help others deliver a superior performance. Managers can do this by creating opportunities for others to develop their talents, and by ensuring the availability of a variety of means from which people can choose how best to apply them to meet agreed goals. They can also lead from behind by only providing advice when requested to by those who seek it out and value their input. They can also do it by ensuring that there are means of feedback on results that are objective, unintermediated, customer focused, immediate and a clear reflection on the requirements for success in an excellence seeking world.

HAVING A PLACE

Tomorrow's organization operates in a world characterized by high levels of uncertainty and where the future cannot be predicted, only created. The scope for getting it wrong is great and no organization can guarantee its future, far less the future of its people. However, the uncertainty and stress that can accompany situations of this kind have their roots not in the fact and certainty of change, but in a lack of preparedness. People and organizations whose skills, assumptions, outlooks and attitudes have not kept pace with the requirements for creating distinctive value in competitive marketplaces, experience anxiety and stress. Organizations and people who have lost their edge can either resort to avoidance tactics – resistance to change (a refusal to acknowledge that change is required) – or they can opt for wholehearted regeneration. Both are stressful: one is the stress of decline, the other is the stress of having to run hard to catch up. The stress-free zone is the point of mastery, where ability equals challenge. It is attained by anticipation and constant attention to skills enhancement and replacement. The stress of change signifies past neglect of the future.

Having a place does not mean having a place in the same organization. As organizations shift from places that offer 'jobs', ranks and positions, to marketplaces for ideas and skills, having a place increasingly means possessing and maintaining the ability at all times to make a valued, distinctive and competitive contribution. Those concerned with having a place will ensure they maintain the necessary abilities and skills. They will not join organizations which compromise their ability to continuously regenerate their skills. Those organizations that cannot attract these people will fade away. In a fundamental sense, leveraging the individual means creating a future for the organization by ensuring that the individual grows and develops and is always marketable inside and outside the organization.

MULTIPLYING POSSIBILITIES

In tomorrow's organization, people are judged in terms of their ability to realize the potential of opportunities, many of which they themselves might identify or create. An important role of all managers is to provide 'venture capital' – the access to the resources, financial or otherwise, and the support and sponsorship required to fund organizational, process, product and skills innovations. Managers are judged in terms of the resulting increase in the capability of the organization to outpace the best competitors – and this means the capacity of the organization to make possibilities realities faster and better than the competition.

It is stating the obvious to say that possibilities have their source in people. But what is critical is that the organization is made up of people who welcome possibilities, can apply them and turn them into value-creating reality. Organizations that insist there is only one right way or who are blind or hostile to other ways, are announcing that they believe that the future has already been invented, and that there is no possibility of it being otherwise.

Possibilities arise when the organization acknowledges that they are the raw material of the future not an unwelcome distraction from a busy present. Possibilities can become realities when rigid organizational structures and boundaries are dissolved allowing the present to be recombined in new ways to meet future needs. They can become realities when steep hierarchical distinctions that mean 'higher up' is and must be better, give way to distinctions based on the 'return on possibilities'. Possibilities can become realities when those able to pursue them have access to the best resources – wherever they are located. Possibilities can become realities when everyone has the scope and authority to shape the role they can best play and with whom to achieve the best result in the marketplace. In an important sense, everyone must be given the space to become entrepreneurs identifying what is possible, valuable and useful in the creation of innovative results in discerning marketplaces.

For the individual, multiplying the possibilities depends on having broad skills – technical, functional, strategic, management and conceptual skills – and an integrative perspective on what needs to be brought together to achieve the desired result. This not only enables the individual to see how things need to work together and overall, it enables the individual to envision how best to make a unique and valuable contribution. Extending the legitimate boundaries of people's interest and contributions creates the space for people to grow. It develops their capabilities, creates a moving horizon of extending possibilities, and clears the path to a new organizational future.

Organizations with the traditional boundaries of rigid territorial structures, 'I'm better than you' distinctions, rigid 'reporting' and control relationships, and static roles and responsibilities cannot dynamically reallocate resources to meet changing needs. Their only possibility is the one they have now. Perhaps more threatening still is the difficulty they have in changing when they ultimately recognize the need for change. Visionary and far-sighted management may mandate the elimination of barriers, rigid structures and distinctions. But what they cannot mandate is an overnight change in the deeply seated conditioned mindsets created over many years – and in particular in those who see and have accepted the traditional organizational game as an organizational and historical inevitability.

CULTURES OF ESTEEM

Nothing limits the individual more than low self-esteem. Organizations which see their people as raw materials, sources of hands, mere factors of production and disposable, are systematically cultivating a work force with low self-esteem. This may have in the past ensured the compliance thought necessary for quick and effective action – but at a massive cost to the energies and innovative capabilities. Organizations that allow their managers to progress through the exploitation and manipulation of others are announcing clearly that their people are there to be exploited and manipulated, and are sharply de-emphasising pride, commitment and self-worth. These same companies then try to introduce total quality programmes. They are expressing a belief that business is solely about procedures and techniques and that these are more important than the people who are confined within them. This is in contrast with the Japanese view where quality is an expression of the inner state of people. Organizations that put integrity and respect for the individual to the fore, and eliminate the many subtle factors which relegate most people to an inferior condition, produce more innovation and more quality.

Tomorrow's organization's goal is to have a place in the future and to influence its shape and character. It believes it can only achieve this if it has people who are willing and able to invest in the future. As such it bases its future on its unqualified belief in its people (see Figure 6.5). Its contract with its people is not the feudal, tribal or paternal one of symbolic or unreserved commitment between the person and the organization. The common bond between the organization and its people is not one born of feudal allegiance but of a shared willingness and ability to invest in and bring about the future. Tomorrow's organization therefore needs people whose place in the scheme of things rests not on their conformance or compliance with the past but on their ability to command a place in the future. It is no longer a reasonable expectation to build the future on the basis of passive people – vitality, creativity, intuition and the human touch are too much a part of the recipe of the future for that to work. Least of all can the future be born of those riddled with fear, uncertainty and doubt.

Tomorrow's organization believes in its people but realizes their growth can be easily held back and stunted, and that the consequences of this are serious for all. The wellspring of ideas and innovative action is a fragile one. Unless ideas generation and problem solving are part of everyone's 'routine', the routine will crowd out the innovative. Unless jobs and roles are to the greatest extent possible redefined to be about improvement,

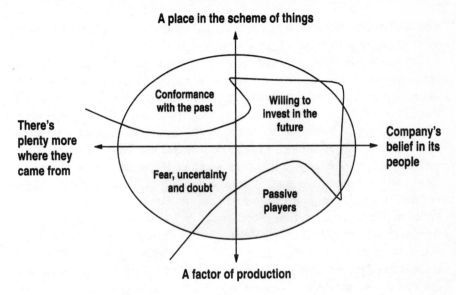

A place in the scheme of things

Conformance with the past

Willing to invest in the future

There's plenty more where they came from

Company's belief in its people

Fear, uncertainty and doubt

Passive players

A factor of production

Figure 6.5 *Cultures of esteem*

innovation and bringing about tomorrow, people will rapidly become conditioned to the ever-decreasing boundaries of yesterday. The benefits of the current management vogue for business process re-engineering will be lost if advantage is not taken of the opportunity this presents to redefine jobs and roles. There is a very real opportunity to move from the past approach of engineering people into processes – and only into those parts which machines or computers could not do – to turning everyone into process, service and experience designers and engineers.

REWARDS FOR DEVELOPMENT

Bureaucratic carrot-and-stick rewards based on narrow measures of performance have little place in tomorrow's organization. The incentive is a place in the future, or the ever-present now, whether with the organization or not. The means are the continued development and regeneration of value-creating capabilities. Organizations with little future will only attract those with little concern for it, compounding their problems. Organizations committed to building the capabilities to succeed in the longer term will attract those with the abilities to make the vision possible. The reward is a win-win outcome. The organization creates markets for its offerings, it attracts the right human capital and retains it by developing it in ways which increases its value.

The relationship between tomorrow's organization and its people is a developmental one. Incentives for loyalty are avoided as these can incentivize allegiances to things other than the conditions for tomorrow's market success. Rewards for conformity risk incentivising yesterday's winning formula. Rewards for long service do not incentivize rocking the boat. All rewards which are not developmental are fragile. In the West, the security enjoyed by the professional and middle-classes is almost universally a thing of the past. Where once the opposite was true, the risks of development-sapping loyalties and conformities now far outweigh their benefits. The security that they once promised has been reversed. Anything which incentivizes anything other than development, incentivizes oblivion.

Continuous development in meaningful value creating directions is the only route, to the extent that one exists, to security. As the individual grows so will the organization. The reward for continuous development is for both the individual and the organization to have a place in the future. This does not mean having a life-long place in any one organization; indeed no one can afford to stay with an organization beyond the time it is able to create conditions which preserve and enhance their asset value. Anyone who does, has given over responsibility for their own futures to those least likely to guarantee it.

PROFILE OF THE NEW PARADIGM

The approaches to individuals in the old and new paradigms can be contrasted in the following way:

Old paradigm		New paradigm
Top-down initiative	⟶	Bottom-up initiative
Segmented culture	⟶	Integrative culture
Exploitative	⟶	Cultures of esteem
Pigeon-holing	⟶	Role renewal
Rewards for advancement	⟶	Rewards for development
Know your place	⟶	Create the future
Top-down appraisal	⟶	Open appraisal
Need to know only	⟶	Intensive, open dialogue

Corporate knows best	$\longrightarrow$	Self-development
Committees	$\longrightarrow$	Dynamic teaming
Functional focus	$\longrightarrow$	Dynamic recombination
Go through channels	$\longrightarrow$	Fast direct access
Tight control of resources	$\longrightarrow$	Creating space for innovation
Direction and control	$\longrightarrow$	Coaching and enabling management style
Uniformity an asset	$\longrightarrow$	Diversity an asset
Only one way	$\longrightarrow$	Generating multiple possibilities

7 Living with Continuous Change

'*It is stupid to predict and it is not possible to predict. The possibilities of life are too great and too varied.*' (Karl Popper)

THE MANAGEMENT CHALLENGE

Tomorrow's organizations will continue to move in environments of great turbulence and uncertainty. Those that will succeed are those which are more adaptable, innovative, fast moving and customer-oriented than the competition. Uncertainty, and the required responses to it, challenge traditional management approaches. Traditional linear long-cycle strategic planning approaches are particularly inappropriate if the only certainty is uncertainty, and the organization is operating in a real-time world that is only satisfied by real-time action.

As innovation, creativity and human initiative become the vital organizational resources in the challenge of thriving in the face of unpredictability, innovation has to become continuous and real-time. If the organization is going to be in a position to deliver unique customer value it will increasingly have to be able to redefine both the ends and the means in something close to real-time. Planning approaches which take up to a year or more to produce, and which result in a three to five year plan, are working at the wrong wavelength. Perhaps worse, they tend to confine the creativity vital to survival to a select few – planning is seen as something special and not the concern of most people. For tomorrow's organization, the issue is not planning, but creating the conditions for creativity and for the belief to take root that creativity is a vital concern of all and a vital contribution all can and must make.

In a very real sense, all organizations are now vehicles of discovery. The future is there to be discovered and created. Planning approaches which project the past onto a future which bears little resemblance to the past are at best misconceived. Planning approaches which do not challenge, and get underneath assumptions, perceptions, fears and hopes can never be part of the creative process. Approaches that do not re-engineer managers and their world-views – or better, allow managers to re-engineer

142

themselves – and equip them with an entirely new toolkit and world-view, are at best superficial.

Management is now a process of challenge – one of redefining the status quo, not one of staying as close to it as possible. The practice of management can now no longer be confined to running a tight ship, but must be extended to include the continuous redefinition of processes, products and services, structures, systems, skills and sometimes cultures. The aim of all managers must now be to build the capacity to prosper tomorrow when the conditions for prosperity are likely to be very different from those that shaped their careers to date. As information technologies grow in their capacities to take over the performance tracking and reporting routines of management, the true value-added of management – moving the capabilities of the business forward – will come increasingly to the fore. As management movements such as business process re-engineering ultimately result in the complete reconceptualization of the entire organizational architecture, the caging of people within low-scope and stultifying physical and cultural boxes will end freeing up vast creative potential. Working with and realizing this potential will require new managers and entirely new forms of management. Realization of potential will also be the sole criterion against which effective management is judged.

The challenge of creating success in an uncertain world is compounded by the challenges of finding and applying the new forms of management appropriate to turning organizations into creative processes. For this, managers need the skills of organizational and collective exploration – and the ability to use them to identify sources of wealth-generating dynamic stability. They need new holistic guidance systems to enable their organizations to track fast changing conditions in real-time and to continuously simulate the potentials of possibilities in real world conditions. They also need the ability to realize the future from increasingly confident, self-directed and able people – people who will not tolerate the squandering of the future (see Figure 7.1).

The management agenda of tomorrow's organization is dynamic and full of uncertainties. Success in the uncertain world of tomorrow depends on the continuous regeneration of the organization, its internal structures, processes and relationships while maintaining the ability to do the new exceptionally well quickly and first time. A key management challenge therefore is to maintain a complex and rapid form of organization learning. In tomorrow's organization, rapid organization learning replaces the traditional forms of strategic direction development – the old paradigm single-goal one-outcome quasi-military forms. Managers in

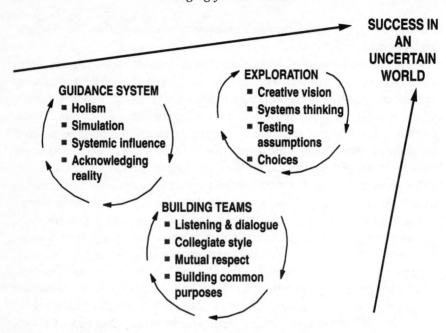

Figure 7.1 *A context for living with continuous change*

tomorrow's organizations add value when they are ensuring the capacity of the organization to progress and evolve through rapid learning. They add value when they are building the capacity of people to explore the future and to develop views of what needs to be done to ensure continued relevance. They add value when they ensure that their organizations are continually exposed to the best challenges rather than to the challenges of fire-fighting and survival. They add value when they strive to guide their organizations to meet the total requirements of the most demanding customers and the most imaginative and capable competition.

Tomorrow's organization replaces traditional management processes with processes intended to stimulate individual initiative, and team-based actions between the most relevant skills, experiences and outlooks wherever they are located. The principles and practices of organizational learning are already being introduced as organizations strive to transform the assumptions about how to succeed. They are being introduced to ensure that the organization is always engaged in an active search for new standards of value and new ways of creating it better than the competition. They are making the identification of the real issues and opportunities the responsibility of all as it becomes increasingly clear that finding and putting into practice appropriate responses to real-events requires the involvement and initiative of all, not just the few.

Organizational learning is not an academic abstraction. Not only is it profoundly important, it centres the future of the organization firmly in the growth and development of the individual. Tomorrow's organization recognizes that the development of the organization rests ultimately on the individual. The contribution of management is not to develop the individual in the passive sense – with only proven organizational wisdom between them and hopelessness. Managers of tomorrow's organizations have two responsibilities. The first is to create the conditions that assist the individual fulfil his or her growth needs. The second goes beyond co-ordinating individual abilities to meet the overall needs of the organization – important as that is. This wider and perhaps more challenging role of management is to continually work to realize whatever organizational purposes can be achieved by continuously developing individual capabilities.

SELF-DIRECTED LEARNING

As the rate of new product, technology and process introductions accelerates, and competition from all corners of the globe intensifies, all are confronted with direct challenges to their assumptions about what it makes sense to do and why. Already the dramatic effects of complex change are affecting everyone. The successful companies will be those that recognize that survival and growth depends not on resisting change, but on their ability to continuously renew their know-how – and to apply it quickly. The winners will be those who recognize that it is only the continuous regeneration of know-how and the ability to apply regenerated know-how, that will allow them to secure a place in the future.

Competitive progress is fast coming to be seen as a learning process whose cornerstone is the rate at which organisations can change the way they view things and their assumptions about what is the best way to do things. Organizations unable to sustain learning are in great danger of obsolescence. All organizations encounter new ideas and new practices but in some this encounter causes a change and in others it does not, or if it does it is far slower than the fast learners. The rate at which organizations learn increasingly determines their prospects for survival. As rapid change affects more and more aspects of organizations – their processes, technologies, management approaches, cultural formulas, and customer relationships – those that are unable to learn quickly, or do not recognize its importance, will be the losers left to wonder what happened and what went wrong.

However, organizational learning is not an abstraction or something that abstractions like 'organizations' do. It is people who learn and the rate at which they learn is on the critical path to 'organizational learning'. Organizations facing the prospect of continuous transformation, can only do this if they consist of people who are able to generate ideas and new insights and who have the ability to work with others to turn them into distinctive organizational performance. Without this, the organizational learning on which living with continuous change depends, cannot and will not take place. All managers can do is create the human, structural and technical conditions which encourage, support and make rapid individual learning possible, and which turn individual learning into improved organization capability.

The conditions that enable individuals to learn, are therefore a primary concern to tomorrow's organization. This is not about making individuals more receptive to received organizational wisdom, it is about fostering individuals who are concerned with the pursuit of learning. The conditions that enable enhanced individual learning to result in increased collective capacity to pursue organizational purposes are also important and of equal concern to those who carry the designation of managers. In an important sense, tomorrow's managers are organizational architects concerned with designing and continuously regenerating the management, structural, social and technological context necessary to enable the organization, through its people, to continuously increase its capacity for delivering original world-class responses in a global, knowledge-intensive competitive arena.

There are two key questions for organizations aiming to be tomorrow's success stories. The first is, what are the management priorities, attitudes and approaches that will ensure that the organization's people continually generate a widening range of possibilities from within and from their constant searches for the best ideas from whatever source? The second, and perhaps more important, is what management concepts and approaches will ensure that the organization has the capacity to change as required to ensure that possibilities become the realities of world-class capability and performance? In other words, how does an organisation continually extend its genetic diversity – its latent survival and growth potential – to the point where its people represent an infinite reservoir of ways of dealing creatively and successfully with a future which will always be dramatically different than the past? A key management issue is how to make learning real-time and not locked into rigid long-cycle formal systematic approaches which frequently serve little purpose other than to march the organization gracefully into history.

CREATING THE CONDITIONS

In a world where success is dependent on the rate at which individuals learn, organisations must not insulate the individual from the challenges of change. The challenge of change is rapid learning. Only individuals can learn. The individual is at the centre of the future.

In an important sense, organizational learning is not the acquisition of skills or technological, professional or process know-how – however up-to-date it may be – it is the ability to change organizational behaviour in ways which are consistent with the success requirements as they change in a rapidly transforming business world. The continuous transformation of organizational behaviour is the key to living with continuous change.

In conditions of continuous change the future of the organization depends on creating the space for individual learning and turning this into increased organizational capacity for adaptive change. New organizational behaviours expressed in terms of innovation, adaptability, fast responses and a world-class customer orientation are the goal. The management and developmental approaches must therefore centre on attaining organizational behaviour which ensures continued relevance and distinction. This concern with organizational behaviour goes beyond that of individuals and groups. It must embrace the ability of the organization to adapt as a whole – adaptable people and teams are of little use if it takes three to five years to change the systems that determine how they actually work, or the products and services which substantially define how they interact with their customers. While organizational learning is essentially about people, overlooking the totality of the architecture of organizational adaptation can relegate an important idea to mere rhetoric.

Traditional approaches to training and development have little to do with creating the conditions for individual and organizational learning. Many traditional approaches to training and development assume that the aim is to impart the knowledge or skills required for the recipient to play a part or fulfil a prescribed role. To a limited extent this is useful, but the risk is that the individual is relegated to a passive role in the development own their future, and that their own original contributions are relegated to secondary or irrelevant status. What is more important than the 'pouring in of skills' is the development of the urge to inquire, solve problems and apply new insights through organizational change. Placing a priority on this urge and equipping people with the associated skills announces that the answers to the future are not known, but are yet to be discovered. It announces to people that it is their responsibility to find such answers to the future as can be found. This is a very powerful and energizing message. Management whose people are actively engaged in finding problems, solving them and continuously moving the business forward, must acquire new management skills. The skills they must acquire are those concerned with enabling people to apply their spirit of inquiry and increased capacities towards achievements which are greater than they themselves could. In other words, their evolving purposes must be enabled to find expression in evolving organizational purposes. As people grow in their capacity to innovate and take on challenges, management's role increasingly must become one of ensuring that fast-learning people and their organizations realize the return on their increased capacities – as reflected in improved business performance, a growing certainty of being able to deliver world-beating performance into the longer term, and a growing certainty of having a place in the future.

Perhaps the essential resource in tomorrow's organization is the growth potential and the growth urges of people. It is a vital management responsibility to make sure that human growth is not stifled and the energies that growth brings are not squandered. Traditional organizations do both, sometimes intentionally and most times because its importance is not understood. Unless an organisation's developmental philosophy is able to stretch each and every individual, leading to a positive and self-reinforcing cycle of continuous growth, it is wasting perhaps the only resource that can propel it into the future – positive, future creating human growth. Unless the organization is able to create a positive framework within which the individual can through personal growth make his or her distinctive contribution to wider organizational purposes, the organization can never evolve far beyond its starting point. It cannot move with the times, and it certainly can never surprise the competition.

The conditions for learning turn the traditional management paradigm on its head. Few developmental programmes recognize that learning is a very personal experience and that it is the experience of growth that keeps it alive. Few recognize that the ideal conditions for learning vary from individual to individual, and that learning is less about gaining 'knowledge' thrust in from outside and more about making sense of personal experience. Many developmental programmes overlook the uniqueness and breadth of what each individual brings with them as potential and experience. And indeed some, by implication at least, reject individual experience as unworthy alongside received and approved organizational wisdom. Very few developmental programmes take individual experience as the starting point and are designed to help the individual make sense of their experience. However, effective individual and organizational learning depends on developmental approaches which help the individual understand their experience in a new light.

Learning is not substantially outside-in but substantially inside-outside. It takes place when there is a felt need. The tension of a felt need creates the push or pull necessary for learning to occur. Tomorrow's organization works to maintain this tension. Its management processes are concerned with the continuous exploration of a changing reality, with redefining what it is important to be doing, and redefining the best ways of doing it. In this way it and its people are always aware of the gap between where they are and where they need to be. And an important management responsibility is to ensure that the organization and its people are always in a position to close the gap – having destiny but no means, is like having the arrow but no bow.

SURFACING THE ISSUES

The progress of tomorrow's organization depends on facing the prospect of continuous transformation. The implication is that the competitive progress of the organisation has its foundations in continuous changes in assumptions, goals, values, norms and processes that arise from a process of continuous challenge.

The management process must therefore become one of facilitating the turning of the ideas arising from fast-learning people into new formulas of organisational success. This not easy for organizations which almost by definition exist to preserve a winning formula. The cultural immune responses of organizations can be powerful and new ideas, skills, outlooks and approaches can be rejected simply because they are not self. Given that this is real, perhaps the big management issue surrounding living with continuous change is how to deal with the fact that organizations have a strong tendency to reject it.

Tomorrow's organization needs more than a simple tolerance of diversity. In tomorrow's organization, challenging the status quo is expected and actively encouraged. All managers need to be equipped to be engaged in a constant search for the need to change and for what needs to change – structurally, technically and behaviourally. They also need to be equipped to deal with the human and political aspects of change – helping others to deal with the perceived and real threats, hopes and fears associated with change (see Figure 7.2).

A primary role of managers becomes one of helping others learn and to turn individual learning into greater organizational capacity. The role of the manager shifts to one of facilitator of organisational learning. This means that opening the organization and its people to new possibilities becomes a basic requirement, as does encouraging people to put ideas forward and assisting them to reflect on their own assumptions about the present and the future. It means that a key management role becomes the fostering of a spirit of continuous experimentation – encouraging people to try out new ways of doing things, and to show initiative in deciding how best to apply new ideas. It is also important for senior managers to be seen to acknowledge that individual ideas and contributions are essential to the future of the organization and that the questioning of the present, and a willingness to try out new ways of doing things is essential, welcomed and highly prized.

As continuous transformations are required if organizations are to grow and prosper and support the lifestyles people want, competitive progress becomes a process of changing assumptions about what is the best way to do things and increasing the organization's ability to act in new ways. Management increasingly have a key role in challenging the way things are done – what might be called 'cognitive re-engineering'. Progress increasingly requires a continuous rethink of the organization and how it goes about things. The future is fundamentally about the 'soft'

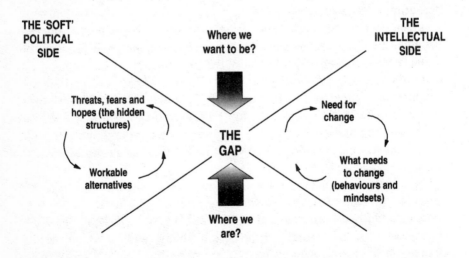

Figure 7.2 *Surfacing the issues*

side of the organization – it is about people, how they see things and about how views which are no longer relevant can quickly be replaced with those that are. As such the ability to transform is about more than the 'hard' side of organizations, the structures, business and management processes, skills and technologies – important as they are. It is about how organizations become able to continuously manage the relevance of their assumptions, structures and behaviours in ways that will ensure meaning, survival and growth.

This task of challenging assumptions about the present and the future is a complex one. However, as it becomes increasingly clear that tomorrow's organizations will bear little resemblance to those of the past, the ability to creatively challenge assumptions becomes an essential management skill. As if that was not challenging enough, the urgently required fresh perceptions of what it makes sense to do and why, require new multidisciplinary concepts and perspectives – the successful enterprises of the 21st century cannot be understood piecemeal. Tomorrow's organization looks very different, and to understand it, it needs to be understood from the point of view of how it behaves as a total 'system'. Only from there can managers proceed to describe how it needs to be able to function to deliver and sustain those behaviours. Approaching tomorrow's organization purely from the structural, process or technical perspectives – from the point of view of what it looks like – reveals little about how it will need to behave and how it characteristically deals with situations. Still less does it capture the essence of how it will feel to be part of tomorrow's organization. These fresh perceptions require managers who can both combine and transcend the traditional disciplines of strategy, general management, sales and marketing, operations, finance, systems theory, psychology, sociology, philosophy, human resource management and information technology.

Enabling the organization to challenge its present and future, and enabling the organization to move ahead with entirely new perspectives, requires a revolution in management thought and practice.

CREATIVE INTERACTION

Creative interaction is concerned with two major issues. The first is to ensure individuals are exposed to, stimulated and changed by, direct experience of a changing world. The second is to ensure that people interact in ways which constructively solve problems, resolve differences, and change the way the organization works.

Staying in touch with a fast moving world requires the fullest interaction between the organization and the external world. Real-time data reflecting the full complexity of events is required. Attempting to manage using historical accounting abstractions is equivalent to piloting a plane using last year's passenger revenues as flight control data. Narrow sources of data, data which are predominantly internal, not customer focused, and not linked clearly to required standards of excellence, are of little use.

Information that is not shared is information wasted. Unlike money, sharing information multiplies its value. Not sharing information prevents the organization as a whole from understanding what is going on, what is critical, what the priorities are, and cuts it off from the operating realities. The organization will then inevitably become more concerned with itself than with what it there to do. Not only will it drift dangerously off course, course changes will become impossibly slow, and when they do occur, they will be dangerously disruptive.

Tomorrow's organization depends on a sense of shared purpose – not just because that may be more efficient in achieving a particular end, but because it makes fast change and fast responses possible. It believes that the foundation of shared purpose is continuous open discussion and dialogue about what is happening in the outside world and its significance for current practices and the future of the organization. Continuous dialogue based on a real-time understanding of the operating realities is a form of continuous simulation of the world and what it takes to prosper within it. This continuous simulation is a process of constant preparation. And those organizations that are constantly prepared are the ones best placed to respond first, most effectively and most creatively to opportunities and threats.

Change does not occur through elaborate but detached 'ivory tower' planning mechanisms – though some approaches such as scenario-based approaches may have a place. Change occurs when the organization is sensitized to the environment. The more organizational surface that is exposed to the outside world and the more that the 'inside' is concerned with what is sensed from beyond its boundaries, the sooner that the need for change becomes obvious – and the sooner the adaptive response can take place. In tomorrow's organization all people have a primary responsibility for learning from customers, competitors, suppliers and other companies. Managers have a primary responsibility for ensuring that information is shared within the organization and in particular between groups, functions and geographical locations.

Increasing all forms of feedback and accelerating the rate at which organizational learning occurs is a key management responsibility. Failure to anticipate and respond in a meaningful way to a changing environment can never be anything other than an indication of a management process that has failed.

Information is the primary co-ordinating material of tomorrow's organization. The unnecessary control, restriction or rationing of information deprives people of involvement at a time when organizations need not just involvement – to enable them to move quickly and together – but informed commitment to programmes of action which mean something personal to every individual. Information rationing also implies distrust and or a patronizing attitude. Both are profoundly demotivating, and ultimately deprive the organization of the opportunity to deal confidently with the competitive realities.

In tomorrow's organization, the primary mission of its people is to connect the organization to its environment. To do this all the human senses and faculties are required but perhaps empathy is amongst the most important. Empathy with customers is a basic requirement in all industries if the customer is to feel understood and valued. While perhaps not a quality possessed by all, empathy is required for there to be an emotional bond between the customer and the organization. Empathy is required for the organization and the designer (all must become designers) if they are to chart ways ahead which anticipate customer's changing needs. In tomorrow's organization, feelings not just 'facts' are data. Fundamentally, creative interaction is seen less as a process of structured communication and 'rational' decision making, and more an aesthetic and intuitive process where the goal is to be tuned into events, where they are leading, and what it takes to ensure relevant organizational behaviours.

REAL-TIME LEARNING

The rate at which the future is rushing towards us all is compressing the time available for effective responses to fast changing events. Basing decisions on obsolete understandings of current data is just as dangerous as basing them on obsolete data.

Real-time learning depends on three things: the availability of real-time information, the ability to recognize its significance, and the ability to turn new insights into new behaviours. It is now technically feasible to provide real-time information about all aspects of business operations from the point-of-sale through to the availability of raw materials such as ideas. Those who have gone down that route find it electrifies the business and that it has an electrifying effect on its people – most people find life in real-time more immediate and arresting. What is more difficult is to be sure that the significance of events is recognized and understood. What is much more difficult is to do something about it quickly.

Much depends on ensuring that people are open to change, used to and able to exercise free will responsibly, and are continually striving for an better understanding of what it makes sense to do in their own best interests and in the interests of the organizations to which they belong. Much depends on the sense that what we know today is at best today's feeble approximation – and that tomorrow perhaps we will know more. This requires that views of people as mere costs or factors of production be replaced by views of people as sources of resourcefulness. It also requires a recognition that to be resourceful, people need opportunities for developing and exercising resourcefulness, and by extending their resourcefulness, increasing their capacities and capabilities.

The ability to question and change assumptions which is so fundamental to real-time learning, requires the individual to accept full responsibility for their own learning. It requires people to be equipped to learn and discover for themselves – to understand their experiences and to draw new insights from them. Developmental inputs that are judgmental or prescriptive, cripple or at best stunt real-time learning capability. Therefore a key concern of managers is to assist people to learn how to learn, to remove obstacles to learning and to help people make their own learning process more effective. To equip itself for real-time learning, the organization must equip its people with concepts, tools and techniques that will allow them to make sense of and respond better to current and future situations and events.

This means that for tomorrow's organization, yesterday's approaches to strategic planning – the ends, ways, means sequence set in stone for three to five years – are obsolete. What replaces them is a continuous process of simultaneous simulation of ends, ways and means designed primarily to continuously regenerate the means. And the aim of the continuous regeneration of the means is to always be best prepared to meet the unexpected challenges and customer requirements of today and tomorrow. Strategic management is therefore something that everyone does. Continuous conscious experimentation becomes the way of life with real-time feedback its guide.

The barriers to real-time learning are not technical, but conceptual and cultural. It is now feasible and becoming ever more so, to bring the realities of the real world immediately to every individual. The operating realities need no longer be dimly communicated through the restricted information handling media of a former age. They need no longer be delayed by management hierarchies concerned more with hoarding and massaging information than passing it on. The operating realities need no longer be muddled by the irrelevant information produced by business processes designed to meet the information-handling constraints of the pre-information technology era. Not only can the design of business processes now reflect the operating essentials, the info-sphere within which they operate can now communicate the essence of what needs to be said and heard for confident action-oriented people to take confident forward-looking action.

In a real-time world of instantaneous feedback, organizations can become sensitized to the nuances and realities of the worlds they inhabit. Instead of stumbling blindly in the dark, they can respond intelligently and quickly. Instead of endlessly repeating previously learned responses long after they have ceased to be useful, they can be continually changed by the very dynamics of being a fully connected part of the real world.

MANAGING DYNAMIC AGENDAS

The only management agenda in tomorrow's organization is the dynamic one, and one which is very different from that characteristic of the past (see Figure 7.3).

For example, managers and the management processes of the organisation must energize and connect the individual with evolving organisation's purposes, and ensure that people believe they are fundamentally central to the continuously evolving means by which the organization achieves its aims. They must continually strive to ensure that people believe that what the organization needs from them goes beyond their time, their skills, their loyalty and their forbearance – and that what is also important is the spirit in which people approach things. In the increasingly quality, values and intangibles-oriented nineties, the approach to things – the process – represents an increasing part of the perceived value-added.

The dynamic agendas of the nineties challenge managers to let go of control-oriented and prescriptive management approaches founded on long since obsolete patriarchal assumptions of an unskilled, immature and

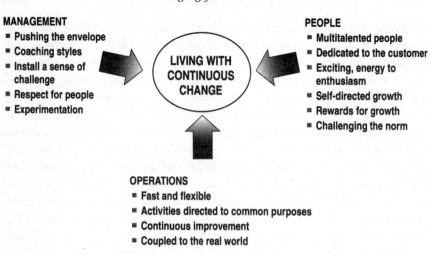

MANAGEMENT
- Pushing the envelope
- Coaching styles
- Install a sense of challenge
- Respect for people
- Experimentation

LIVING WITH CONTINUOUS CHANGE

PEOPLE
- Multitalented people
- Dedicated to the customer
- Exciting, energy to enthusiasm
- Self-directed growth
- Rewards for growth
- Challenging the norm

OPERATIONS
- Fast and flexible
- Activities directed to common purposes
- Continuous improvement
- Coupled to the real world

Figure 7.3   *Managing dynamic agendas*

passive workforce whose physical energies and abilities were the only contribution they could make to drive the industrial machine. Instead, managers now have a vital responsibility to encourage each individual to take ownership and responsibility for the distinctiveness of the organization's intellectual assets, and for its all-round capabilities distinguishing it from even the best competition in the world. This is a dramatic departure from even the near past.

Managers also have to work with, lead and be led by people who are now vitally concerned with maintaining the relevance of their skills to ever changing customer and competitive needs. Such people will insist that management manage in a way which ensures that opportunities are created which continuously reinvent their skills in the face of the rapid obsolescence of existing skills. They have to work with people whose sights are set on developing creativity, energy and imagination at levels high enough to meet current and future challenges, and with people who believe in their vital contributions as sources of experience and potentially important ideas. Perhaps most challenging of all, management must have the goal of working with people for whom the creation of excellence and distinctive customer value is not a matter for compromise.

Continuous change and real-time learning inevitably create tensions. Where individuals are encouraged to have different values, perspectives and points of view, management have to find a way of accepting differences and building convergent views which encompass them. As collaboration is increasingly required to achieve results, management need to replace rival-beating internal competition with a mutual commitment to pushing the organization's envelope to new horizons.

In a fundamental sense, the agenda of tomorrow's managers is an agenda of continuous renewal rather than an agenda intended to preserve yesterday's formulae for success. To do this they must create a supportive climate and environment within which self-directed learning can flourish. Developing the effectiveness of self-directed learning requires that managers make it possible for their people to develop the skills of learning itself and by so doing, develop the ability of the organization to accept and assimilate new ideas and practices. The agenda of tomorrow's managers is to equip the organization to discover the future. Not only must individuals be equipped to direct their energies towards preparation for future conditions – the organization will also have the ability to transform to meet them.

ORCHESTRATION

The growth of tomorrow's organization depends on the real-time learning and growth of its people. A fundamental responsibility, for the individual and the manager, is how to create the real-time learning conditions wherein the routine is discovery. An important aim of management and the developmental process in tomorrow's organization, is to create the conditions wherein the individual will assume personal responsibility for the creation of the future, rather than assuming a passive role or succumbing to fear, uncertainty and doubt. This is in sharp distinction to traditional approaches which often view development as giving people information or giving them skills – what they need to know to do the job. An important point is that it is only by enabling people to increase their ability to create outcomes which are meaningful to them as individuals, that they can and will take the lead and responsibility for shaping their own destinies.

The developmental mechanisms of tomorrow's organizations do not relegate individuals to a passive role in the development of the futures. They do not ask people to hand over their destinies to a paternal institution. The dominant characteristic of their operating style is not the passive transfer of existing values and skills. Far more important than providing access to learning tools and resources, is the ability of the organization to live with people who constructively challenge by asking the simple question why. Questions about the future are more common than the received answers to yesterday's challenges. Constant inquiry about where future success will come from is much more common than acceptance of the myths of the past. As such, tomorrow's organization energizes and revolutionizes. It is a hectic and demanding place to be.

There is a major management challenge inherent in a situation where individuals have assumed responsibility for their own destinies, and where they have embarked on a process of discovery – rather than following the well-worn path. The challenge – and it is a particular threat to traditional management approaches – is to achieve a convergence between individual discovery and organizational destiny. If the organization has no vision and no will to create the future, and is more concerned with preserving past positions and glories, this convergence will be impossible to achieve with the kind of people that inhabit tomorrow's organizations. Traditional management approaches frequently seek to force a convergence by avoiding or outlawing challenges to both organizational goals and the means of achieving them, and by using a variety of coercive tactics – subtle or otherwise. The cost of the traditional approach is little or no fundamental development of the organization's capacities and capabilities. While large organizations can disguise the inevitable slow decline in various efficiency and 'downsizing' initiatives, they are only going one way. If however, the goal is the future and the means is recognized as continuous fundamental regeneration, then continuous challenge from within must become the norm. This requires a new management approach: one whose convergent activities are based on the desire all have to be part of an exciting and worthwhile future.

REWARDS FOR GROWTH

In tomorrow's organizations the reward for participation in them is growth. The absolute measure is a continued and desirable place in the wider scheme of things.

Traditional roles and careers seldom allow for or indeed encourage real growth – the generalist or open-ended role is reserved for very few. Yet this approach reflects an era when educational levels and educational technologies were primitive, and when the ability of computers to empower and create 'technology-enabled generalists' could not even have been dreamed of. Tomorrow's organization requires people to be flexible. Moreover, it believes they should be flexible – because they are better people and more human by virtue of having the scope and ability to grow. Creating the room for growth is not only accepted, it is seen as a foundation requirement for the growth and development on which the ability of the organization to meet new challenges depends. For this to work, jobs and roles, rather than being 'positions' or lifetime confines, must become vital explorations into the present of what it will take that is different to create the future. Careers and career paths rather than being an ascent, must be about the growth and evolution of the individual's ability to contribute in richer, more complete and more rounded ways. Careers must become growth patterns whose evolving form is indeterminate, rather than being comfortable processions to a certain destiny.

Growth is fast becoming the only insurance policy the individual has, and a primary means by which the individual can exercise control over their own destiny. The once safe-havens of life-time skills, organizational careers, and positions in the professions, offer increasingly little shelter to decreasing numbers of people. Organizations that ask people to trade control over their destiny for a career with the organization, will be increasingly scrutinized to see whether they are in a position to continue to offer long-term careers. Few organizations can predict what they will look like and need five years ahead far less their requirements thirty to forty years ahead. Few of the organizations that we see around us now will be around in thirty to forty years. In tomorrow's organization the contract between the organization and its people is one of mutual growth, not the increasingly unrealistic one of the traditional career. As such, tomorrow's organization does not ask its people to give up control of their own destinies. If it did, its people would feel threatened and go elsewhere.

In tomorrow's organization there is no such thing as the standard job. Personal missions will replace standard jobs and relatively static roles. All personal missions will be concerned with the individual making a difference and growing through the challenges inherent in making a difference. This will be assisted by three key trends in the use of information technology. The first is the use of computers to take over inhuman routines. The second is the use of computers to amplify human capabilities, and in particular their inquiring, imaginative, and designing capabilities. The third is use of computers to enable and support alternative organizational concepts. As these trends unfold, instead of being locked into and subservient to the confining structures of yesterday's industrial engines, people will have tomorrow's 'industrial' capabilities at their disposal. For those who chose to work with organizations, they will not be required because their physical energies are required to make it work, but because it is their ideas and other human qualities that enable it to create value, and enable it to move forward in its value-creating capability.

Payment will be increasingly based on capacity, versatility, knowledge, the ability to take on challenges, the array of valuable possibilities the individual presents, and fundamentally, on the ability to make a difference. In conditions where many of the skills and abilities that enable someone to make a difference rapidly obsolesce after the difference has been made, continued payment is a reward for growth and regeneration. Payment for yesterday's skills will be short-lived. Careers based on yesterday's victories in the political jungle will also be short-lived.

In an important sense, money is not a reward for growth, it is one way of measuring growth. Neither is money the sole way that personal growth can be assessed. Independence, broader responsibilities, the opportunity to acquire new skills, and the scope to take on new initiatives and challenges are equally important measures. However, perhaps the ultimate reward for growth is a future-ensuring capacity for continuous self-renewal.

MANAGING WITH DIVERSITY

Tomorrow's organization is not a monoculture. The fact that its environment is one of unpredictability and uncertainty, requires that it have as a basic competence, the ability to deal with diverse, unpredictable futures. The fact that the appropriate organizational response is changing all the time, means that the organization must have the ability to continually generate and apply many new alternative responses which not only meet future needs, but which do not compromise alternative futures. The people who inhabit tomorrow's organizations are the sole source of the innovation and fast well-judged adaptive responses that must come to characterize all organizations if they are to survive. These people are not just flexible, they are change-seeking, fast-learning, leaders in their own right, innovative and demanding in terms of what must be done to satisfy customers and to create a future worthy of the name. This is the management arena of tomorrow (see Figure 7.4).

The big question is how do managers ensure that forward progress results when everything is in a state of continuous flux, and when the organization's energies are generated inside-out rather than top-down bottom-up? The process and approach to involvement is key. Traditional organizations see high levels of diversity as obstacles to involvement and to efficient collective action. Their management approach is frequently one of actively reducing diversity in all its forms. Tomorrow's organiza-

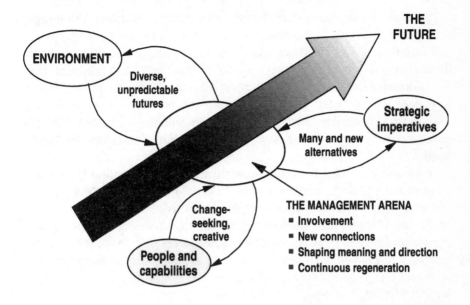

Figure 7.4 *Managing with diversity*

tion needs to maintain a high level of genetic diversity if it is to have the wherewithal to produce the new response to meet new and unexpected conditions. However, this does not dispense with the need for fast and efficient collective action. A core competence of tomorrow's organization is its ability to rapidly assemble whatever is required to produce a wide array of desired outcomes. This applies not just to the business process but equally to the management process.

Fast and efficient collective action requires involvement and commitment. Involvement and commitment are perhaps more vital than the ever, but they can no longer be insisted on. Traditional leadership styles with their use of power, overt incentives, directives, political and social manipulation, and frequently micro-management, are inappropriate for people with a high sense of their own worth, who know what they are doing, and who know their own destinies must and do lie firmly in their own hands. These traditional leadership approaches communicate the message that management believe their people are not committed and able, that they have no sense of what needs to be done, that they lack responsibility and initiative – and that without management's direct day-to-day involvement and decision making nothing would happen. This is not only unacceptable to the people tomorrow's organizations needs if it is to prosper, it will ensure that the vital prospect of continuous learning is destroyed.

Tomorrow's organization demands a new view of leadership. In tomorrow's organization, everyone is a leader. If they are not committed to leading the field at what ever they do, they are the wrong people. If they are not able to take initiative, display resourcefulness and make a difference in everything they do, they are the wrong people. To insist that a leader needs leading is not only inappropriate, it is, in these conditions, insulting.

What is valid, is for managers to work to create the conditions in which people can produce results they truly care about and can be proud of. What is valid, is spending time working with people as equals to clarify goals and to agree how the means of achieving them can be best brought together. In tomorrow's organization, the manager therefore has two primary roles. The first role is one of architect responsible for building and shaping organizations where people can continually expand their capabilities in line with the changing requirements for personal and organizational success. The second role is that of coach, enabling people and groups to reflect on and understand what it takes to extend the boundaries of the possible.

PROFILE OF THE NEW PARADIGM

The assumptions of managers in the new paradigm can be contrasted with the old in the following ways:

Old paradigm		New paradigm
The future is predictable	$\longrightarrow$	The future is discoverable
Visions and plans	$\longrightarrow$	Dynamic agendas of possibilities
Shared organization-wide vision	$\longrightarrow$	Holistic guidance systems
Strongly shared cultures	$\longrightarrow$	Shared commitment to the future
Managers stabilizing consensus	$\longrightarrow$	Managers surfacing assumptions and accelerating learning
Analytical decision making	$\longrightarrow$	Decision making as exploration
Top-down control	$\longrightarrow$	Control as self-directed learning
Strategy as prediction	$\longrightarrow$	Strategy as real-time learning

Preserving the winning formula $\longrightarrow$ Creating the conditions for complex learning

'Ivory tower' planning $\longrightarrow$ Creative interaction with the environment

Missions to preserve $\longrightarrow$ Missions to create the future

8 The Enabling Infrastructure

'You can never have the use of the inside of a cup without the outside. The inside and the outside go together. They're one.' (Alan Watts)

EMBRACING THE CUSTOMER

Dramatic advances in the new technologies of information are combining to enable the transformations required to make tomorrow's organization a reality.

Rapid improvements in the cost and capabilities of communications, data storage and management technologies create limitless possibilities for transforming organizations – most of whom defined what they do, and how, where and with whom they do it, in an age when data was scarce, costly, and difficult to move. The global village is already becoming a reality as combinations of fibre optics, satellite communications, high-power low-cost computers and easy-to-use software make information super-highways possible. As the global gulfs of time and space are eliminated, organizations, their operations, boundaries and their capabilities are completely transformed. Entire industrial structures, their definitions and those of their supply chains – once seemingly static and permanent – are blurring and shifting, and assuming entirely different and hard-to-define alternative forms. Entire geographical markets are being redefined as the resources, experiences and capabilities of diverse and physically distant organizations can be made available instantly anywhere in the world to whoever needs or wants them. As the global becomes local and the local becomes global, the organization becomes virtual. Assumptions about work, careers and relationships that have spanned centuries and civilizations, are being transformed as information technologies take over routine work, call into question the traditional role of managers, and put increasingly powerful capabilities at the disposal of people once confined within narrow, low ranking and thankless routines. As personal computers and low-cost, easy-to-use communications become widely available, work, communications and meetings can be carried out from anywhere with anyone. The organization, its resources, activities and outputs – once largely physical and tightly confined in time and space – can increasingly occur in virtual time and space. Information technologies once used to automate and eliminate people are now combining with the human abilities of creativity, adaptability and flexibility to create new levels of innovation, variety and versatility – paradoxically, the new technologies of information are in the process of transforming the old industrial machine-oriented paradigm into a new human values-centred paradigm.

As the power and capabilities of the new technologies of information have grown, so has the recognition that they are only realized when used to reshape the organization. It is now widely accepted that the new technologies are not only wasted but positively harmful if they are used to automate the organizational approaches, structures and processes of the past. Most important of all, it has now become clear that the new technologies do not determine organizational effectiveness, but that tomorrow's effective organization is very different in all its respects – it just happens to need the new technologies in some form to make it work. In other words, a comprehensive organizational transformation involving paradigm shifts in all organizational dimensions must precede the application of information technology.

Tomorrow's organization requires the new technologies to be used very differently. Instead of a focus on improving business efficiency, management effectiveness and competitive advantage, the new technologies must enable the organization to behave differently, that is with characteristically high levels of innovation, closeness to the customer, fast responses and adaptability – the behaviours on which success in the turbulent nineties ultimately depends (see Figure 8.1). The challenge is to define what the new technologies can do to enable the design and realization of tomorrow's effective organization, and how they need to be organized to enable the behaviours tomorrow's organization needs to prosper in a turbulent world.

Communications, databases and personal computers put organizations and their customers in direct and immediate two-way contact (see Figure 8.2). At a time when the key organizational assets are up-to-date, customer-specific knowledge, a sense of timing, sensitivity to the customer, and the ability to build high quality relationships, databases and communications can be used to give the customer the sense that he or she is being listened to and responded to as an individual.

Information technology can move the customer from being a passive recipient of the product to being its co-producer. Real-time information technology-enabled interaction can rapidly establish a shared understanding of what the customer values. Business processes can be put under

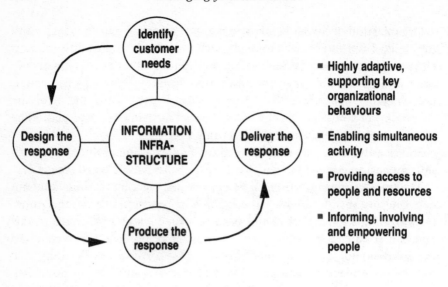

Figure 8.1   *The enabling infrastructure*

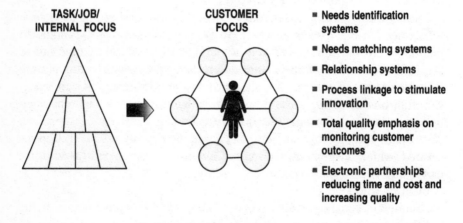

Figure 8.2   *Embracing the customer*

the direct control of the customer ensuring that the product or service is assembled to fully reflect what the customer values. The sense of interaction and self-directed co-creation helps create a memorable experience, moving the basis of the customer relationship from the product to the organization as informed contributor to the customer's highly individual and intangible needs.

Organizations need to be able to bring the best of the company's full capabilities to bear at the moment of customer contact. Information technology enables highly dispersed capabilities to be dynamically concentrated where they can have most effect. By enabling instant networks of interconnections, high levels of interaction between the elements required to meet customer needs can be achieved. The relationship between the customer and the organization's capabilities becomes a dynamic one enabling unique and evolving relationships with shifting customer needs.

The total knowledge of the customer and the customer's behaviour can be made instantly available at the point of contact with the customer. Organization-wide knowledge of the customer's status and current needs makes it possible for the customer to know he or she has been recognized as an individual and their perceptions of value understood. By being able to recognize the customer and his or her needs, the organization can mobilize its resources and capabilities increasing the opportunity for delivering the one solution that will uniquely satisfy the customer. Information technology can become a vital factor in co-ordinating a unique one-time-only customer response.

The time lags usually associated with fulfilling a customer's needs can be reduced. Information technology can shorten the time it takes to identify a customer's need, the time it takes to design the solution and fulfil the need once identified, and the chances of the organization getting it right at the right time. Design, production and delivery can occur simultaneously enabling more factors to be taken into account when defining, designing and delivering the customer's needs. The distances in time, space and thought can be reduced and instantaneous feedback loops created which link identified customer needs and the organization's increasingly real-time response.

Information technology can enable the customer and his behaviour to be understood as a dynamic whole, can put the human back into the concept of customer, and keep the organization coupled to the real world of its customers. It is easy for information technology to track and handle an infinite number of market niches and to shift the economics of business from being in favour of the mass, to being in favour of the individual.

The growing instanteity and bandwidth of information technology-enabled organization/customer interaction greatly increases the rate at which organization learn about their customers. Faster feedback increases the power of what is heard making it more likely that the organization will be changed by its customer interactions. Not only is its knowledge and customer-specific delivery capacity increased, the traditional one-way 'communication' directed at the customer is replaced with a process of learning-oriented inquiry. Every point of contact can be made a vital source of intelligence about what is happening in the marketplace, and the front-line becomes an active listening post in the process of continuously monitoring and updating understanding of the customer and what he or she values. The marketing, design and product development cycle becomes more of a process of joint inquiry involving the customer as a co-designer.

Information technology can avoid customers' time being wasted. It can ensure that stock-outs do not occur and it can eliminate the search for products which are available but whose location is unknown to the customer. By enabling the customer's requirement to be verified in the customer's presence, an organization can immediately confirm its ability to meet a customer requirement. Waiting and queuing times can be eliminated by passing ownership and control of time to the customer. With geographic distance no longer an issue, the time it takes for the company to assemble its resources and ideas on demand to meet customer specific needs can be compressed. By eliminating the time delays that result from physical, psychological and knowledge barriers, the front-line of the organization is enabled to respond dynamically to the dynamic movements of the customer.

Information technology can enable instantaneous support to the front-line. Immediate co-ordinated and simultaneous action throughout the business enables the organization to bring its resources and the resources of others to co-operatively achieve customer value. Fast responses to customers requires any point in the organization to initiate the response. Direct unintermediated communications are key for each point in the network to know the real wants and needs of real customers and what they must do and with whom to fulfil them. By speeding up the process of interconnection required to enable a unique response to be created, information technology enables organizations to reduce the effective distance between what could be achieved and what can be achieved.

DELIVERING THE RIGHT RESPONSE AT THE RIGHT TIME

Organizations are designing vehicles. Their excellence lies in their ability to conceive and design what makes sense for their customers, and the access they have to those who are the best in the world at making it happen through their unique contributions (see Figure 8.3).

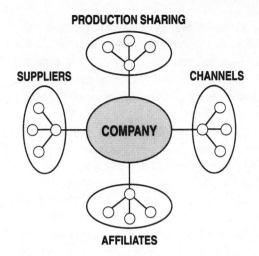

PRODUCTION SHARING

SUPPLIERS

COMPANY

CHANNELS

AFFILIATES

- Production sharing, e.g., electronic subcontracting

- World class affiliations, e.g., co-operative R&D ventures

- JIT supply chain management

- Global sourcing

- Co-ordinating complex inputs

- Transparency to the customer

Figure 8.3 *Delivering the right response at the right time*

Interactive simulation technologies and tools are increasingly being used to rapidly translate ideas, concepts and knowledge into product and service designs. New information technologies focused on the man-design-machine interface enable fast responses to changes in demand. Computer-aided design (CAD) and a growing array of simulation tools allow the rapid development and testing of designs allowing modifications and new designs to be quickly developed. Rapid simulation of ideas and concepts is combining with 'soft', programmable configurations of products, services, and processes to enable the highly customized solutions required to meet individual customer needs. This enables the production and distribution processes required to deliver new products to be rapidly designed and redesigned, and to have their configurations under their direct and flexible control of similar information technology tools. Close links with production facilities – frequently owned by others – enables a fast, responsive, flexible and co-operative production system to deliver what the customer wants, where and when it is required.

The designing capabilities that information technology can bring to an organization, provide it with a vehicle for expressing the energies, imaginations and creativities of people rather than constraining them within the inflexibilities of a world of fixed assets. Information technology can turn the spirit of design into tomorrow's organization's source of energy. By providing the instantaneous access to whatever ideas, resources and components are required, the structures, products, processes and relationships required to create customer-specific solutions can be instantly redesigned. By making resources and assets accessible, and easy to use and reuse across a range of products and services, information technology can enable organizations to become versatile and general-purpose vehicles of design able to reduce their response times to new market demands, and able to provide greater variety to the meet the needs of wide ranges of customers.

The new production paradigm depends on the ability to dynamically co-ordinate many activities spread throughout the organization and its network of partners, suppliers and co-producers. The ability to respond to the needs and requirements of individual customers requires the entire business network of suppliers, co-producers and distributors to be interconnected and enabled to respond instantly. Proliferations of linkages across and between the functions of the business wherever they are located, puts their full potential at the customer's disposal. By reducing the costs of accessing, co-ordinating and transforming diverse resources wherever they are located, the boundaries of an organization's possibilities are extended and redefined. By eliminating the vast separations in time and space between business activities, the possibility of instant access to anything anywhere really does put the world at the customer's finger tips.

By reducing the time it takes to set up and produce new combinations of ideas, information and resources, information technology enables the organization to shift from producing to forecast – to producing to and on demand. Fast information flows compress the time between events and the organization's response, enabling it to respond to its customers in real-time. By so doing, it can track shifting standards of customer value and stay more closely in touch than the competition. The rapid design and assembly of individual customer solutions ensures that every customer gets exactly what they want, not what the organization has in stock. High-speed customized solutions enable the organization to be in a position to achieve higher prices and to maintain its position ahead of the competition. Faster and more precise information enables the organization to rapidly respond with its best ideas and designs, evaluate the response and accelerate the regeneration of know-how, knowledge, skills and assumptions.

Very short information feedback loops combine with instant unintermediated responses to enable the right response at the right time – creating dynamic stability from apparent instability. Instead of ineffective control, continuous adjustment becomes possible. By being closely in touch with events the organization has the ability to discard configurations as soon as their usefulness diminishes. By having unintermediated responses, and 'soft' processes not linked to one product specification, tomorrow's organization is enabled to maintain its relevance to changing circumstances as they arise. Adaptation, rather than being occasional event, becomes part of the routine of seizing new opportunities.

The continuous delivery of customized products at similar cost and quality as mass production is enabled by information technology. 'Soft' configurations of an organization's capabilities are possible, enabling structures, products and processes to be flexible and responsive to fast changing circumstances. Flexibility based on an ability to rapidly reconfigure means that the entire organization and its processes do not need to be redesigned to meet the needs of each new product – the costs of change are reduced. The enabling of rapid reconfigurations and fast high quality information flows provides the organization with the ability to behave quickly and intelligently in an uncertain world.

Information technology enables economies of scope by extending access to global niches and by extending the number of uses to which resources can be put. By enabling the rapid reconfiguration of information, components and skills, very short runs of any particular product or service are made possible. The ability to generate variety from the available resources, provides the overall volumes which change the economics of individuality. The falling costs of technology are not so much the issue as the fact that their availability changes the economics of co-ordinating activities – this is what is creating new possibilities and bringing these possibilities within reach of every organization and everyone.

Information technology enables a redefinition of the organization's idea-to-delivery capabilities by making its capabilities systemic – a function of the possibilities of the business and its network as a whole – rather than the limitations of the individual parts. By increasing the integration and co-ordination of resources throughout the various parts of the business, information technology can eliminate the under-utilization of resources characteristic of the traditional functional boundaries, and amplify their synergies.

Sustained demand for capabilities, not products, is the basis of success. New process technologies (such as flexible manufacturing systems and computer-integrated manufacturing techniques) are making it increasingly economical to deliver a continuous stream of new products. The capability to pursue ever-changing definitions of customer value is created ensuring a continuing demand for the company's capabilities.

In services and manufacturing, the response to the need for new capabilities increasingly draws on the integrative possibilities of information technology. Concepts with parallels in technologically-based computer integrated manufacturing are being applied to use the combined capabilities of computers, software and communications to enable all parts of any organization to operate simultaneously. Each productive cell or node in the organization's process may have its own unique application of technology – but within the context of an overall architecture for the organization's capabilities as a whole. For example, computer-aided design ideas and tools may be used to assist in the identification, design and development of product and service ideas, computer-aided engineering ideas and principles may be used to assist in the design of the production process, and concepts and techniques drawn from computer-aided manufacture or assembly may be used to integrate a unique response to the customer.

Information technology enables organizations to thrive in fragmenting markets. Better, continuous and immediate sources of customer knowledge enable the organization to see each individual as unique. Soft-configurations enable business processes to produce great numbers of different, high-quality products and services in ever shorter production runs. The time to reconfigure the organization's wider network of suppliers and alliance partners can also be reduced extending the possibilities of what can be delivered at very short notice.

There have been countless billions spent to introduce the new technologies of information into organizations with the objective of achieving 'competitive advantage'. With a few well-known exceptions these expenditures have failed to achieve a result. Those that have succeeded, have done so because they did not use the various technologies to electrify existing organizational structures and processes. They used information technology to reframe and transform of the entire organization and its processes – recognizing that the new technologies themselves did not equal transformation. For information technology investment to be successful, the aim must be to enable a new paradigm of assumptions, practices and goals. The correct aim of investment in the new paradigm therefore becomes to arrive at the best organization – the dynamic configuration that has the capacity to produce an individual solution for each customer every time.

CREATING ENTREPRENEURIAL STRUCTURES

Tomorrow's organizations depend on amplifying the contributions their people can make. Structural and attitudinal obstacles which stifle initiative confine the organization to what made sense yesterday. Slow,

low capacity, hard-wired organizational nervous systems moving at snail's pace stultify and produce an air of resignation and acceptance of the status quo. Specializations which allow the parts to play one role only reduce the organizational repertoire to one routine. The new technologies of information challenge all of this (see Figure 8.4). Intelligently applied, they can dramatically increase the entrepreneurial capacity of organizations.

Information technology is being used to reduce the inertia often bred by long lines of communication, layers of management, the compartmentalization of expertise, job de-skilling and narrow roles. Information technology is being used to flatten the management hierarchy, to replace top-down control with customer-oriented self-control, and to focus attention on outcomes as well as tasks. Information technology is being used to extend and redefine inter-organizational boundaries. It is enabling the creation of entrepreneurial structures.

The fact that information technology is enabling a transformation of the structures of the organization – and how they behave – is a consequence of the fact that information technology is tending to push the costs of information transfer and storage towards zero. This enables the information required to co-ordinate business activities to be made

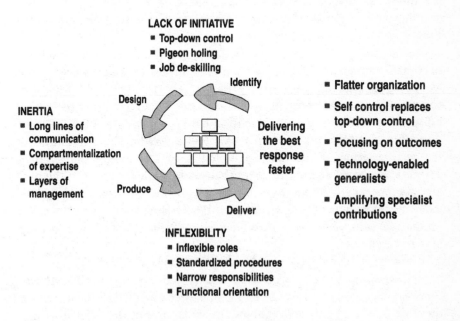

Figure 8.4 *Creating entrepreneurial structures*

available instantly anywhere and anytime – and as many times to as many locations as are required without multiplying the costs of co-ordination. The costs of co-ordinating business activities are falling in line with advances in communications and the emergence of communications network standards. The growing networks of high-bandwidth data communications are making time and distance transparent and can extend direct human contact and relationships to any corner of the globe. The distinctions between internal and external business spheres of communication and co-ordination disappear, creating limitless boundaries for the organization and binding it and the wider world together.

Activities which in the past could only be done internally, that is in close physical proximity, can be done anywhere. Communications, management, influence and control which in the past could only be done quickly and effectively enough if management and employees were within earshot, can now be carried out independently of distance. One result was that the organization and all its resources needed to be clumped together in the one place. Whether or not better resources existed outside, the only ones that it was feasible to use were those available internally – the time and cost benefits of co-ordinating internal activities outweighed the time and costs penalties of using resources located elsewhere – however good they were. Generations of assumptions about what organizations, and cities, are and what they look like have been greatly influenced by the high costs and limitations of pre-modern information technology data communications.

For the most part, the familiar political, social and physical structures of organizations are the sensory, communications and co-ordination technologies available before the arrival of the computer and computer communications. As most of a business and its activity is made up of information-intensive and information-based transactions, the costs of doing business with pre-modern technologies was high and limiting. As the relative costs of the new technologies of information have fallen dramatically, most of the structures that made up the business of the past are disappearing. Previously impossible forms of time and space-independent organization are now possible. Organizations can now focus on and develop their core capabilities, expand their scope, and open up new possibilities.

Information technology enables the close co-operative integration of organizations and their operations. Fast, high-bandwidth communications enables collaborative relationships between operations wherever they are in the world, and enables the collaboration to behave as one system. Individual organizations can become a part of network of actual and potential synergies, giving them scale and scope way beyond their own capabilities. The new technologies bypass the need for information to be handled and interpreted by middle managers or other intermediaries. Experts in one part of the network can be transparently linked to others in other parts. The expertise of marketers, designers, production specialists, distribution and sales specialists can be brought to where it is needed quickly and at low cost. Global and local responses to global competitors are possible as the organization is able to reconfigure, reallocate and adapt to mount the most effective response. Valued customers can be recognized as such wherever they are encountered. By eliminating internal and external boundaries, time and space, information technology can ensure the quality, responsiveness and efficiency required to ensure that excellence is delivered to the customer. Electronic markets able to instantly connect those who know and those who need to know can enable the organization to achieve its results with an extended pool of resources. Each part of the organization can see the customer and what needs to be done to satisfy his or her needs, and the information necessary for shared decision making and commitment building can be made rapidly available. Information technology becomes the vehicle for participation in a world of dramatically compressing cycle times, ever more exacting market conditions, and customer defined configurations of operations and capabilities. Fast communications can enable the organization to respond quickly and in concert with others to deliver the required response.

Information technology replaces management's traditional organizing and controlling role with resource allocations determined by the dynamics of shifting demand. This is creating opportunity for those not conditioned to managing within a narrow organizational space and who are able to dynamically create and re-create cross-boundary, cross-disciplinary and cross-cultural relationships. Decision-support software enables decision making to be pushed out to those who are directly in contact with the customer. The same software can be put in the hands of the customer enabling the organization to meet customer defined criteria for success. Close connections at the point-of-sale multiply the points of contact the organization has with the fast moving market realities. Rapid feedback exposes every function, process and activity to the market realities, stimulating innovation and enabling the continuous competitive calibration of business activities against shifting standards of excellence.

Information technology enables niche-specific communities of shared information and co-operative capabilities consisting of whatever skills, resources and experience are required from wherever in the world. Collaborations can be made possible as communications infrastructures enable the dynamic sharing of physical assets, distribution networks or sales operations. The same infrastructures provide access to world-class alliances ensuring world-class inputs and offering the potential to reduce costs. Direct links with world-class designers can increase the rate of product and service introduction. Distribution scope can be greatly extended through electronic means and the direct connection to many network alliance partners can make it possible to meet individual customer needs flexibly.

The new technologies of information are putting the future-building capacities of people to the fore. The structural obstacles presented by the information handling deficiencies of yesterday's information technologies are being relegated to history. The old organizational structures are yesterday's information handling technologies. The new technologies of information work because they entirely supersede them. The new structures work not because of new technology, they work because they amplify the human.

CHANGE-SEEKING CULTURE

Information and communication networks are increasingly bringing the organization and its people into closer contact with real events as they occur. The widespread availability and sharing of information throughout the organization brings the immediacy of the competitive world direct to the individual even in the largest of organizations. By directly confronting and expanding the individual, information technology can increase the organization's capacity to receive signals of change from the environment and its ability to use them to change the assumptions and behaviours of the organization. The potential for the ready and widespread availability of information increases the capacity of the organization to translate the need for change into new priorities, and the ability of the organization to generate the new behaviours which will enable it to stay in touch with a fast-moving real-time world.

Real-time information systems focused on customer behaviour, customer satisfaction and a rich picture of competitive performance, increasingly force the pace of change (see Figure 8.5). Real-time systems make it possible for people to operate in real-time. Instead of operating on information which partially tells them what happened a long time ago, they can use their knowledge of what is happening now to influence events before they are beyond influence.

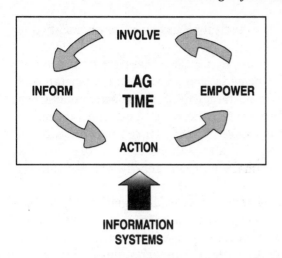

- Vastly superior internal and external information
- Increased ability to test probable outcomes
- Reducing the time to turn ideas into action
- Immediate feedback on the consequences of actions
- Overcoming conservatism with intelligent control
- Enabling organizations to master change

Figure 8.5   *Change-seeking culture*

The focus of the information being provided within the organization is shifting from an historical perspective on narrow financial information – and from one restricted to management – to a richer base designed to enable individuals to form their own views about operating and competitive performance, and enabling them to question organizational assumptions about performance and how it can be improved. The immediacy of feedback encourages the questioning of assumptions. The availability of tools which test the implications of feedback increases the probability of different action the next time the situation is encountered, and increases the speed with which the response can be generated. As the sense of dealing with something real and immediate increases, so does the need to do something real and immediate about it. As what is happening and what it means become clearer, the prospect is of spending more time dealing with what needs to be dealt with, and less with what does not.

The open access to information that reflects real events in real-time, enables tomorrow's organization to seek change. Uncensored and unfiltered information facilitates individual inquiry and the discussion of the issues. More importantly, it prepares individuals and the organization for new practices and new priorities. By allowing people to evaluate situations for themselves, information technology can widen perspectives and can generate new levels of initiative. The open availability of information enables the organization to move faster. All can be part of the process of reflecting on circumstances and of preparing themselves to deal with it. The organization increases the originality and speed of new responses.

Information technology can create real-time operating feedback and provide an immediate sense of being in contact with the real world – and of being directly affected by it. In this way, information technology can enable the organization and its people to see the world as it is – and to keep close to events as they evolve. Close inter-connections between functions and other organizations – and with customers – can ensure a source of constant challenge to existing and prevalent assumptions and capabilities.

The real world requires real-time responses. Information technology can create close connections between sources of information and those individuals and groups who can together make sense of it. By sorting through complex information more quickly, organizations can be put in touch with real-time. Time-compressing technologies enable organizations to operate in real-time. Technologies such as groupware, enable new practices, ideas and innovations to be quickly transferred around the organization enabling organizations to realize their collective capability.

The continuous renewal of tomorrow's organization depends on the organization's people being closely in touch with the evolving competitive imperatives. Direct, immediate and broad-based feedback requires, of itself, that assumptions about how the world operates and how it should best be approached, should be examined. By making the drivers of change self-evident, and experienced at a visceral level, the organization's ability to stay connected with and to the real world is transformed.

Tomorrow's organization requires high levels of involvement. Tomorrow's organization depends on everyone having an interest in the future. Strategic learning – the wish to have a future – is energized by individuals reflecting on the issues, the opportunities and what can be done with them, and developing shared purpose with others. The use of information technology to inform, involve, and to enable people to exercise choice can enable them to develop internalized commitments to a shared purpose. People can be active participants all the time – not just occasionally. Open information provided by widely available personally empowering technologies can encourage and enable people to explore, examine and initiate changes in how work is done – and to develop their own commitments to change. Preparation for the future can be the continuous, and active concern of all.

Information technology shortens the loop between the new and the ability to do it routinely. The immediacy of feedback from operations, markets and the competitive environment increases the rate at which individuals and organizations can replace and reconfigure their assumptions and practices. It also transforms the rate at which behaviours can be changed to enable the organization to create distinctive value.

Tomorrow's organization depends on the rate at which its people learn. Information technology-enabled links with suppliers, customers, strategic partners – and competitors – can increase the volume and variety of information transferred, and directly expose the organization to what the best in the world are doing. Computer-based training and increasingly CD-ROMS can increase experiences and developmental possibilities. The availability of simulation tools to managers and others can accelerate their ability to deal creatively with the situations they face and with the changes their organizations must make.

Open information creates the space for initiative. Informed people can take action, reflect on the consequences, and be prompted by that to find ways of doing it better next time. Rather than being confined to the perspectives inherent in a single job or task, they can develop new perspectives on the required outcomes and on what needs to change for them to be achieved better than ever before. By seeing the organization and the issues it faces in a broader sense, and by having the space to show initiative, people can apply their initiative to finding ways in which they can make their own best contributions to the future – and to those who follow them.

In a time when there is no more serious organizational disability than being confined to the past, organizations now have the prospect of being part of the making of tomorrow's story. The new technologies of information have the potential to enable organizations to ride at the edge of a fast moving real-time world. They have the potential to make it possible for people to participate through their actions today in the shaping of their organization's destiny.

LEVERAGING THE INDIVIDUAL

Instead of turning work into a sub-human activity, information systems are increasingly being used to increase the human element in products and services. The human element in organizational responses is increased when individuals are provided with the information they need to understand immediately and accurately what they and their organizations can do for the customer. In tomorrow's organizations, everyone and everything they do is in the front-line (see Figure 8.6). Everyone is a vital point of contact in the delivery of customer satisfaction. To have the ability to play their full part they need a clear and immediate window on what the customer wants, the ability to work with the customer to confirm this, and the means to assess how well the last performance met the customer's expectations. Equally, they need a window on what the organization can do and the ability to commit the organization to it. The new technologies of information provide the means to inform, advise and involve.

In the past, the individual was limited to and by what he or she knew or had acquired in the form of skills. The manager was limited to and by the abilities of those he or she directly controlled. The organization depended on its ability to make its many specialist human parts add up to a greater capability. The role of the manager was to be sure that the parts added up to something useful internally or in the market. The dramatically increasing capabilities of micro-processors, communications and database technologies are fast bringing about the situation where everything that the organization knows, can do and has access to, will be available to and usable by any individual. The organization will no longer be a relatively fragile and unadaptable structure constructed of hard-wired human raw materials, it will be transformed into knowledge-based organization whose abilities are mirrored in everyone. Rather than being a small and

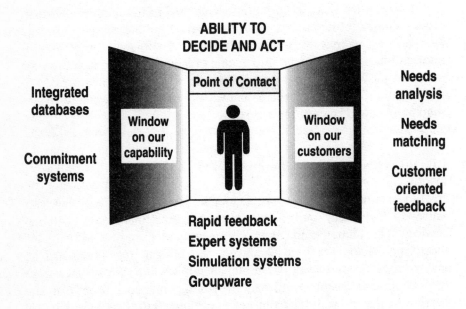

Figure 8.6 *Leveraging the individual*

static part of the organization's capability, the individual will become the means of expressing the organization's total capabilities in unique ways to meet unique customer needs. Rather than being limited by inaccessible knowledge, the individual will become dramatically more powerful. Instead of being limited to what each part can do, what the organization knows and can do will amplified not attenuated by its people. No longer is what the organization knows and can do confined to the particular configurations represented by the mindsets, skills and actions of individuals – the explosive growth in accessible organizational knowledge allows highly adaptable organizational behaviour – the organization can look at what it knows in many ways and from many perspectives. It can also combine what it knows and is capable of, with new insights in new ways to create highly original responses every time new circumstances are encountered.

The role of the individual changes and broadens. Instead of being 'merely' a contributor of a limited set of skills, the role of the individual becomes one of ensuring that the capabilities of the organization are used to best effect. In contrast to the former paradigm where managers had the sole rights of resource allocation, in an important sense information technology can enable everyone to become 'managers' – those charged with making the optimal use of the available resources and knowledge. The issue is less one of 'expert' know-how becoming available to everyone through 'expert' systems. The transformation occurs when individuals are enabled to move from the narrow confines of traditional roles, and by so doing are able to amplify the contributions they can make within their organizations, and perhaps more importantly, able to amplify the capabilities of their organizations.

Information technologies cannot turn inexperienced people into sophisticated, highly experienced people – computer-based procedures with a human voice attached will always make the customer feel like a transaction rather than a person. Computers can only amplify what is there already – amplified inexperience or lack of concern has only the obvious effect. The design issue is one of amplifying the human and personalized element in the customer relationship – the product or service – and by so doing increasing the space for the unique human contributions of innovation, originality, empathy and concern. The mindset shift that needs to be accomplished is the one from people as the 'deliverers' of the product or service – people as conduits, to people as the creators of services and products – capable, confident and innovative people who have the total capabilities of their organizations at their disposal at all times.

The purpose of information technology is not to replace people or to limit their contributions. In other words, the information technology revolution is not about carrying forward the era of industrial automation. The purpose of the information technology revolution is to amplify the human. This is occurring in two ways. The first is by relegating sub-human repetitive and narrow routines – routines that do not require thought – to the non-human silicon world. The second is to provide tools with which to leverage human capabilities and which can accelerate the development of human potential.

Leveraging the individual depends on eliminating the distinction between those that think and create and those that do. Thought in its many forms – such as speculation, curiosity, exploration and learning – is what is characteristically human. To systematically eliminate thought from the work of many if not most people, is to corrode the organization's creative capital and increase the dead-weight of the organization. As human creativity, imagination, diversity, energy and enthusiasm increasingly become the sole basis on which an organization can distinguish itself, organizations which diminish the human through the misdirected use of information technology will squander their futures.

The new information technologies are fundamentally important because they enable a change in perspective. Technologies such as electronic mail, video conferencing, and groupware extend the boundaries of collaboration and teamwork. Issues that once appeared local, or had to be local because of technical constraints, can involve and draw upon a wider range of views, ideas and experiences. Organization-to-organization links such as those enabled by electronic data interchange (EDI) can extend collaborative relationships beyond organizational, geographic and time boundaries and offer new opportunities to all participants and new approaches to once adversarial relationships. Modelling and simulation tools extend perspectives beyond what is to what might be and what can be. Teams and groups, once susceptible to arriving at stable self-referential norms, can be dynamically extended and continuously recreated as information technologies create unlimited possibilities for team membership, participation and interaction.

Fundamentally, the goal when 'engineering' new relationships between information technology and people has less to do with concepts such as 'empowerment' – putting more capability and authority at the disposal of the individual – important as that is, and more to do with enabling the customer to see and experience what the organization is capable of. Information technology, well applied, enables the 'front-line' to be experience designers – intelligent judges of the customer requirement 'empowered' with the tools to create original, once-off customer-specific designs from the vast resources and capabilities of the organization.

LIVING WITH CONTINUOUS CHANGE

The survival of organizations depends on the speed at which they can adjust to new situations. Real-time feedback of the effects of actions and events is increasingly a basic requirement for staying in touch with fast moving customers and competitors. At the operational level, information technology is already making possible instant feedback and enabling instant responses, tuning organizational reflexes to the demands of a real-time world. At the management level, information systems are increasingly capable of generating real-time insights into the whys, whats and hows of business performance, enabling management to focus on what needs to change for organizational responses to get better all the time. Modelling and simulation systems enable managers and teams to question their assumptions about what is happening and what is the best way to respond. Systems providing end-to-end and holistic views of the business process and the industry value chain, are being used to ensure that all aspects of the performance generating equation are considered, and to increase the probability that the response will be the most relevant and most effective one possible. (see Figure 8.7).

Organizations need to be able to deal with the world as it happens. Those dealing with only parts of it – and after the event – are at best fumbling in the dark. Planning processes tuned to the organizationally convenient quarterly and annual cycles, are left behind in a real-time world. Information technologies are increasing in their capacity to bring the urgency of the immediate to the attention of those who need to respond. By supporting rapid communications, dialogue, and simulation of complex situations and events, they are accelerating the ability of managers to initiate and respond to new situations. Information technologies are enabling the replacement of traditional planning with real-time continuous simulation – tuning the organization to fast changing operational realities.

Information technologies change which answer is the right answer. As the costs of information transmission decline dramatically, the distinctions between local and distant locations and markets blurs and the global market becomes the only market. What price can be offered to a customer or market depends on identifying the best source at the lowest cost which can deliver in the fastest time. What is the best source is changing all the

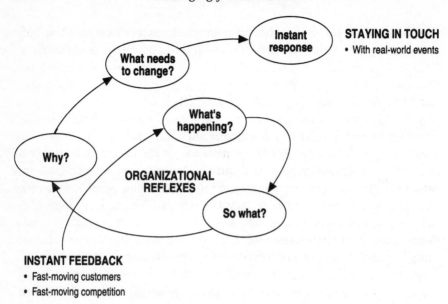

STAYING IN TOUCH
• With real-world events

INSTANT FEEDBACK
• Fast-moving customers
• Fast-moving competition

Figure 8.7 *Living with continuous change*

time, and any organization locked into one configuration for too long will be bypassed in the global information technology-enabled search for the most competitive offerings. The dynamics of the global marketplace are being reshaped by the rapidly growing capacities of information technologies to eliminate previously insurmountable, geographic, cultural and information barriers. Being a player in any market means being in and active in the market. In a world where the only market is a fast changing, highly competitive global market, success increasingly depends not only on the customer-sensitive intelligence gathering capabilities of information technology, but on the fact that information technologies can enable organizations to deploy their decision-making abilities and operational capabilities anywhere at any time.

Without the new information technologies the growing complexity of increasingly global business operations will limit the ability of organizations to change continuously. As business processes become increasingly integrated and required to operate in real-time only, information technology can provide the means to ensure simultaneous action between many activities in many markets. Information technology does not eliminate this complexity, it has the potential to allow organizations to operate at higher levels of complexity. As increasing levels of intelligence become embedded in computers and their software, what is complex to the human can be made routine. The increasing sophistication of simulation systems can be used to assist managers and professionals examine and evaluate alternatives and possibilities, ensuring the best result is assembled from the best wherever it is located, and delivered to wherever it is required.

Fast and continuous change requires real-time learning by the organization and its people. This can only take place if information about what is happening is immediate and vivid, the situation can be evaluated quickly, a decision made and the consequences of the decision seen quickly and in close conjunction with the original event. Information technologies can enable these learning loops and drive the individual and organizational learning process.

The powers of information technology are primarily those of co-ordination not those of automation. Automation reduces the need for things, co-ordination enables them to work together. Effective co-ordination is essential if the organization is to be able to bring the best together from wherever in the world to achieve world-class results. As low-resistance interdependence within and between organizations becomes a basic requirement for fast and flexible responses, the ability to co-ordinate things, people and information easily, quickly and at low cost, will distinguish the successful from the failures. The continuing dramatic increases in the cost/performance of communications and microprocessing technologies, the growing convergence towards widely accepted technical standards, and the increasing sophistication of applications and data management software, are fast reaching the point where co-ordination ceases to be a constraint on the operations and designs of organizations. As this takes place the organization will increase in flexibility, multiplying the options an organization has and the configurations it can adopt to meet fast changing needs. Managers will become less the guardians of static structures and static arrangements of resources, and more dynamic combiners of identified customer need, solution design ideas, the best available resources, and the best means of delivery.

Perhaps surprisingly, the essence of the information technology revolution is human. Information technologies are dissolving long established organizational structures and organizational and physical boundaries. By so doing, perspectives and psychological boundaries are being extended. Not only is the power to act and apply initiative being extended, the roles of people are shifting fast from being the machine fodder of the past to the highly empowered experience designers of tomorrow. Information technologies are fast making possible the conditions for continuous change – learning, growth, development, inquiry and creativity – these most human of characteristics are becoming the vital organizational resource. Organizational structures, controls, procedures and cultures designed to secure the organization against individual limitations, and to minimize the variability inherent in being human, are being reconceived in the face of information technology-enabled transformation to allow the brand-bounded expression through people of not only the organization's total capability, but of the capabilities inherent in the organization's value chain and wider network.

Ultimately, information technology is putting human cognitive skills to the fore. The current widespread phase that emphasises 'computer literacy' is perhaps misplaced. The challenge for most is not how to programme computers or to understand how they work, but how to acquire the conceptual skills that make it possible to use increasingly powerful information technology tools to change how we understand ourselves and our organizations.

Computers disintermediate. The human relays, filters, co-ordinators, and communicators that were necessary when information transport was limited slow, expensive and defined by earshot, are no longer required. Entire organizational and industry structures have been designed around the limitations of information transport along with generations of assumptions about management and operational roles. These are now entirely obsolete – to keep them is choose to limit what we know, and the speed with which we know it. High bandwidth multi-media communications technologies are combining with a proliferation of audio, text and visual information storage and retrieval technologies, and user specific interfaces, to bring those who need to know into direct and immediate contact with those who know. Armies of intermediaries within organizations and industries are already being swept away by the new technologies, and as they do, continuous change will become not a threat, but easy and natural.

Continuous change requires continuous observation, evaluation, action and feedback. Information technology makes the necessary information available to all with dramatic implications for accountability, influence and control. Immediate feedback from customers, markets and actions taken, enables individuals and teams to self-evaluate and self-redirect to achieve better results the next time. The time-lags inherent in traditional management planning approaches and cycles are not shortened but rendered obsolete. The time-lags inherent when control of information is used as a means of exercising hierarchical authority, are swept away as information technologies increasingly provide more information, more immediately to more people than could ever have been provided by any hierarchical management information masters or relays. As real-time and interactive multi-media information systems develop, they will be able to present situations for what they are, eliminating the time-lags of guesswork, procrastinations over uncertainty, and immobilising uncertainty. As new technologies of information empower people through widely available information and the availability of tools to support effective actions by everyone, accountability for results becomes a wider responsibility. This makes the organization's problems and opportunities everyone's problems and opportunities, and makes the need for action everyone's imperative. Local responses to challenges as they are directly encountered can be immediate and therefore faster responses. Where the local issue requires a global response, the resources of the organization can be brought to bear quickly. As accountabilities diffuse, management's role shifts to one of creating the conditions for fast responses. And this means new information technology-enabled non-hierarchical measurement systems, organizational constructs, management philosophies and perspectives on the potentials and capabilities of the individual.

In most organizations today, the only reality is a virtual reality – only very vague images of what's going on can be discerned, and the only actions that can be taken are slow and hesitant. As dinosaurs limited by their information processing capacity, organizations can only proceed through a dimly-lit world and hope that they do not bump into extinction. The management process of tomorrow's organization is the info-sphere enabled by the new technologies of information. As the new technologies advance, they will make reality available to all, not just to the chosen few. Instead of the blind being led by the one-eyed man, confident people will be able to make their own decisions on their own account, and be able to do so quickly. As participants in the real world – and empowered to change it – confident people can continuously re-invent the future of the organizations and the communities to which they belong.

In tomorrow's organization, the info-sphere created by the technology infrastructure becomes the means by which the organization co-ordinates its activities in tune with the dynamics of its environment. The traditional management processes – the approach to yesterday's co-ordination challenges – are already obsolete. To cling to them in a world of continuous change is to drown, not to wave.

PROFILE OF THE NEW PARADIGM

The new information technology paradigm can be contrasted with the old in the following way:

Old paradigm		New paradigm
Restricts collaboration	⟶	Enables collaboration
Reinforces the past	⟶	Enables continuous transform-ation
Dehumanizes	⟶	Empowers and extends
Delivers data	⟶	Delivers knowledge
Obscures operations	⟶	Generates insights
Reinforces status quo	⟶	Forces the pace of change
Isolates the company	⟶	Opens it to the world
Generates big learning curves	⟶	Eliminates learning curves

9 The Soul of the Organization

'*We are entering a time when the future, in so many areas, is to be shaped by us and for us; a time when the only prediction that will hold true is that no prediction will hold true; a time for bold imaginings, for thinking the unthinkable and doing the unreasonable.*' (Charles Handy)

CREATING SOCIAL REALITY

Tomorrow's organization depends on its ability to create meaningful futures (see Figure 9.1). Its products and services are increasingly intangible and designed to appeal to the intangibles of customer value. Its raw materials are increasingly the intangibles of ideas, imagination, knowledge, commitment, purposefulness, enthusiasm, care and values. Only for as long as people see the future in what they do can they be the source of the necessary intangible raw materials. Tomorrow's organization's unwritten contract with its people is its commitment to the creation of future-generating possibilities.

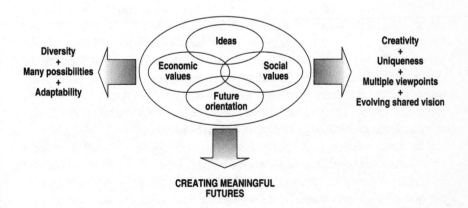

Figure 9.1 *Creating social reality*

189

Tomorrow's organization's unwritten contract with its people is fundamental. If the future is not in an organization it has nothing more than the structures, technical and economic resources which are increasingly available to all. Without the ideas, imagination, knowledge, commitment, purposefulness, enthusiasm, care and values that only future-believing people can provide, its inability to regenerate its resources will soon mean it is without them. Resources, technologies, organizational design and management approaches do not create the conditions for success – although they can limit it. The most that resources, technologies, organizational design and management approaches can do is to amplify the human. The worst they can do is to destroy it.

For as long as the primary means of exchanging what is needed and available is economic, tomorrow's organizations will have an important and centrally economic mandate. This does not conflict with its primarily being in the intangibles business. The apparent conflict between the economic mandate and human and social mandate arose in the earlier stages of 'industrial' evolution when it was possible to create capital by simply using the physical energies of people. This simple formula had the unfortunate side effect of atrophying the human. When this happened the human spirit revolted. The now absolute centrality of the human to the creation of 'capital' means that creating the future means creating the conditions for abundant human spirit.

Tomorrow's organization reverses the equation that says that people are there to fulfil prescribed organizational purposes – just as the traditional strategic planning process of ends, ways, means has been challenged by approaches which suggest that the process should really be turned around to be means, ways, ends. The deterministic view of the world – the future can be controlled from the present – is already being rapidly replaced by the indeterministic view – the future will always be a surprise. Tomorrow's organizations are indeterministic. What they will be doing, making and selling in the future is to a large extent unknown and unknowable. But they operate on the principle that chance favours the prepared mind. And organizational preparedness is the ability to amplify the possibilities created by open-ended individuals.

The organizational psycho-sphere – its 'culture' – is not somehow external to the organization's people. It is an expression of a complex interplay of many factors such as values, beliefs, aspirations, assumptions, energies, hopes and fears. The management paradigm in play can thwart the full and positive expression of the social, psychological, and spiritual needs of each individual. Structures and strictures which subjugate the individual to the needs of a particular role or to the traditional precepts of the process of creating 'capital', announce that the individual is a mere factor of production – there to meet organizational needs without thought, and whose developmental concerns can only be a distraction from the narrowly defined economic purposes of the organization.

Perhaps paradoxically, tomorrow's organization is not there to meet people's needs – and its people are not there to meet the organization's needs. Tomorrow's organization is there to create the future and by so doing uncover the new possibilities required to sustain valued life-purposes, experiences and lifestyles. When it does so, not only are material needs met, but people's social, psychological, and spiritual needs are met too.

Organizations with missions to create the future, and which recognize that its realization depends on conditions which find expression for the human, cannot afford to cling to the separation of economic man from social and spiritual man. Nor can they afford the myth that the economic task requires them to be separated. Where this myth might once have been functional – at least within the sense and narrow definitions and confines of short-term material economics – it is one which is now profoundly dysfunctional. A challenge for modern Western organizations is not to somehow reconnect the economic, the psychological and social, but to transcend what is a false dichotomy. The economic 'result' is increasingly intangible, and one which is increasingly but one expression of a richly human state.

The West cannot afford for most of its people to leave most of themselves behind when they walk into their organizations. It cannot afford the destruction of the human that subjugation to the narrow and de-humanizing old paradigm definitions of work and jobs and roles required. The increasingly intangible economy is increasingly a direct expression of the higher selves and abilities of people. Success is increasingly dependent on sophisticated customer responses to the higher expression of human talents and sensitivities. And this is happening at a time when it is becoming increasingly clear that technology can do nothing other than amplify the human psycho-spheres into which it is introduced. Technology cannot create value, meaning or success. Indeed technology is moving fast in directions in which it can only give expression to the aspirations, energies and capabilities of people. As technology reveals the inner life and orientations of the organization, those organizations whose mission is other than to create the future, will find themselves alienated from the societies to which they belong.

ENERGIZING IDEALS

Tomorrow's organization does not see its value solely in terms of the value of its products or services to its customers. It sees itself not in terms of its outputs at a particular time – important as high quality 'outputs' are – but as a process through which societies and its human and other resources are continuously cycled and regenerated. The wider standards of living – the economic definition is too narrow – of a society and its people cannot be advanced, except in the short term, if it is achieved at the cost of reducing or underdeveloping human capital. On one level, the value of human capital depends on the skills people acquire and the extent to which these are continuously regenerated to avoid quickly inevitable obsolescence. On another level, the value of human capital lies in its ability to make a difference – and one which increases the possibilities of a future with more potentials.

Tomorrow's organization exists to make a difference. It is a 'process' of making a difference. The process and the product are not separate things. In the increasingly intangible world of values and experiences as the 'product', the process is the product, and unless the process makes a difference for the customer it is of little or no value. Neither can the process and its means be considered as separate things. The procedures and technologies that have characterized the business processes of the past, are already becoming increasingly secondary to processes designed to express human qualities – the primary means is becoming more human. But the shift will not stop there. As the old and frequently oppressive technological/industrial paradigm rushes into the past, technology is being recast as a means of empowering the individual – extending what the individual can do to an extent undreamed of even in most science fiction. As these technological tools become more transparent and seemingly natural extensions of the human, the distinction between the means and the process will blur. At this stage, the means, the process and the end become expressions of the same thing – human 'capital'.

The vital process of tomorrow's organization is the creation of possibilities through the upward regeneration of human capital. It cannot create life-enhancing possibilities for its customers and the societies to which it belongs while diminishing them in the process. The organization which does not form human capital is playing a negative-sum game – whatever an accounting interpretation of performance might suggest. This is not an argument for socialism. The argument surrounding human capital is not the either-or, black-or-white one of capital versus labour. Nor is it one which overlooks the disciplines required for necessary monetary capital formation. What it is, is an argument for extending the definition of capital and the long-term means for its creation.

CHALLENGING THE HUMAN SPIRIT

As a process designed to create meaningful futures through creation of human capital, tomorrow's organization encourages its people to grow. 'Traditional' motivational devices are seen as manipulative rather than expressions of a concern for growth – they still say that someone else knows best, and by typically continuing to encourage a very limited repertoire of behaviours, they tend to continue to reinforce the industrial 'keep it simple for simple folk' mentality. Perhaps worse, they reinforce the myth that motivation is extrinsic and reducible to a narrow economic principle. Other devices such as providing people with options in when they work, their working conditions, and the compensation packages they choose, can be seen as minor concessions by a management paradigm intent on preserving its existence long after its sell-by date. Creating meaningful futures depends on getting the past out of the way, not on carrying as much of it forward as is possible. It means making it possible for good people to do great things, not on making them dependent and helpless. It means weeding out the tangles of the industrial management past, letting in the future, and allowing people whose basic instinct it is – unless strangled – to inquire, learn and grow in the open spaces of future possibilities.

Tomorrow's organization is committed to developing capabilities that express values such as quality, excellence, service, and elegance. Its activities are not planned in the sense that it creates plans and procedures and management controls to ensure that quality, excellence, service, and elegance result. This would be to impose the industrial model which assumed that by building the cage, bird-song would result. At the heart of its commitment, is the belief that quality, excellence, service, and elegance are expressions of the human spirit, and that the best hope of achieving them lies in allowing the human spirit to be challenged by the disciplines intrinsic to them. As the cornerstone of tomorrow's organization is the human spirit, it is uncompromising in its respect for the dignity and rights of each person in the organization. And it is everyone's right to be challenged by quality, excellence, service, and elegance, and it is a foundation of human dignity that each person possess the skills that enable them to respond.

Tomorrow's organization does not owe anyone a living, nor does it owe anyone a future. Dependency, by whatever euphemism it is known, is not part of the contract. Instead, it is committed to the creation of the future and to providing the means for meaningful whole-person contributions. This requires providing the opportunity for the mastery of quality, excellence, service, and elegance in the direction of future-valued customer experience. The recognition is that mastery of the future is ultimately about self-mastery and that this cannot be gained when the individual passes control – gives up personal responsibility – to another. Tomorrow's organization is about people who have mastered themselves, and who by so doing, possess the art of the future. Management which is about mastery of others, denies the organization of the vital energies of those intent on mastering the ever-changing disciplines of quality, excellence, service, and elegance.

SHAPING THE FUTURE

The apparent turbulence and uncertainty of the nineties will continue well into the next century. In an intangible and virtual world where the nature of the productive process, its 'products' and the means of their production has been transformed, the full implications of continued change for nations, societies, industries, individuals and their lifestyles can only be speculated upon. Longer term, assuming the many and varied challenges inherent in transiting from the old to the new are achieved successfully, the world will be a very different place. And who can say what challenges will be presented then. Perhaps they will be a better class of challenge. But whatever the specifics of a particular snap-shot of the future at a point in time, it is likely to be a space where individual human capabilities can be greatly amplified and where the potentials arising from dynamic individual/group/societal synergies are likely to be unbounded. Tomorrow's organization believes its role in shaping the future of 'society' is not one it should ignore or avoid. Indeed it aims to become a major force in the realization of a changed world, not through developing and selling a philosophy, or through 'taking its fair share of social costs', but by responding to the wishes of its customers through the changing and the surprise-full evolving capabilities and potentials of its people.

Tomorrow's organizations do not adopt predictive planning approaches when determining how best to shape the future. This does not mean that they yield to paralysis and immobilization, or that they resort to the development of resolute plans that specify the direction to be pursued at all costs, and whatever happens. Its approach to the future is not just aspirational, it is an evocation of a deep sense of in what the future lies (see Figure 9.2). Its approach to the future is not a prediction of the future, but an expression of a deeply considered visceral belief about what approach to things is required to ensure that how things are approached always makes sense at the time. And what makes sense at the time is not just what is dictated by short-term economics, it is also what is consistent with the realization of ideals – something better than what we currently know. In a very real sense this does not mean living in the future – and therefore not in the present – it is about living in and approaching the present in a way which uncovers the future through everyday action. The underlying perspective is that organizational life is a process of constant simulation through which direct experience, aspiration and imagination interplay to make tomorrow of necessity different to that which it might otherwise have been. The goal is the creation of a better future through continuous regeneration. The means is the continuous reinvention of today's organization.

The process of continuous simulation is an important means of releasing energies in the direction of the future. It is an important means

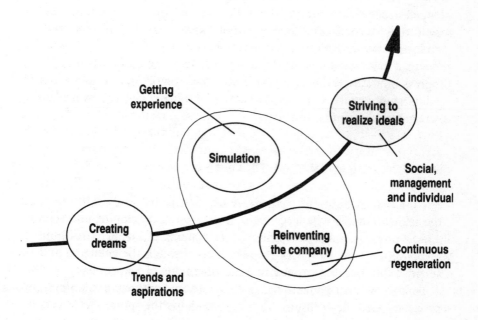

Figure 9.2 *Shaping the future*

of releasing the future from the bonds of managing the past in the present, and shifting the emphasis to managing for the future in the present. Continuous simulation is not a process of prediction which tries to pin down the future, it is a process of examining the implications and possibilities arising from changes in nations, societies, industries, individuals and their lifestyles and the business opportunities they will bring. It is a process of understanding the implications of complex, industrial, technical and social evolutions for the total organizational capabilities required to survive and prosper, and for how these capabilities can be created. And simulation is not an abstract activity confined to the few, it is a widespread and fundamental part of enabling the individual to develop a bond between what is coming and their connectedness with it.

A reluctance to change predictions, and the plans with which they are closely associated, is to misunderstand the nature of prediction. Prediction as an expression of management capability and courage, and of what management is, is a widespread but nonetheless a dangerous phenomenon. And perhaps just as serious as prediction as management machismo, is the avoidance of prediction altogether. The starting point must be a recognition that the future is unknowable but that the conditions for success in it are becoming clearer. How clear they become depends on the intensity and breadth of the continuous simulation of the relationships between technology, people, what they value and the communities to which they belong. Prediction is not, as it can be in the macho-management approach, a once and for all activity. It is a continuous process of constant adjustment guided by a keen sense of what it takes to progress minute by minute. As such, for tomorrow's organizations, prediction as a process of once-in-a-while learning is replaced by a process of continuous real-time learning.

CREATING MEANINGFUL FUTURES

Creation of meaningful futures depends on its essentially human dimension. Tomorrow's organization is one that uses technology to amplify human capabilities – both in the products and services its offers to its customers, and in the essentially human means by which they are created. In an important sense, the old paradigm dichotomy between the means and the end disappears. As such, the organization is its products and its process – both together are the engines of social value it is able to create. Information technology in particular is accelerating the organization towards the human and to the human scale. Not only is dehumanizing activity being taken over by an increasing array of information technology applications, the potential for shifting people's contributions to the creative and human is accelerating. On the wider scale, the massive, resource intensive, exploitative and insensitive industrial paradigm is already being replaced by technologies whose capabilities can only move organizations ever faster in the direction of low mass, intangible resource use, regeneration and greater sensitivity.

The organizations of the future live in a world of discontinuities. If they are to base themselves on entirely new virtual and intangible foundations, the consequence is that they will require great innovative and regenerative capacities. In unpredictable times, the capacity to be unpredictable assumes great importance. Tomorrow's organization sees its progress as an open-ended process whose outcome is to a large degree inherently unpredictable. It depends on people's fundamental desire for progress – however defined. A future-oriented management approach requires a real feel not just for the technological advances which will cause change, but also for organizational and social innovations it must be part of the process of bringing about. As the emphasis of management increasingly becomes one of making it possible for people to generate possibilities, management perspectives on reinventing the entire organizational paradigm will be required. Rather than bringing about one particular future, or predicting what happens at the end of the 'information age' – if that is what we are in the midst of – the important thing is to be continually extending the organization's boundaries in both space and time. The greater the pull of the future, the more it energizes the advance from the past.

REDEFINING MISSIONS

Tomorrow's organization sees its greatest challenge as being able to create meaningful futures through its daily activities. To this end, it defines the role of managers as explorers. Technological advances already make it possible to hand over the routine to computers and machines, and as work is redefined to tap into the human rather than the sub-human, all people will be involved in making a difference. Where managers are engaged as explorers, their role is to uncover new challenges and opportunities which constantly explore, develop and expand the horizons and capabilities of their people.

Uses of information technology which reinforce the old management paradigm, not only serve to drain the human out of the workplace, they serve to confine the organization to the routine – that which has been learned and mastered in the past. Perhaps more dangerously, it continues the man/technology conflict which dominated the old industrial era. The answer lies not in balancing the human and technology – achieving a truce or compromise – it lies in the use of technology to amplify the human. This is now possible and already commonplace in many areas of many industries.

To a considerable extent, technological advances have greatly enhanced the material living standards of most people. In the West at least, most people have everything they need in the material sense, and they also have growing amounts of so-called 'leisure time'. Perhaps for many this has been achieved at the cost of alienation. Many expressions of the industrial age philosophy encouraged people to leave most of themselves at the factory gate, and insisted that they hand over their destinies to the organizations they joined. The enforced exclusion of that which is most human – inquiry, learning, creativity, variety and the urge to make a difference – understandably led many to believe that technology was of itself a force or vehicle for domination of human values and concerns. For many, the experience of the workplace and its technological revolutions, was an experience of rejection, domination, and inevitably one of alienation. In the process, the workplace lost its meaning and society-creating functions. Another source of alienation in the workforce was the extraction of decision making and choice from work by the management paradigm in play at the time. Deprived of a primary means of psychological engagement too many people descended into a form of industrial ennui. Perhaps the final source of the believed-inevitable industrial soul-crushing process, was the confinement of people to small repetitious tasks defined by the organization and methods of the scientific management principle. This is not to question the material gains of the industrial age, nor is it call for the end of industrial activity. It is a call to see the industrial 'process' as much as a product as the end product. Just as in tomorrow's organizations the purpose of a product is to enhance and extend possibilities for the customer, the purpose of the 'industrial process' is to extend and enhance possibilities for the people it engages. The old industrial paradigm created a lot, but at great cost to the human spirit. At best it could be said that its conversion efficiency was low. At worst it could be said to be a serious negative-sum game.

Information technology, applied intelligently, is rapidly evolving to the point where it can enable considerable positive-sum games. It is now possible to take big steps towards transforming the old industrial paradigm. Its complete redefinition is not a distant prospect. The human-spirit-sapping industrial processes can be and increasingly must be redefined to be fuelled by the many expressions of the human spirit. And better still, the capabilities of the new technologies of information are daily increasing in their capacity to amplify the human spirit.

In the organization of tomorrow, technological innovation and a people and socially oriented approach are not in conflict. One is not achieved at the cost of the other. The optimum 'position' is not the both lose but not too much position. There is a real opportunity in close prospect where technology and new concepts of organization and management can redefine the realistic missions of organizations in terms which until recently might have seemed esoteric and perhaps mystical. Organizational missions which are concerned with giving wings to the human spirit, will at some not too distant point, be the only ones that make sense.

CHAOS AND INNOVATION

The essence of tomorrow's organization is its role as a shaper of the future. Its belief is that creation of the future can only take place when the past is let go. As the future requires continuous creation, tomorrow's organizations inhabit what can be called the chaos zone – the interface between what no longer works and what is too soon for it to be useful. The dynamics of this zone are potentially very stressful. As the innovations required can no longer be treated as purely technical in their nature and scope, they grow in their effects on every aspect of business processes, long-held assumptions, patterns of work and working relationships. As the capabilities required for successful innovation become more important, they become more challenging to acquire, master and live with. If it ever was the case, the time when successful innovation and change could be carried out through periodic management or external interventions, has passed. Nor is it enough to 'simply' extend the span of organizational innovation to go beyond the traditional Western fixation with technology, and to include business processes, people, the workplace, culture, and management approaches. Innovation as an external intervention – or something to be responded to – must be replaced with innovation as an everyday expression of the character of the organization and its people.

Tomorrow's organization needs people who are skilled in recognizing, managing and living through the cycle of change (see Figure 9.3). Innovation must become the way that people instinctively go about things – innovation is not something to be directed or made to happen. As such,

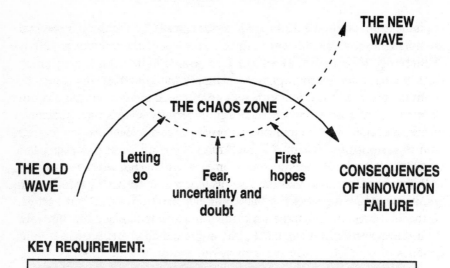

Figure 9.3   *Chaos and innovation*

organizational innovations depend on all, to the greatest practical extent, having a mission to make a difference.

Tinkering with the corporate culture – to the extent that this is possible – and specifying desirable cultural attributes such as change-seeking or tolerance for originality and ambiguity, is on its own not an effective way to bring about a shift towards a greater spirit of innovation. Communications programmes and various forms of management-led innovation management are also largely ineffective because they continue to announce that innovation is something that happens to people, and that it is management who make it happen. Management processes or exhortations which attempt to forge connections between management's ambitions and employees' motivation are also largely ineffective. These manipulations frequently tend to be rooted in the belief that it is management's prerogative to get things to happen differently. It also frequently reflects the view that most people are not inherently innovative, that they are inherently afraid of change, and that they need to be dragged screaming into the future.

For tomorrow's organizations, the distinction between bottom-up and top-down innovation is meaningless. Rather innovation is inside-out and the issue is how to make it more contagious. Most management processes do not make innovation more contagious. Openness helps, and this is facilitated by the removal of management assumptions and reflexes which are founded in the old paradigm of management which sees managers as conduits in a command and control structure – one whose origins lay in the very specific and unusual conditions of military conflict. Communications campaigns which merely embroider management's identification with its historical role as information relay, inevitably and invariably fall on deaf ears. Other devices such as (some) quality circles, management by walking about, and many of the various forms and guises of participative management, are also ways in which management only pretend to let go of the old paradigm. Unless and until management recognize that the future does not lie in their hands, but in the hands of the organizational societies of which they are but a part, innovation will never be anything more than an occasionally noisy tumble into inevitable decline.

It is not enough to insist that the perspective on innovation must be the organization as a whole – that is a meaningless abstraction that takes us nowhere. Or that management must create the flux of ideas necessary to energize the entire organization – that reinforces the view that managers are the energizing principles within organizations. The argument that management should concentrate its resources on establishing the foundations for long-term organizational innovation, merely reinforces the old paradigm view that management are the one and only source of innovation – and that everyone else is at best a spectator at the best show in town. What is required is the fundamental redefinition of everyone's role. Everyone must be seen – irrespective of their perceived capacities – as co-creators of the future, and not as the incidental audience in some wider drama. The basic requirement is a fundamental transformation of the organization – one that moves everyone away from being cogs in the machines and towards being people whose only role is to make the biggest difference they possibly can.

In a world of inside-out innovation, management can only work to ensure that the resources for change – such as information, influence, endorsement, technology and finance – are sufficient to maintain organizational evolution at its critical, chaotic stage.

PEOPLE-ORIENTED MANAGEMENT

The mission of tomorrow's organization is to unfold the future. Its ability to fulfil its mission depends entirely on the personal growth needs of its people – however large or small these may appear to be (see Figure 9.4). Growth and development are not something which is done to people. It is a result of their energetic pursuit of the future through meaningful action today. Human resource policies which work on the basis of helping people along, can appear to imply to those being helped, that growth is not the natural condition of healthy well-adjusted people. Education, training and development, if seen as necessary 'inputs' for the individual to perform, can inadvertently reinforce the corrosive view that the recipient is somehow inherently deficient, and has little to offer in the 'raw' state. Much traditional training reduces rather than increases the contribution the individual can make. It may impart technical skills, but seldom does it touch the individual by imparting challenge. Tomorrow's organizations are primarily in the business of finding new challenges. Not because this is easy, but because they are profoundly people-oriented. If the mission of tomorrow's organization is to help shape a better future for all – which it is – then it must uncover challenges. It is the tensions produced by challenge that fuel the natural desire people have for growth and development. People faced with challenge, and whose desire for growth has not been stultified, will push aside all obstacles to source all the inputs – knowledge and otherwise – that they feel they need.

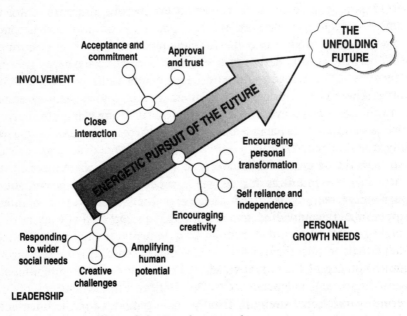

Figure 9.4 *People-oriented management*

Self-reliance and independence are prerequisites for growth to take place. If organizations encourage dependency, even with the best of intentions, they end up depriving themselves of the human energies which can only be released when the individual is engaged in pursuit of that which has personal meaning. To encourage dependency is to deprive the individual of the means of personal transformation – the source of growth and creativity. In tomorrow's organizations, respect for the individual is based not on judgement of what they are, or where they have come from, but on an admiration for the unexpected things a person might be. The future requires the unexpected. To cut off the source of the unexpected, is to make an irrevocable commitment to the past.

People-oriented management is achieved by turning conventional management styles upside-down. Much of the changes in management approaches to date have only gone as far as permitting people to do more. For the most part, people are now allowed to interact more with their bosses and with their colleagues within and across functions. They are sometimes given authority to allocate resources at their own discretion. But the real effect of many of these often well-intentioned efforts is to create the sense of being on parole, and of having been granted a form of conditional liberation.

Until information technologies and their implementations get to the stage of making everyone a powerful technology-enabled generalist, organizations in some form will serve recognizable purposes. Until that time, involvement of the individual in ways which ensure that working together results in more than working alone, will be important. Involvement is key, if the term 'organization' is to have any meaning. However, involvement campaigns that are not truly devolvement campaigns, achieve little – they are seen as expressions of management's unwillingness to go even as far as conditional liberation. In tomorrow's organizations, involvement has its basis in an individual's personal psychological contract with the future – and one which is realizable through the scope to fulfil individual personal growth needs. Management's right to intervene in the process of personal involvement is not one earned through rights of office. It is earned through a fundamental approval of the individual, and in particular an approval of what he or she might become. It is earned through a fundamental trust in the potential of individuals to turn themselves to what makes sense. It is earned through an acceptance of their right to self-determination and a commitment to self-reliance and independence as the only secure foundations of long-term organizational strength. Finally, management's right to intervene in the involvement process is earned by enabling the fullest possible interaction between the individual and the organization's internal and external realities.

Having earned the right to be involved in the individual's involvement process, management in tomorrow's organizations can only exert that right through leadership. Leadership in tomorrow's organizations is unlikely to be that of the 'over-the-top' kind, or indeed of the charismatic kind. It is more likely to be an expression of total integrity with respect to the creation of meaningful futures. As such, management must be intent on responding to and fulfilling the wider social implications of what it does and how it does it. In other words, management must be committed to a positive-sum approach based on developing and amplifying human capital. Management must be seen to be clearly intent on being in the business of creating meaningful challenges, and not content with mining the backyards of history. Perhaps above all, they must be seen to be in the business of amplifying the human potential of their people and their customers.

CREATIVE DESTRUCTION

The important and informal psychological contract between tomorrow's organizations and their people, is that of a shared commitment to the future and to the uncompromising quest for the capabilities to bring it about. Survival and pay are amongst the important consequences of being in the business of future-creation.

Creating the future requires the creative destruction of the past – the positive reconfiguration of what is still valuable with what is new – to create new possibilities. The process of continuous change that this involves has the potential to be painful and to be resisted. The pain-of-change equation is a simple one. It is a direct relationship with the sense that there is a future. Tomorrow's organization requires all its people to be creative people, not just a chosen few in the 'creative' functions. To be creative, engaged in discarding the past as well as adding to it, they must be independent of what is being changed, and self-reliant in the sense of seeing themselves as only dependent on their own growing abilities to create the future. These conditions are challenging to create and are only the result of a new management philosophy expressed over a considerable period of time. Organizations that have to change in response to the unanticipated crisis or who have not prepared for continuous change, will find themselves managing the pain of loss, not the pain of gain, and doing so without the human raw material required to bring the organization out the other end.

For the organization to have the independent and self-reliant people it requires to be engaged in creating the future – the management structures, assumptions and philosophies acquired during the industrial era need to be rolled back. Creating the conditions that will give rise to future-building people has got little to do with more management intervention or sophisticated embroidering of management baggage. Going part way does not work. Advocating a friendly and positive management/staff relationship, introducing creativity management programmes, advocating personal growth and innovation, or whatever, does not face up to the fact that able, independent and self-reliant people need nor want little or any management. The paradox of creating the conditions for creative destruction is that management and managers – in any widely recognized sense – are not required.

Growth-oriented people cannot be developed, the growth impulse of people can only be stifled. Structures and atmospheres conducive to the achievement of growth cannot be created. Management cannot stimulate creativity nor can management manage an individual's creativity. What management – to the extent that the term will exist in the longer term – can do is to uncover challenges which will stretch individual capabilities and which cannot be fulfilled without the individual seeking out the resources and like-minds required to achieve the specific mission implied by the challenge – and which further the organization's ability to tackle new challenges. What they can also do is make sure that the necessary resources are available or accessible, and that avoidable obstacles, organizational or otherwise are minimized as far as possible.

The fundamental organizational transformations required to keep the organization on the move through the present to the future, can only be sourced in people who are confident in their belief in their stake in the future. This is stake is not for organizations to dole out, or to promise to dole out as a reward for good behaviour. It is a stake that the individual owns by virtue of possessing distinctive human capital.

MANAGEMENT TRANSFORMATIONS

Complex waves of change and their complex interacting effects, are not only constantly combining to create instability, fast change and uncertainty – they are increasingly calling deeply rooted management assumptions into question. Most of the key beliefs about organizations and how they work are no longer valid. Yet, today's managers are all continually faced with making investment in the future, a future that looks very different from the past. Perhaps more challenging still is the fact that the past patterns no longer provide guidance, and managers are now faced with making investments in something that doesn't yet exist. Clearly, new management approaches are required – ones that create new dynamic stabilities, and new certainties in a world where flux and change will remain at characteristically higher levels.

The problem however with investing in the future is that the turbulent conditions of the nineties require much more than simple technical or structural changes. Instability, fast change and uncertainty have made fast responses, innovation, adaptability and customer orientation key behaviours of tomorrow's successful organization. Fast responses, innovation, adaptability and customer orientation require the ability to rapidly reconfigure products, processes, capital, human and other resources. The fundamental challenge is the radical changes required to the entire management paradigm.

The roles of managers are being reshaped as the front line becomes the moment of truth at which the organization and its abilities converge to deliver distinctive customer satisfaction. As every customer encounter must become a real-time learning experience, keeping track of all customers, what they do and what they might do next, requires a remarkably capable front line – and not one deprived of the will and ability to do so by the historical divide between those that think and decide and those that do. Streamlining communications with customers and eliminating confusing and frustrating communication problems which can destroy the increasingly intangible relationship between the organization and customer, means taking the external management approval and control loops out of the customer/organization interaction. The need for everyone who comes in contact with the customer to have comprehensive information and capabilities at their disposal requires the redefinition of management's role as the provider, controller and filter of information. The continuous development and fast delivery of new products and services that better meet fast changing customer needs, increasingly depends on the effectiveness of the business process as a whole. All have their part to play in that process of fast regeneration – and the starting point is the predisposition to continuous reinvention brought about by open interaction between the internal and external realities. The implication is that management need to turn their organizations into info-spheres – self-co-ordinating structures attuned to the realities of value creation.

As continuous process innovation becomes a basic survival requirement, continuous, and frequently fundamental, reinventions of value-creating processes are required. Not only must business processes be characterized by a high degree of flexibility and very short response times, the wider organizational and management processes of which business processes are a part, must also be fast, innovative and highly attuned to what needs to change and why. As organizations must become continuous sources of unique experiences, the organization must be capable of continuous flow of original ideas, originally applied to the high levels of discipline required to deliver world-class standards of cost and quality. Management is therefore required to manage with much greater variety than was permitted or possible in the monocultures of the past. Management must master the new disciplines of the unique – most of which mean letting go of much, but not all, of what good traditional management was held to be.

Decision making is not just being pushed out closer to the customer. The aim of tomorrow's organization is to intimately link itself to the criteria for success in the market. Dynamically transient coalitions of resources are replacing high-inertia functional and bureaucratic structures. Industries, companies and their structures are being completely redefined and entering into entirely new co-ordinative relationships. The widespread acceptance and emergence of flatter organizational structures and the shift to direct co-ordination by the imperatives of creating value in fast changing markets is rendering generations of middle-management planners and schedulers obsolete. Management, once secure and evaluated within the boundaries of their organization, are now being fully exposed to direct competition from a growing range of external service providers and strategic business partners. Management is no longer centrally an activity of control over resources – human and material. As technology-based assets and resource ownership become of decreasing relevance, the value-added of management is held up to the searchlight of return on possibilities.

Organizations intent on being those of tomorrow are already reworking their cultures to ensure they are open and responsive to changing conditions. They are working to increase the capacity of their organizations to receive and interpret changing signals in the environment. At the same time they are working to increase the capacity of their organizations to translate these signals into internal behavioural changes –

and by so doing increase their chances of survival, growth, and development. They are also concerned with how each member of the organization can become a vital source of the energies and capabilities required to ensure the present is sourced in the future. This is against a background where management have little to gain, in most circumstances, from resorting to commands and directives.

Tomorrow's organization transforms the roles and management of its people to enable them to make their fullest contribution. As people, as individuals and as groups, are increasingly being seen as the key to success, management are increasingly required to master the many issues involved in encouraging creativity, innovation and experimentation. The importance of expanding people's perspectives and redefining inflexible roles is already becoming widely recognised. Standardised jobs and narrow responsibilities are already being replaced with roles and missions which are centred on the individual making a difference – not on maintaining the status quo. Management as a process of preserving the status quo, shifts to one of enabling those intent on making a difference, make a real difference.

Instead of being the preservers and defenders of existing perceptions – yesterday's success formulae – managers are having to cope with a role which is becoming centrally one of challenging existing perceptions. They are having to adjust from dictating the perceptions required to achieve today's outcomes, to promoting the conditions in which new perceptions can emerge. As the nineties progress, the need grows for managers who can 'step outside the box' and find genuinely innovative ways of approaching and dealing with problems and opportunities. Instead of minimizing, or perhaps tolerating, ambiguity, they need to become adept at seeing ambiguity as a signal of the closeness of new possibilities. Instead of developing the ability to pull diverse ideas together, they need to develop the ability to transcend their apparent paradoxes, and by so doing redefine differences into fresh insights into how best to approach the goal of creating meaningful futures. Very different paradigms of management are required. As they emerge and take root, management as an institution will fast become unrecognizable from the still dominant inherited model.

The architecture of tomorrow's organization is fundamentally different. Its primarily psychological constructs bear no resemblance at all to those of the past. While information technology will silently and invisibly co-ordinate its routine activities, its primary value will come from the elimination of the barriers to a real-time understanding of real-world events, their significance, and the abilities of individuals and groups to deal with them. The organizational info-spheres that will emerge will render management assumptions about what it means to manage and be managed – themselves the result of the limitations of previous information-handling technologies – entirely redundant. The psychological environment that will result will be a self-adaptive one, able to transparently and dynamically combine resources and talents to meet fast changing customer needs, without the psycho-baggage of a past era.

The concern with might be called the soul of the organization is at the heart of the management transformation already happening in our midst. It is a range of social, philosophical and psychological factors that will give shape to and energize tomorrow's organization. The management of tomorrow will be deeply concerned with how the wider dimensions and purposes of 'business' organizations can be achieved without bringing economic and human purposes into conflict. This will not be achieved by simply combining them, but by exploring how that which is uniquely human can be amplified in ways which meet the many challenges organizations will face as they strive to succeed in shaping the future. The challenge is not how to 'balance' the human with the institutional, but how to redefine a value system which sees them as somehow different. For tomorrow's managers, the key factor in the tomorrow's success will be how successful they are at fuelling the creative purposes of the organization.

COGNITIVE RE-ENGINEERING

As a discipline, organizational transformation is maturing fast. It is already moving from its pioneering phase. Proven methodologies and tools are rapidly becoming available to enable organizations to identify and get the benefits of their transformational efforts by approaching them in a disciplined and structured way. As tomorrow's organization is really more about we think about ourselves and our futures, a wealth of 'envisioning' techniques are arriving to make it possible for individuals and organizations to explore radical futures. And since change is painful, change management techniques are now getting the point where they are very effective in ensuring that individuals and organizations can successfully make multiple transitions from discontinuity to discontinuity.

A fundamental transformation is needed if organizations are to grow and prosper, and support the lifestyles its peoples will look forward to. Structural, technological and management approach changes are a good place to start, but what is required is to see competitive progress as a process of changing assumptions about what is the best way to do things and increasing the organization's ability to act in new ways. As such, the transformations facing those who aspire to become tomorrow's organizations are perhaps fundamentally cognitive – concerned with the psychological and social dimensions of organizations. And of equal importance must be the requirement to see competitive progress as an expression of a commitment to the constant improvement of the organization's ability to create wider definitions of value.

The effective organization of tomorrow clearly depends on a wider transformation and therefore is about a complete rethink of the organization and how it goes about things. As such it is fundamentally about the 'soft' side of the organization – it is about people. It is about more than structures and the business process and about more than a set of management techniques. It is about how organizations become able to continuously manage the relevance of their assumptions, structures and behaviours in ways that will ensure meaning, survival and growth.

This task of looking afresh at organizations, current and future is a complex one. As it becomes increasingly clear that tomorrow's business organizations will bear little resemblance to those of the past, a revolution in thought is required. The urgently required fresh perceptions of what it makes sense to do and why require new multidisciplinary concepts and perspectives – the successful enterprises of the 21st century cannot be understood piecemeal. Tomorrow's organization looks very different and to understand it, it appears we need to start from how it behaves as a total 'system'. Only from there can we proceed to describe how it needs to be able to function to deliver and sustain those behaviours. Approaching tomorrow's organization purely from the structural, process or technical perspectives – from the point of view of what it looks like – reveals little about how it will need to behave – how it characteristically deals with situations. Still less does it capture the essence of how it will feel to be part of tomorrow's organization. These fresh perceptions must both combine and transcend the traditional disciplines of strategy, general management, sales and marketing, operations, finance, systems theory, psychology, sociology, philosophy, human resource management and information technology.

For those companies determined to be participants in the future that is rushing towards us all, a key issue is to understand how the required behaviours can be produced: how Tomorrow's Organization will look, feel and function; the specific transformations which are required; and how each of several dimensions of radical organizational change can be addressed simultaneously.

IMAGINEERING

Imagination is one of the most powerful resources an organization can have. It is the flight simulator of the future and the testbed for those possibilities that will one day give concrete expression to the future. The people who will inhabit tomorrow's organizations will increasingly be concerned with shortening the gap between ideas and customer experience. In a world where intangibles are an increasing part of customer value, the scope for real-time applied imagination is increasing. In a world where virtual reality – in more than its current pop-marketing forms – is fast becoming a reality, real-time applied imagination is fast becoming a reality. As business process, technological and organizational and management transformations accelerate, the capacity of organizations to turn ideas into tangible products and experiences is fast moving towards the instantaneous.

Tomorrow's organization is fundamentally concerned with 'engineering' unique experiences – how long it takes for that to be accomplished in real-time is not the concern. Imagination is not seen as the gap between what might one day be possible and what can actually be done or achieved. Imagination is the raw material. The design issue for tomorrow's organizations is how to accelerate the transformation of their capabilities to bring forward the day when imagination can be transferred to be directly experienced by the customer.

The soul of tomorrow's organization is what will set it apart. It is that indefinable something which recognizes the human in everything and everything it does. It is that something which plays the positive-sum game.

PROFILE OF THE NEW PARADIGM

The characteristics of the old paradigm and the new can be contrasted in the following way:

Old paradigm		New paradigm
Individuals as units of production	→	Production as a means of realizing human values
Splits personal and productive	→	Creates meaningful social reality
Motivated by 'narrow' profit	→	Energized by ideals
Technology dominates man	→	Enables man to be creative
Management by control	→	On purpose by growth

Alienated	$\longrightarrow$	Cheerful, creative and enthusiastic
Meeting identified needs	$\longrightarrow$	Realizing the ideal society
Linked together	$\longrightarrow$	Holistic perspectives
Innovation on the margins	$\longrightarrow$	Innovation as a pervasive force
Everything in its place	$\longrightarrow$	Everything dynamically interrelated
Narrow economic perspectives	$\longrightarrow$	Working for a better world
Impersonal efficiency	$\longrightarrow$	Human relationships and development
Administering resources	$\longrightarrow$	Enabling creativity

10 Resolution

'The whole difference between construction and creation is exactly this: that a thing constructed can only be loved after it is constructed; but a thing created is loved before it exists.' (G. K. Chesterton)

FIELDS OF POSSIBILITIES

Tomorrow's organization exists in the space created by its ability to extend and realize the possibilities available to fast-moving and fast-growing customers. Its resources are discontinuous change, accelerating technological developments, and open-ended people intent on creating radical new futures. Its opportunity is that the rules of the game are being completely redefined – the possibility-seeking organization has the opportunity to make the future happen.

Making the future happen depends on creating the space for the possibilities of tomorrow today – playing catch-up is too slow. Only organizations that can create customer-specific experiences of value in the right place at the right time will find a place in the future. Growth will depend on more than flexibility and the ability to adapt incrementally to continually changing circumstances – important as adaptation is to everyday organizational life. More important will be the ability to break out of the confines of the known and familiar, and the mindset which sees stability as a static condition. Those who seek comfort in the structures designed by and for the past will be overtaken by a fast-moving front of what no longer produces value. Unless pulled along by the urge to inquire, experiment and learn, they will be passed by the moving front of new possibilities.

A challenge for organizations is to create space for themselves through people who are adept at growing through recurrent breakdowns (see Figure 10.1). Tomorrow's organization depends on people who know how to deal with discontinuous change – the stages in organizational evolution where the past has little to offer the future other than to put the organization in the position to face the challenge.

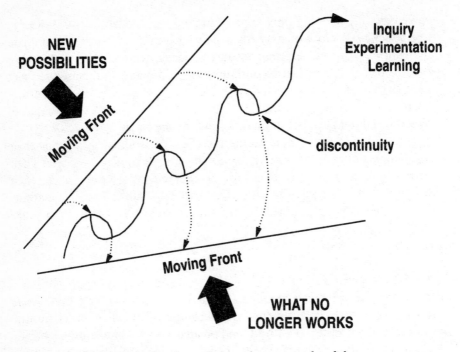

Figure 10.1 *Growing through recurrent breakdown*

THE ADAPTIVE SYSTEM

Adaptability and discontinuous change require the recurrent breakdown of structures, assumptions, processes and practices. New situations require new ideas expressed through new organizational behaviour. What the organization has tended to do in the past it will tend to do again unless the powerful influences of hidden cultural assumptions, values and beliefs are understood. Success in the future requires the levers of organizational change to be understood – and in constant use.

Tomorrow's organization is a change-seeking process designed to extend its space for possibilities. In the old paradigm, structure followed strategy – the particular configuration required to meet a particular forecast of the future. Now, any organization concerned with the future cannot allow itself to be the consequence of a particular objective or of a particular organizational structure designed to achieve it. What it must be is a means capable of expressing highly dynamic, variable and complex behaviours in the pursuit of human purposes. For tomorrow's organization, its future is defined in terms of the number of possibilities that can arise from where it is today.

New possibilities can only arise where old assumptions and knowledge can be replaced more quickly than their inevitable tendency to dominate the future. New and existing resources, ideas, technologies and people need to be capable of fast reconfiguration – disengaging themselves from the past faster makes them available to play a part in the future. Continuous regeneration enables the organization to express its capabilities through whatever form makes sense at the time.

These new adaptive systems derive their capabilities not from their flexibilities but from their ability to qualitatively change their state. Their permanence and identity does not lie in their structures, but in their continued ability to identify with what customers value. Their state at any point in time is determined by the transformations required to make customer value possible.

FLICKERING FLAMES

Tomorrow's organization has few of the physical and structural appearances of stability – and indeed it may have none. It only exists in the minds of its customers. The moment its identity is defined more by its physical means and presence than what its customers think it knows about their needs and values, is the moment it has chosen the relative stability of history.

The physical appearances of tomorrow's organization are snapshots of human energies in motion. Its reality is only apparent and lies in the behaviours it produces over time and at the time. Its physical appearances have no meaning or value except to the extent that they allow human ideas, knowledge and energies to be expressed in a continuous flow of customer satisfaction. Its continuity lies in its ability to transform itself at each moment of its existence as required by shifting definitions of customer value. It does not seek permanence as permanence seeks to freeze time. Rather it seeks to continuously unfold the possibilities presented by change, new ideas, knowledge and technology, and the creativities of people.

What we can see from time to time tells us little about the abilities of an organization to change and redefine itself. Understanding tomorrow's organization requires seeing its reality in terms of its ability to dynamically regenerate and recombine ideas, resources and assumptions – not in terms of any one particular combination. Its reality lies in its ability to express itself in a variety of ways and not in what can be seen or experienced at any point in time. Its ability to sustain itself lies in the capabilities it has to undergo complex change continuously, with purpose and in pursuit of the customer.

Tomorrow's organization is a dialogue with the future. Its essential discussion is how to fuel the creative process without tying its destiny to any one creative output. The output is key to the present and near future, the creative process is the key to the meaningful future.

Whatever the apparent industry, products and services are the tangible expressions of the creative process – at the present time, some creative processes are longer cycle than others. As the demand for any one product or service reduces, perhaps to volumes of one, each becomes the results of a temporary configuration of the physical parts, structures, skills, knowledge and equipment required to create them. The product or service becomes only a particular expression of the dynamic capabilities of the organization. The particular structures, resources, technologies, skills, information, assumptions and outlooks available to an organization are not the organization – unless it is confined to one configuration of them. The issue for tomorrow's organization is the extent to which structures, resources, technologies, skills, information, assumptions and outlooks are at the disposal of the creative process. The dynamics of tomorrow's organization are a function of its human abilities and energies and the extent to which the means at their disposal confine them or amplify them.

Tomorrow's organization is not what you see – it is what you experience. If it is frozen in time then that is what you will experience. If it is a thing in process or in progress then what you might see is the future.

INQUIRY AND SPECULATION

Our assumptions, values and expectations determine what we see, think is possible, and believe we can do about it. Whenever past organizational legacies impose themselves on today's actions and decision making, the past casts its shadow over the future, and how we act or could act is determined before we start. When the legacies of the past can no longer be accepted as obviously useful as signposts to the future, to be determined by them is to steer forward by looking back.

An organization in a changing environment is doomed if it does not continually examine and understand the abilities of its means of perception, and the assumptions it uses to determine what conclusions it should draw from them.

The power and influence of assumptions, values and expectations makes it necessary to have the ability to diagnose them, understand them and their operation, and the ability to transform them. The replacement of the notion of assumptions, values and expectations as static, sacrosanct and fixed, with the idea that they are resources like any other, and like any other capable of being altered and managed, enables tomorrow's organizations to take charge of its own destiny. The ability to renew assumptions, values and expectations opens the door on entirely new ranges of possibilities. Instead of being givens and immovable constraints, assumptions can be changed to create new spaces for people to generate and introduce new value-creating alternatives.

The ability of tomorrow's organization to push forward rests on its ability to create the conditions within which people can generate ideas, possibilities and results, without the constraints of possibility-sapping legacies. The tools of tomorrow's organization are less the machines of old and more the means to identify limiting assumptions, create and test new assumptions and possibilities, and express them through whatever technological and organizational innovations are required.

The spirit of inquiry is a fundamental process in tomorrow's organization. Removing the boundaries and obstacles to inquiry is of fundamental importance. The spirit of inquiry cannot be imposed, nor can the changing of assumptions and values be manipulative – inquiry depends on the will of people to find better ways forward, and on the inquiry-enabling tools placed at their disposal. The possibility-generating energy of tomorrow's organization depends on the spirit of inquiry turned to confident and unbounded search for what will work tomorrow, and make sense in terms of amplifying human potential.

REFLECTION AND ACTION

Tomorrow's organization depends on intelligent and fast responses to complex and unstable conditions. Its natural habitat is an indeterministic world where the future lies in the hands of those determined to make the future a better place, and who are able to apply creativity to turn the balance of probabilities in their favour. Where all organizations will be on the narrow and fast moving boundary between what no longer works and what will work tomorrow, everything depends on the detection of many subtle and complex signals, and on rapid responses to them.

The management process becomes very different. Progress becomes a process of continuous learning based on making the best sense out of current experience, developing theories to explain it and testing them by enacting them. In an indeterminate world, progression is about redefining the present to make way for the arrival of the future.

As direct participants in the real-time frontier of events, moving ahead requires making sense of events as they happen. Real-world events need real-time responses to direct experience, and existing knowledge needs to be rapidly changed by it. In tomorrow's organization, the future is shaped by living with it as it happens, empowered by unbounded horizons on what is possible. Organizations are freed to participate in the future when they realize that what they know is no more than a theory under test, and that learning ability is as relevant as what is 'known'.

CONVERSATIONS FOR POSSIBILITIES

Organizations cannot survive for long when their guidance systems are blinded by assumptions that can only see things as they once were. Any organization that aims for a future can only hope to have one if it always has a real-world image on its radar screen and the skills to recognize fast-moving patterns for what they are. The issue is not one of information overload. It is one of developing useful cognitive models of how the world works. There is a need to ensure the usefulness of assumptions and the behaviours conditioned by them. 'Cognitive re-engineering' tools are required if assumptions are to be surfaced, challenged and renewed. The management process shifts from oiling the wheels of the known to the continuous redefinition of how we see the world.

In tomorrow's organization, a central role of managers is to help the organization prepare for the future – empowered people and the intelligent use of automation will run the show. As the continuous generation of new possibilities becomes increasingly vital, working with people to think through how the world works and might work differently becomes the basis for organizational renewal. Readying them for step-change positions the organization to glide through the transitions which throw others into chaos and turmoil.

Management becomes a challenge to the present – not a defence of the status quo punctuated by periodic correctional or directional interventions. As a process of challenge, management becomes a joint process of finding new ways to approach things. The agenda is always the future, what is possible and what needs to be made possible. Shared understanding of new possibilities is what makes future success possible – not enforcement of what was required to exploit past possibilities. Tomorrow's organizations can only move forward if there is a shared awareness of the possibilities and what is possible.

NEW MODELS OF REALITY

For tomorrow's organization, the issue is not how to second-guess the future, but how better to pursue it. And for this, learning skills, challenge, regenerative thinking, openness and spirit are required. Historical assumptions, structures and behaviours are not. The resulting spirit of inquiry and choice ensures that models of reality endure the passage of time (see Figure 10.2).

In tomorrow's organization, the management emphasis will be on maintaining the organization's ability to perceive and deal with reality in a way that ensures success. This does not mean imposing a view of the future, it means exploring for things which appear to make sense in terms of getting there – the arrival will always be different. Searching for things that make sense requires multiple points of view and many ways of thinking. Multiple perspectives extend the range of the search and allows the thing sought to be brought into sharper focus. Where the commitment is to the pursuit of a better way, the future will always be a surprise. The only future that will be recognized as making sense will be recognized for

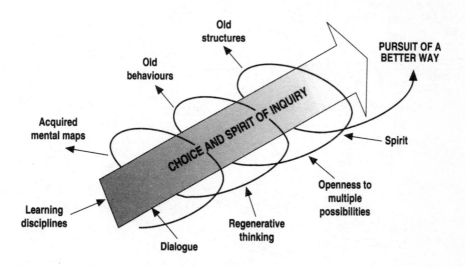

Figure 10.2 *The passage of time*

what it is – the latest theory which must be tested through practice. The future never arrives but the pursuit is what makes every day an arrival of new possibilities for a better world. How the day after next is approached is determined by what was learned from the last theory to explain today. The goal is not to find what works for all time but for that which appears to be the best way forward at the time – in full knowledge that the best way has not yet been found.

Tomorrow's organization is an organization committed to what makes sense for the future. It is not in the business of prediction, it is in the business of shaping the future by challenging, extending and redefining the boundaries of the present. Its journey is into the future and its challenge is to create boundless possibilities by navigating accelerating waves of change. There is no end point. Ultimately the only organizations that will be around to see tomorrow will be those whose people are able to see a rapidly changing world as it unfolds, and who are empowered to act with vision and energy in ways which are relevant to the realization of their ideals – and to their evolving realizations.

Sources and Further Reading

Although not mentioned in the text, many authors and their works have been influential in the shaping of this book. And in most cases their influence has spanned many of the chapters.

Abegglen, J. C. and Stalk, G. Jr., *Kaisha: The Japanese Corporation* (New York: Basic Books, 1986).

Ackoff, R. L., *Redesigning the Future: A Systems Approach to Societal Problems* (Chichester: John Wiley, 1974).

Ackoff, R. L. and Emery, F. E., *On Purposeful Systems* (Chicago: Aldine, 1972).

Aldrich, H. E., *Organizations and Environments* (Englewood Cliffs, N.J.: Prentice-Hall, 1979).

Allen, B. R. and Boynton, A. C., 'Information Architecture: In Search of Efficient Flexibility', *MIS Quarterly* (December 1991).

Ames, B. C. and Hlavacek, *Market Driven Management: Prescriptions for Survival in a Turbulent World* (Homewood, Ill.: Dow Jones-Irwin, 1989).

Ansoff, H. I., *Strategic Management* (London: Macmillan Press, 1979).

Ansoff, H. I., *Implanting Strategic Management* (Englewood Cliffs, N.J.: Prentice-Hall, 1984).

Ansoff, H. I., *Corporate Strategy* (London: Penguin, 1987).

Argenti, J., *Corporate Collapse: Causes and Symptoms* (New York: McGraw-Hill, 1976).

Argyris, C., *Organizational Learning: A Theory of Action Perspective* (Reading, Mass.: Addison-Wesley, 1978).

Argyris, C., *Reasoning, Learning and Action* (San Francisco: Jossey-Bass, 1982).

Axelrod, R., *The Evolution of Co-operation* (New York: Basic Books, 1984).

Barker, J. A., *Discovering the Future: The Business of Paradigms* (St Paul: ILI Press, 1988).

Bateson, G., *Steps to an Ecology of Mind* (New York: Ballantine, 1972).

Beckhard, R., *Organizational Development: Strategies and Models* (Reading, Mass.: Addison-Wesley, 1969).

Beckhard, R. and Harris, R. T., *Organizational Transitions: Managing Complex Change* (Reading, Mass.: Addison-Wesley, 1977).

Belasco, J. A., *Teaching the Elephant to Dance: Empowering Change in Your Organization* (London: Hutchinson Business Books, 1990).

Best, M. H., *The New Competition: Institutions of Industrial Restructuring* (Cambridge, Mass.: Harvard University Press, 1990).

Blau, P., *The Dynamics of Bureaucracy* (Chicago: University of Chicago Press, 1963).

Blauner, R., *Alienation and Freedom* (Chicago: University of Chicago Press, 1964).

Boisot, M., *Information and Organizations: The Manager as Anthropologist* (London: Fontana, 1987).

Camillus, J.C. and Datta, D.K., 'Managing Strategic Issues in a Turbulent Environment', *Long Range Planning* (June 1991).

Chandler, A.D. Jr., *Strategy and Structure* (MIT Press, 1962).

Child, C., 'Information Technology, Organization, and the Response to Strategic Challenges', *California Management Review* (Fall, 1987).

Cyert, R.M. and March, J.G., *A Behavioural Theory of the Firm* (Englewood Cliffs, N.J.: Prentice-Hall, 1963).

Davenport, T.H., *Process Innovation: Re-engineering Work Through Information Technology* (Boston, Mass.: Harvard Business School Press, 1993).

Davis, S.M., *Future Perfect* (New York: Addison-Wesley, 1987).

Davis, S.M. and Davidson, B., *2020 Vision: Transform Your Business Today to Succeed in Tomorrow's Economy* (New York: Simon & Schuster, 1991).

Deming, W.E., *Out of the Crisis* (Cambridge University Press, 1986).

Denison, D.R., *Corporate Culture and Organizational Effectiveness* (New York: Wiley & Sons, 1990).

Drucker, P.F., 'Managing for Business Effectiveness', *Harvard Business Review* (May–June 1963).

Drucker, P.F., *Management: Responsibilities, Tasks, Practices* (New York: Harper & Row, 1974).

Drucker, P.F., *The Practice of Management* (London: Pan Books,1983).

Drucker, P.F., *Managing for Results* (New York: Harper & Row, 1986).

Drucker, P.F., *The Frontiers of Management* (London: Heinemann,1986).

Drucker, P.F., 'The Coming of the New Organization', *Harvard Business Review* (January–February 1988).

Forrester, J.W., 'Industrial Dynamics: A Major Breakthrough for Decision Makers', *Harvard Business Review* (July–August, 1958).

Fuller, R.B., *Synergetics: Explorations in the Geometry of Thinking* (New York: Collier Books, 1982).

Galbraith, J.R., *Organization Design* (Reading, Mass.: Addison-Wesley, 1977).

Garratt, B., *The Learning Organization* (London: Fontana, 1987).

Garratt, B., *Creating a Learning Organization: A Guide to Leadership Learning & Development* (Cambridge, England: Director Books, 1990).

Gleick, J., Chaos: *Making a New Science* (London: Sphere Books, 1987).

Goffman, E., *Presentation of Self in Everyday Life* (New York: Doubleday, 1959).

Gray, D.H., 'Uses and Misuses of Strategic Planning', *Harvard Business Review* (January–February 1986).

Hamal, G. and Prahalad, C.K., 'Corporate Imagination and Expeditionary Marketing', *Harvard Business Review* (July–August 1991).

Hampden-Turner, C., *Maps of the Mind* (New York: Macmillan, 1981).

Handy, C., *The Gods of Management* (London: Pan, 1985).

Handy, C., *Understanding Organizations* (London: Penguin Books, 1986).

Handy, C., *The Age of Unreason* (London: Business Books, 1989).

Hayes, R. H. and Abernathy, W. J., 'Managing Our Way to Economic Decline', *Harvard Business Review* (July–August 1980).

Heilbroner, R. L., *The Future as History* (London: Harper & Row, 1960).

Hertzberg, F., *Work and the Nature of Man* (Cleveland: World Publishing Co., 1966).

Hirschhorn, L., *Beyond Mechanisation: Work and Technology in a Postindustrial Age* (Cambridge, Mass.: MIT Press, 1984).

Hirschhorn, L. and Gilmore, T., 'The New Boundaries of the "Boundaryless" Company', *Harvard Business Review* (May–June 1992).

Jaikumar, R., 'Postindustrial Manufacturing', *Harvard Business Review* (November–December 1986).

Jantsch, E., *Design for Evolution: Self-Organization and Planning in the Life of Human Systems* (New York: George Braziller, 1975).

Jantsch, E., *The Self-Organizing Universe* (Oxford: Pergamon, 1980).

Kanter, R. M., *The Change Masters: Corporate Entrepreneurs at Work* (London: Unwin Hyman, 1983).

Kanter, R. M., *When Giants Learn to Dance* (New York: Simon & Schuster, 1989).

Kask, D. E., *Perpetual Innovation: The New World of Competition* (New York: Basic Books, 1989).

Katz, D. and Kahn, R. L., *The Social Psychology of Organizations* (New York: Wiley, 1966).

Keen, P. G. W., *Shaping The Future: Business Design through Information Technology* (Harvard Business School Press, 1991).

Koestler, A., *The Act of Creation* (London: Hutchinson, 1967).

Kohn, A., *No Contest: The Case Against Competition* (Boston: Houghton Mifflin, 1986).

Kolb, D., *Experimental Learning* (Englewood Cliffs, N.J.: Prentice-Hall, 1984).

Kuhn, T. S., *The Structure of Scientific Revolutions* (Chicago: University of Chicago Press, 1970).

Land, G. T. A., *Grow or Die* (New York: John Wiley, 1986).

Lawler, E. E., III. *Pay, and Organizational Effectiveness* (New York: McGraw-Hill, 1971).

Lazonic, W., *Competitive Advantage on the Shop Floor* (Cambridge, Mass,: Harvard University Press, 1990).

Leavitt, H. J., *Managerial Psychology* (University of Chicago Press, 1978).

Levitt, T., 'Marketing Intangible Products and Product Intangibles', *Harvard Business Review* (May–June 1981).

Likert, R., *New Patterns of Management* (New York: McGraw-Hill, 1961).

Lynch, D. and Kordis, P. L., *Strategy of the Dolphin* (New York: William Morrow & Company, 1988).

Magaziner, I. and Patinkin, M., *The Silent War: Inside the Global Business Battles Shaping America's Future* (New York: Random House, 1989).

Maturana, H. and Varela, F., *Autopoiesis and Cognition: The Realization of the Living* (London: Reidl, 1980).

McGinn, C., *Wittgenstein on Meaning* (Oxford: Blackwell, 1984).

Miles, R. E., Snow, C. C. and Coleman, H. J. Jr., 'Managing 21st Century Network Organizations', *Organization Dynamics* (Winter 1991).

Mills, D. Q., *Rebirth of the Corporation* (New York: John Wiley, 1991).

Mintzberg, H., *The Nature of Managerial Work* (New York: Harper & Row, 1973).

Morgan, G., *Images of Organization* (Beverley Hills, California: Sage Publications, 1986).

Morton, M. S. M., *The Corporation of the 90s: Information Technology and Organizational Transformation* (New York: Oxford University Press, 1991).

Naisbitt, J., *Megatrends* (New York: Warner Books, 1982).

Naisbitt, J., *Reinventing the Corporation* (New York: Warner Books, 1985).

Noori, H., *Managing the Dynamics of New Technology: Issues in Manufacturing Management* (Englewood Cliffs, N.J.: Prentice-Hall, 1990).

OECD, *Information Technology and New Growth Opportunities* (OECD, 1989).

Ohmae, K., *The Mind of the Strategist* (New York: McGraw-Hill, 1983).

Ortony, A, (ed.), *Metaphor and Thought* (Cambridge: Cambridge University Press, 1979).

Pascale, T. R., 'Zen and the Art of Management', *Harvard Business Review* (March–April 1978).

Pascale, T. R. and Athos, A. G., *The Art of Japanese Management* (New York: Simon & Schuster, 1981).

Pedler, M., Burgoyne, J. and Boydell, T., *The Learning Company* (Maidenhead, England: McGraw-Hill, 1991).

Peters, T. J. *Thriving on Chaos* (New York: Alfred A. Knopf, 1987).

Peters, T. J., 'Part One: Get Innovative or Get Dead', *California Management Review* (Fall 1990).

Peters, T. J. and Waterman, R. H., *In Search of Excellence* (New York: Harper & Row, 1982).

Piore, M. J. and Sabel, C. F., *The Second Industrial Divide: Possibilities for Prosperity* (Cambridge, Mass.: Addison-Wesley, 1987).

Popper, K. R., *The Open Universe: An Argument for Indeterminism* (London: Hutchinson, 1982).

Porter, M. E., *Competitive Strategy* (New York: Free Press, 1980).

Postle, D., *Catastrophe Theory* (London: Fontana, 1980).

Quinn, J. B. and Pacquette, P. C., 'Technology in Services: Creating Organizational Revolutions', *Sloan Management Review* (Winter 1990).

Rappaport, A., *Creating Shareholder Value: The New Standard for Business Performance* (New York: Free Press, 1986).

Reitz, H. J., *Behaviour in Organizations* (Homewood, Ill.: Irwin, 1977).

Robson, G. D., *Continuous Process Improvement: Simplifying Work Flow Systems* (New York: Free Press, 1991).

Roeber, R. J. C., *The Organization in a Changing Environment* (Reading, Mass.: Addison-Wesley, 1973).

Sakai, K., 'The Feudal World of Japanese Manufacturing', *Harvard Business Review* (November–December 1990).

Schein, E. H., *Organizational Psychology* (Englewood Cliffs, N.J.: Prentice-Hall, 1980).

Schein, E. H., *Organizational Culture and Leadership* (San Francisco: Jossey-Bass, 1985).

Schlesinger, L. A. and Heskett, J. L., 'The Service Driven Service Company', *Harvard Business Review* (September–October, 1991).

Schon, D. A., *Beyond the Stable State* (New York: Random House, 1971).

Schonberger, R. J., *Building a Chain of Customers: Linking Business Functions to Create a World-class Company* (New York: Free Press, 1990).

Schwartz, P., *The Art of the Long View,* (New York: Doubleday Currency, 1991).

Sculley, J., *Odyssey* (New York: Harper & Row, 1987).

Senge, P., *The Fifth Discipline: The Art and Practice of the Learning Organization* (New York: Doubleday Currency, 1990).

Stalk, G. Jr. and Hout, T. M., *Competing Against Time* (New York: Free Press, 1990).

Thomas, P. R. and Martin, K. R., *Competitiveness Through Total Cycle Time: An Overview for CEOs* (New York: McGraw-Hill, 1990).

Thomas, P. R. and Martin, K. R., *Getting Competitive: Middle Managers and the Cycle Time Ethic* (New York: McGraw-Hill, 1991).

Thurow, L, (ed.), *The Management Challenge: Japanese Views* (Cambridge, Mass.: MIT Press, 1985).

Thurow, L. C., *Head to Head – The Coming Economic Battle Among Japan, Europe and America* (London: Nicholas Brealey Publishing, 1992).

Toffler, A., *The Third Wave* (London: Pan Books, 1981).

Toffler, A., *The Adaptive Corporation* (London: Pan Books, 1985).

Turkle, S., *The Second Self: Computers and the Human Spirit* (New York: Simon & Schuster, 1984).

Van Doren, C., *The Idea of Progress* (New York: Frederick A. Praeger, 1967).

Von Hippel, E., *The Sources of Innovation* (New York: Oxford University Press, 1988).

Watts, A. W., *The Way of Zen* (New York: Pantheon Books, 1957).

Welles, J. F., *Understanding Stupidity: An Analysis of the Premaladaptive Beliefs and Behaviour of Institutions and Organizations* (New York: Mount Pleasant Press, 1986).

Whitely, R. C., *The Customer Driven Company: Moving From Talk to Action* (Reading, Mass.: Addison-Wesley, 1991).

Williamson, O. E., 'The Modern Corporation: Origins, Evolution, Attributes', *Journal of Economic Literature* (December 1981).

Wriston, W. B., 'The World According to Walter', *Harvard Business Review* (January–February 1986).

Yoshino, M. Y., *Japan's Managerial System* (Cambridge, Mass.: MIT Press, 1973).

Zuboff, S., *In the Age of the Smart Machine* (New York: Basic Books Inc., 1988)

Index

unique
  design 39
  experience 39
  responses 35
unpredictability 1
upward regeneration of human
    capital 192

value
  added of management 88, 207
  adding capabilities 53
  creating capability 139, 159
  of time 48
  seeking dialogue 43
values 216
vehicles of discovery 105, 142
venture capital 136
versatility 65
video
  conferencing 182
  on-demand 59
virtual
  markets 40
  networks 59

organization 81, 84, 85, 89
  reality 48, 60, 66, 187, 211
vision of tomorrow's organization 114
visionary companies 12
vital organizational resources 142
voice of the customer 11, 98
voyages of discovery 7

war of movement 9
wavelength
  defined markets 40
  defined marketspaces 40
waves, from the future 2, 6
world of the blip 54
world-class
  capabilities 89
  resources 84
  responses 146
  suppliers 93
Wriston, Walter 8

yesterday's mindset 9

zone of the possible 13, 23